The Inner Workings of a LEGO® Mind

Steven James Erickson

The Inner Workings
of a
LEGO® Mind

Steven James Erickson

Dedication

This book is dedicated to the
LEGO® community, all of you,
every single one, are incredible.

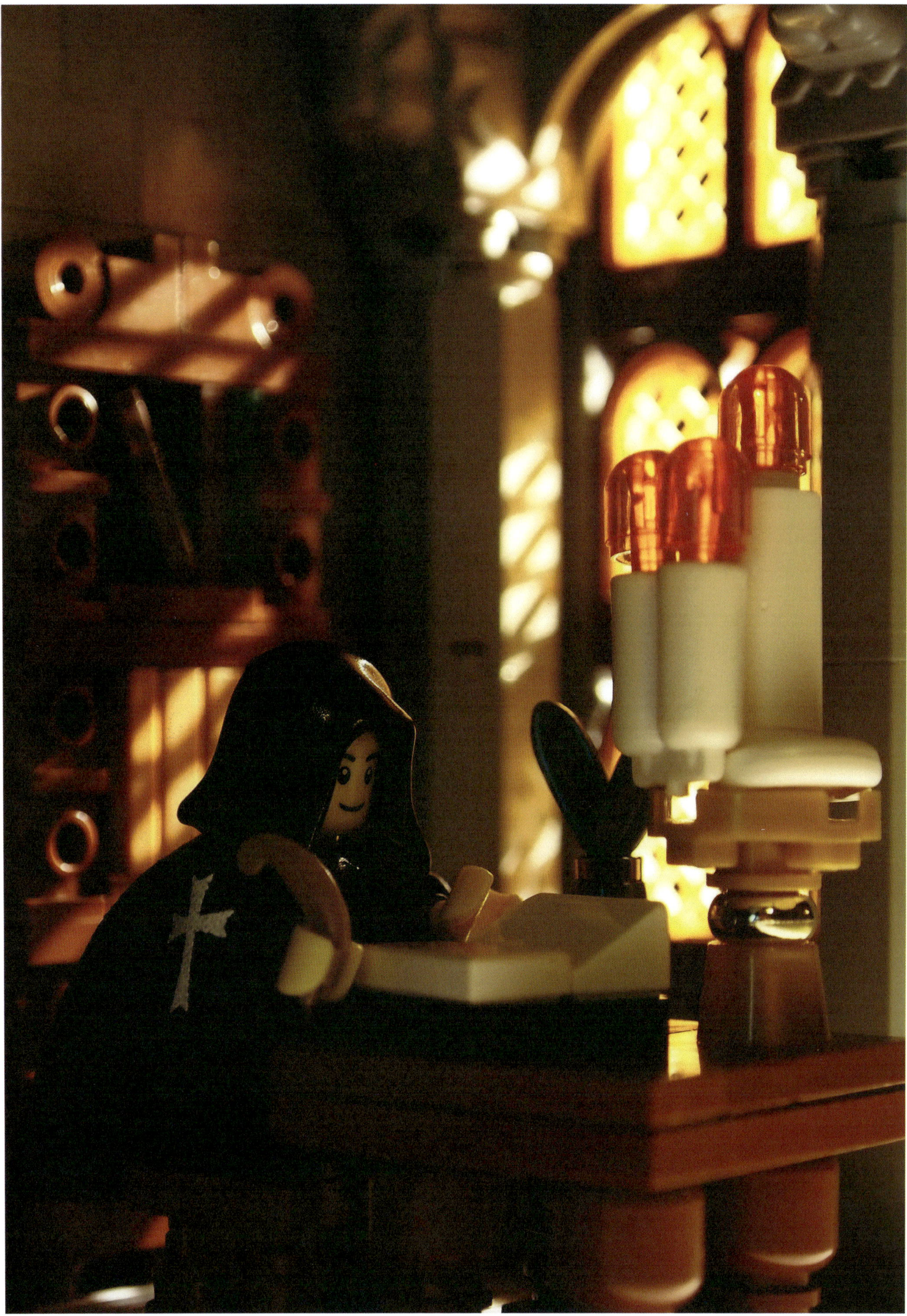

CONTENTS

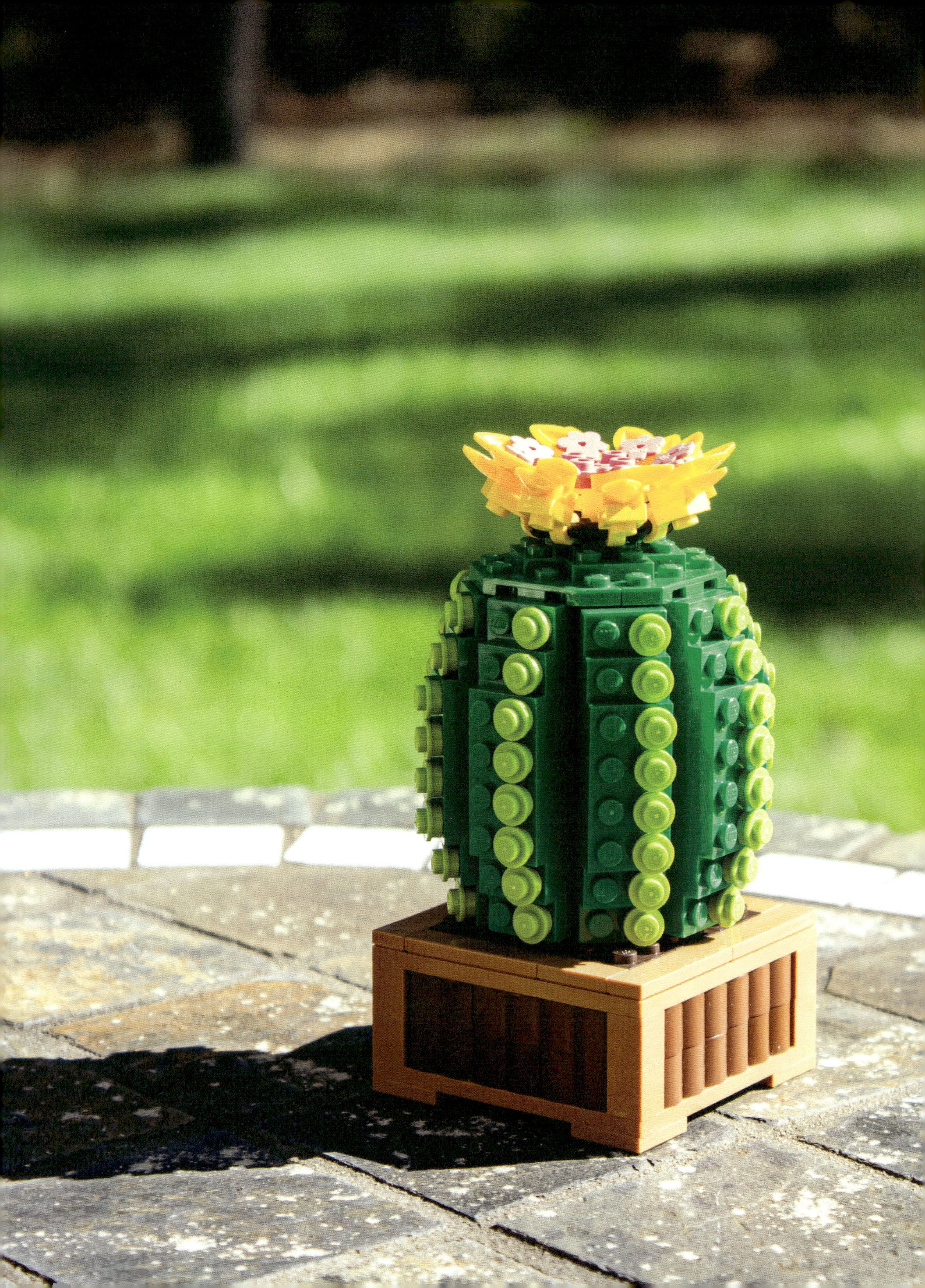

INTRODUCTION

When most people think of art, they think of famous artists like Leonardo di Vinci, Michaelanglo, Van Gogh, and Picasso – masters who had achieved the summit of their talent. And, they would be right.

But, art may not always be a masterpiece instead, art can be a very personal expression.

I believe that art is about telling your story and expressing who you are and where you've been. For me personally, art, in this case – LEGO® art – is my story. LEGO® is a wonderful, artistic medium because you are never too young or too old for LEGO®.

Your art is your interpretation of your experiences that are completely unique to you. I've heard many people say, "I could never do that." or "I could never create that." when they have seen my work in person. That's because it's my story and not theirs.

Those famous masters had a starting point in their artistic journey. Everyone has potential inside of them that can start out small and grow with practice. Art is a way for all of us to speak a universal language and show the world our incredible individuality. That is the purpose of this book. Enjoy!

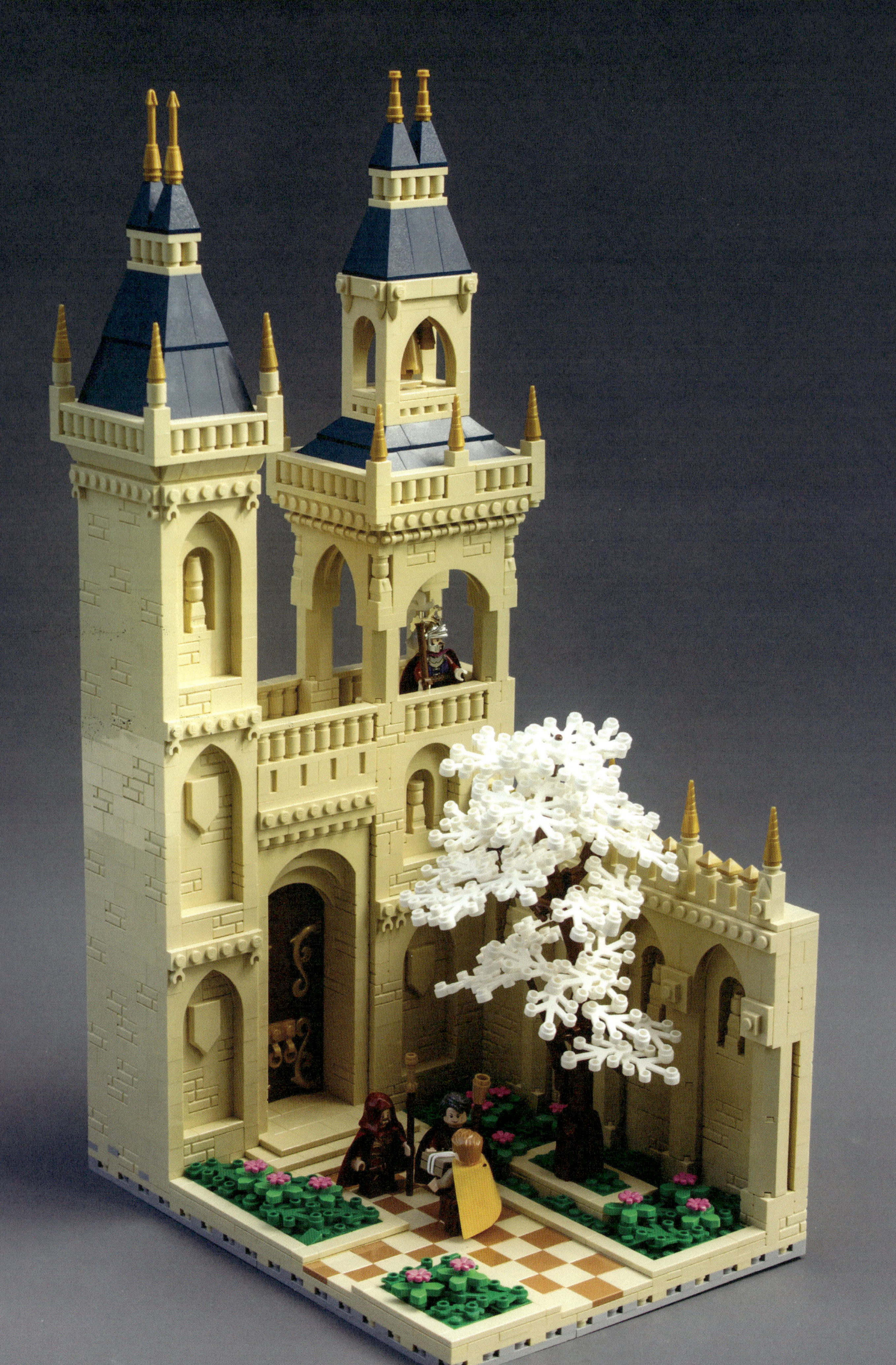

CASTLE

Out of the many almost limitless themes of LEGO®, Castle stands head and shoulders above the rest as my enduring favorite. To me, Castle and LEGO® go hand-in-hand and are virtually inseparable.

Though on the surface it sounds somewhat straightforward, with muted colors and basic blocky structures, this theme is incredibly inspiring and in-depth. LEGO® Castle can mimic real-world architecture on a smaller scale.

There's a theoretical database of ideas, spanning thousands of years, different cultures, and eras of Castles.

Not to get too wordy, but Castle ... RULES.

Balancing the color of a castle is one of the most enjoyable parts of castle building. You have the walls, the roofs, the doors, and separate buildings that all need harmony, and color can be used effectively to achieve this.

Another feature to note is the balance of texture. Exquisite details really make the whole creation pop to life. Different elements working together can tell a visual story about the creation without saying a word.

In the following section, we will be discussing all these elements further, including the castle you see on your left!

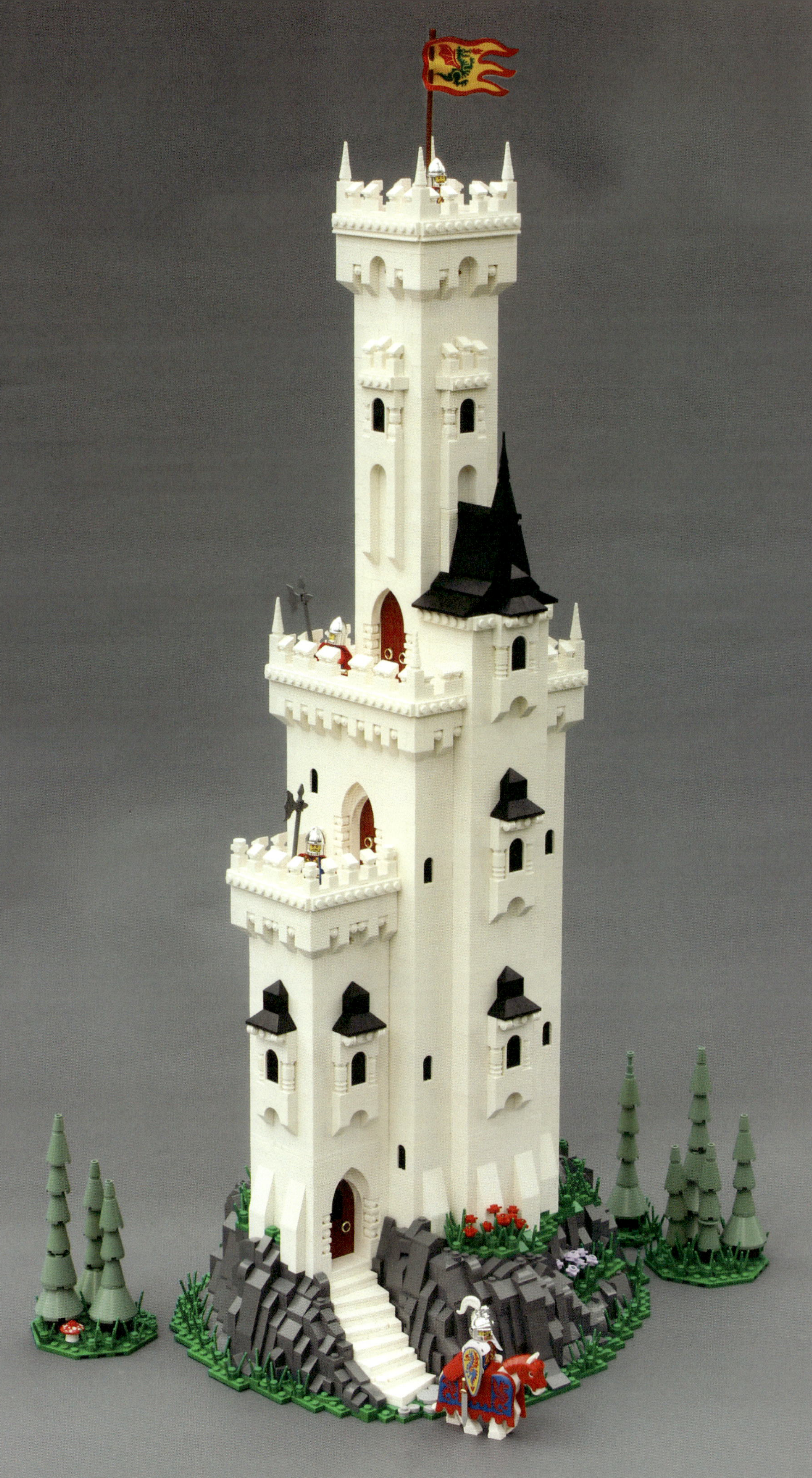

Aldingham Keep

One of my most favorite and recent castle examples, **Aldingham Keep** has some key details that are definitely worth highlighting.

The first is color. Black and white are as sharp a contrast as you can find. These polar opposites make any other colors stand out like crazy. The red doors, chrome elements, flowers, and grass appear even more vibrant.

The next aspect is the cleanliness. This tells a story of wealth and power, as if the occupants of this castle needed not to trouble themselves with the problem of warfare, but were able to enjoy this as a peaceful, elegant residence. The smooth walls act as a canvas for the architectural details to rest on.

I always loved how the rest of this landscape behaved with the castle. Most nature is chaotic, but here it appears orderly while it retains a natural feel.

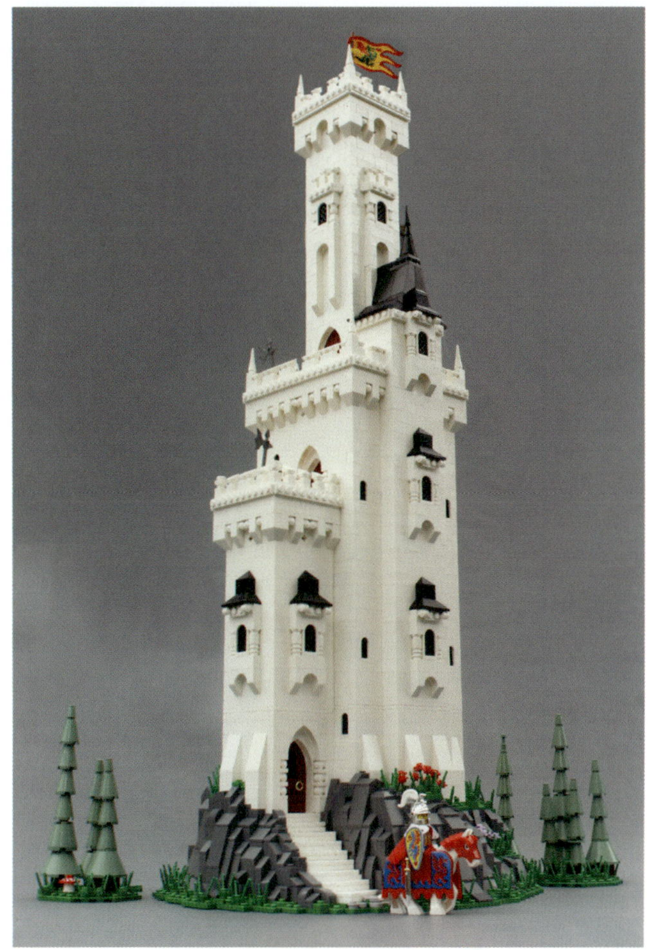

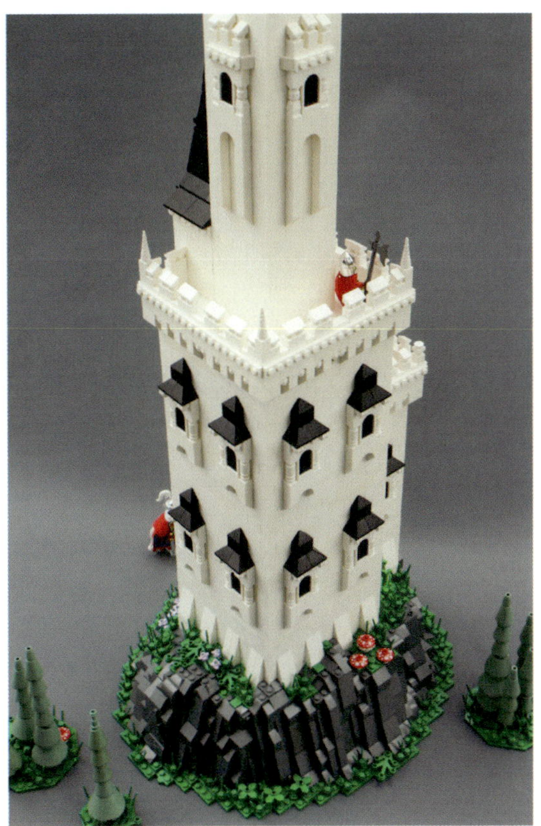

Lastly, the composition of this castle is what brings everything together. It's all proportioned correctly for the size of a minifigure. Every floor and window is aligned just right which gives it consistency.

Also to mention, the tower dimensions match. The tower on the ground level that meets the curving staircase is the exact dimensions (8x8 studs) of the tower sitting at the top.

This castle was based on late German architectural style and was loosely inspired by the Neuschwanstein Castle of the 1800's. It was also a residential castle not intended to withstand warfare.

Overall, the aesthetic for Aldingham Keep was simple, yet refined elegance and I think it worked very well.

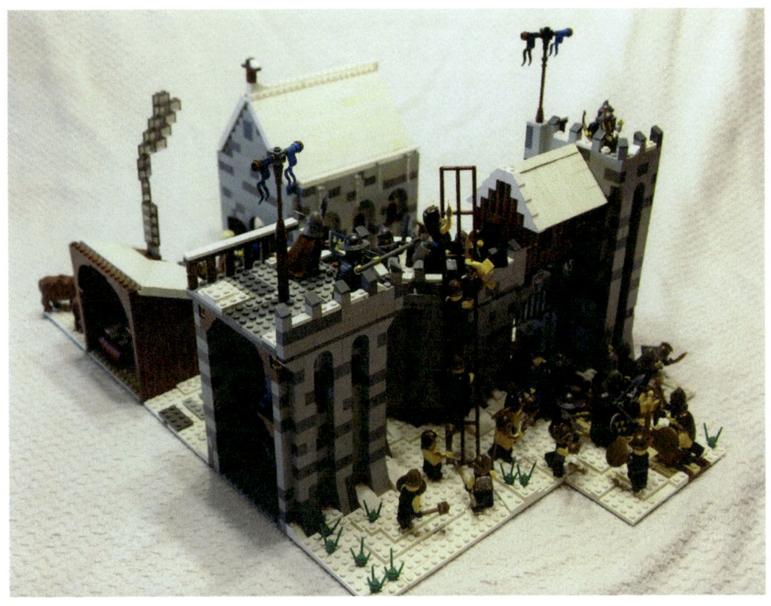

You have to start somewhere! For me, that somewhere was a long time ago. My earlier castles are almost painful to revisit, however - there are things in here that hint at what was to come in my building style.

In **Rothburg**, (top) you can tell that the concept is there. The whole build is a great example of a good idea that was executed without much previous experience.

The color palette is boring and all wrong, a sad lack of detail (especially in the paths and landscape) is glaring, but there's a lively energy in the build despite the unconcern for the viewer's perspective. It's hard to see between the buildings in one glance.

Bronzewick Castle (bottom) is where things start to take shape. The details are more even, the color brighter and more pleasant and the landscape, despite still being a bit blocky, flows more gracefully. (Landscape would become a much greater feature for me in following years.) There's notable variety in the trees and foliage, including small prefab LEGO® trees with light and dark green. There are also standard green trees to give everything a more diverse palette.

Also, the castle narrowly escapes the dreaded "Big Gray Wall" syndrome - a term used to describe a wall that is too plain with not enough interest. Fortunately, we have some inset arches here. The colors of the flags and windows also help to add a much needed visual punch that distracts from all the gray.

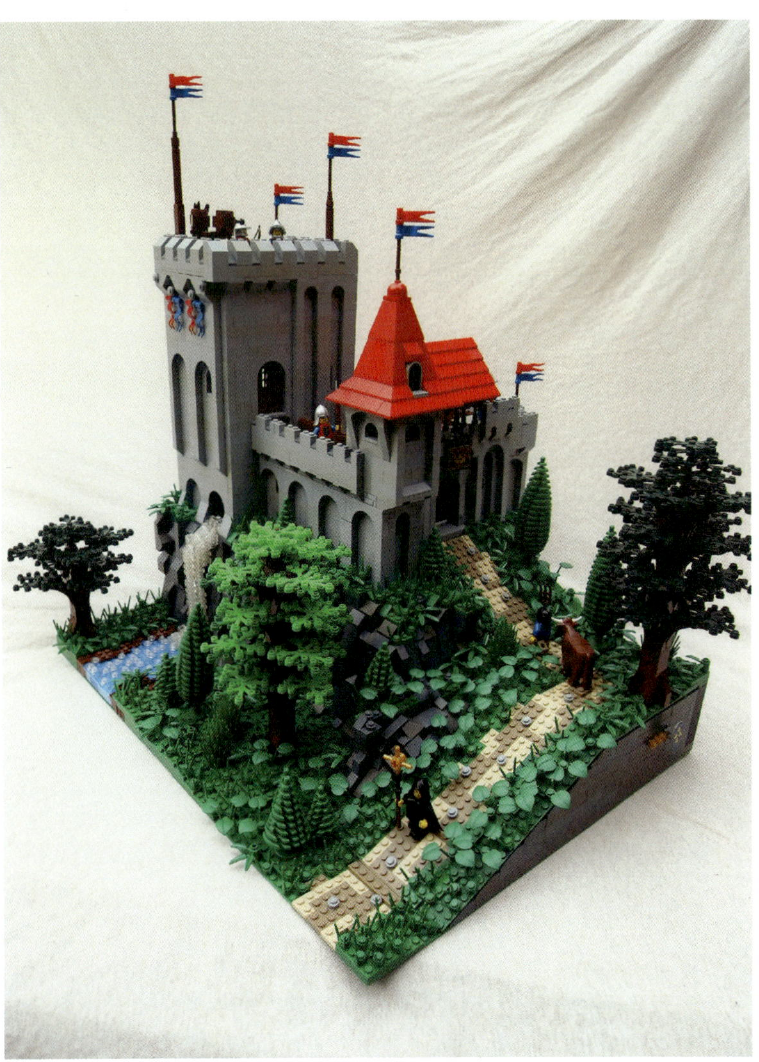

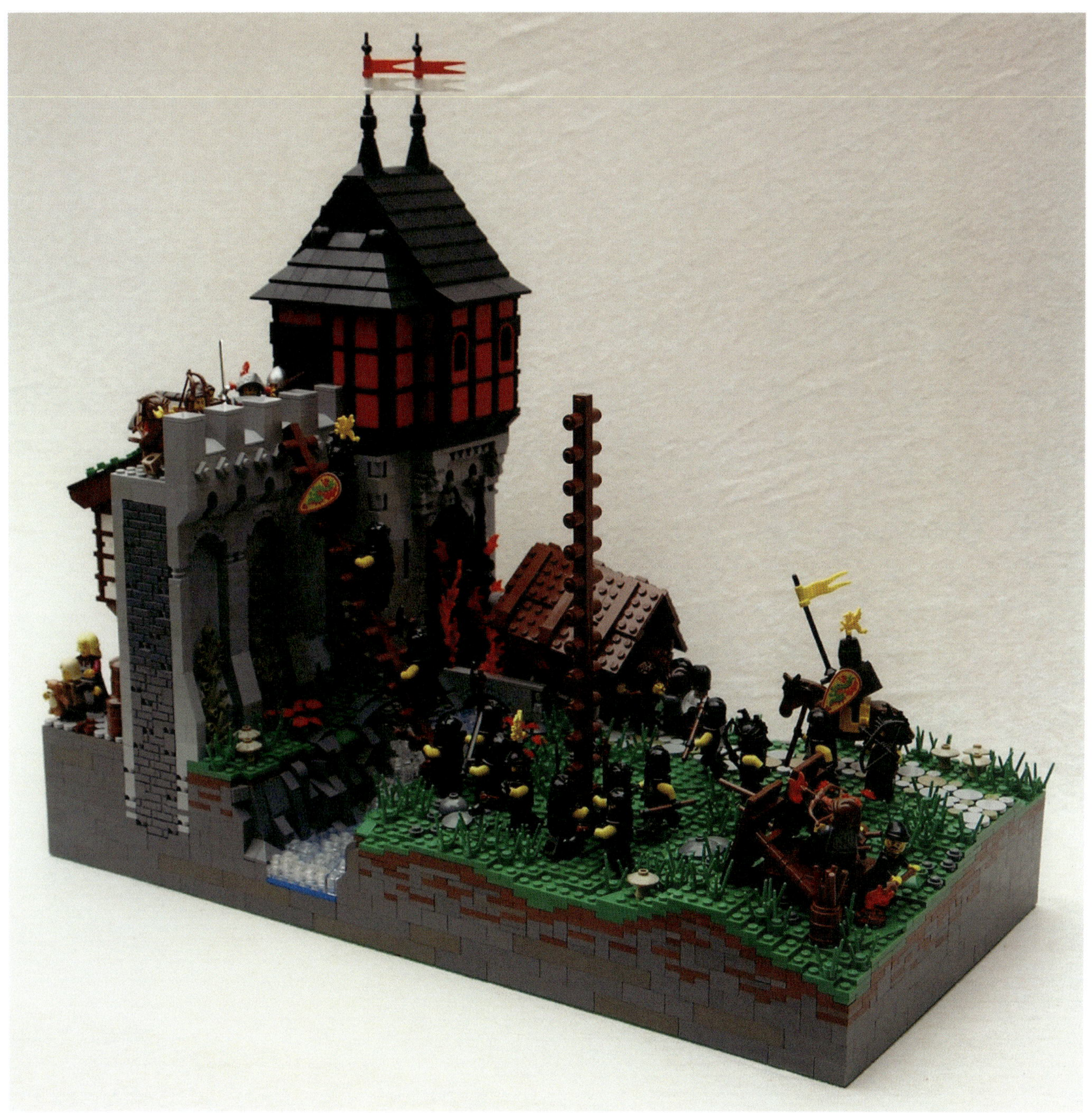

Avremarus - Here's where the balance of a creation starts to come to life. At this point, I had made great strides in castle architecture, including lion's heads and decorative crenells (which are the fortified railing at the top of the walls), more vines, and different types of arrow slits. The most notable feature here is the cutaway wall, giving a unique glimpse that makes it feel more realistic.

I was beginning to fine-tune various aspects of my creations. The landscaping has an improved flow but also more tidiness to it. Smaller plant elements and more color have been added. The cutaway also shows the dirt at different elevation levels.

Another improvement is the overall layout. Everything is far easier to see in this build in one glance and the groups of the attacking army are spaced out well and realistically organized.

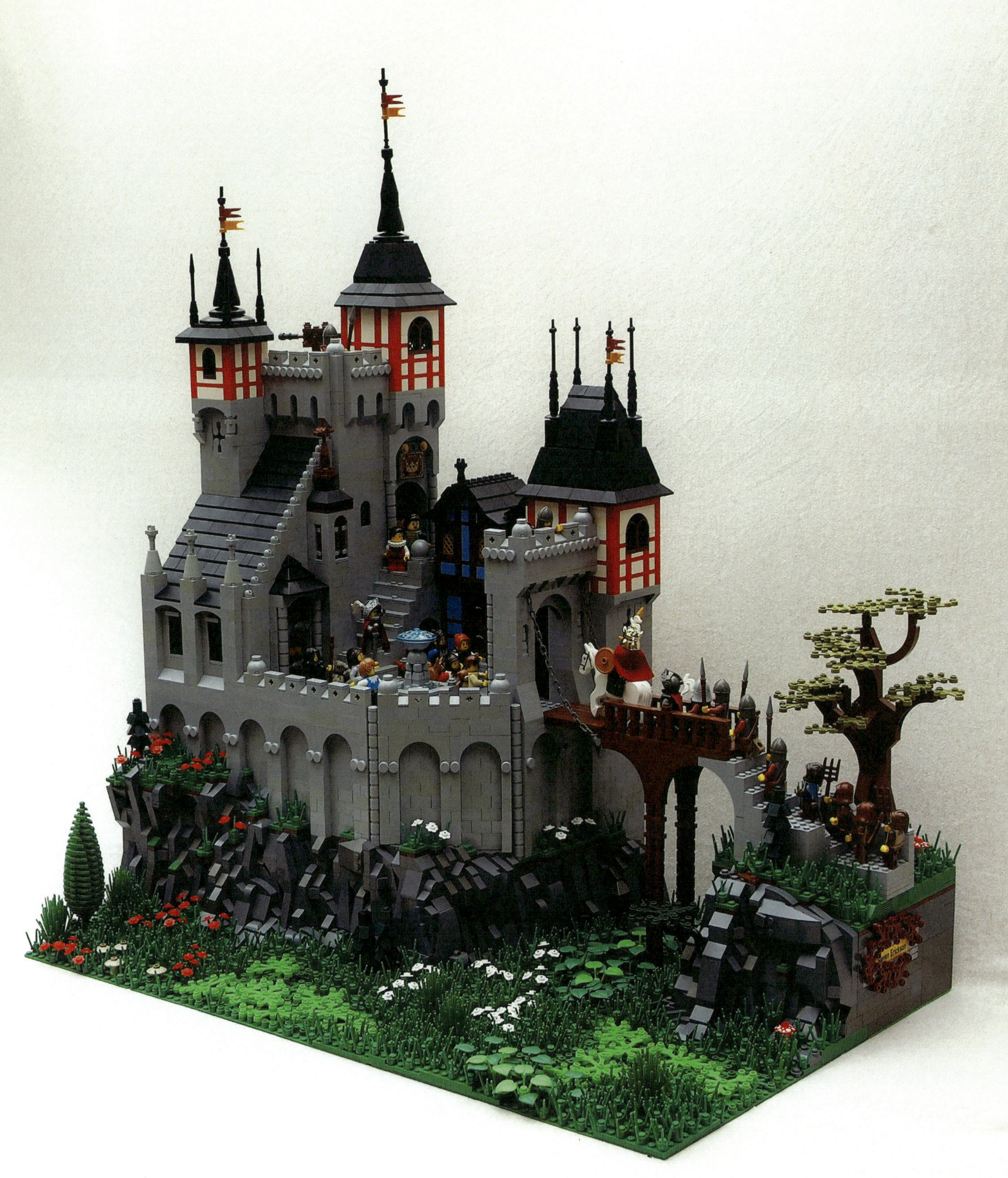

Ald Wickeraus - A personal favorite of mine, this castle is an accumulation of the things I learned with Avremarus and other builds, only on a much more amplified and grand level.

Let's start with the walls. There are many eye-catching details, like the rounded crenells and the round studs decorating the insets. The circular theme is echoed throughout the architecture. There are also many subtle details like the bricks stacked half on top of each other, just like real-world masonry would be. This can be seen especially in the curved castle wall at the base.

One major feature of this creation is the beautiful landscaping which really helps to bring the entire MOC to life. (MOC means My Own Creation.) The colors and textures of the grass give a hint of elevation, brighter colors for lower, darker and leafier for higher ground. The red and white flowers also match the color of the tudor towers of the castle.

At this point in time, the olive green leaves of the tree (see right) were unbelievably rare and extremely difficult to come by - sold in only the most expensive of LEGO® sets. This one tree alone contained my entire collection of them! (In later years, they became more common and can be seen more frequently in different creations in this book).

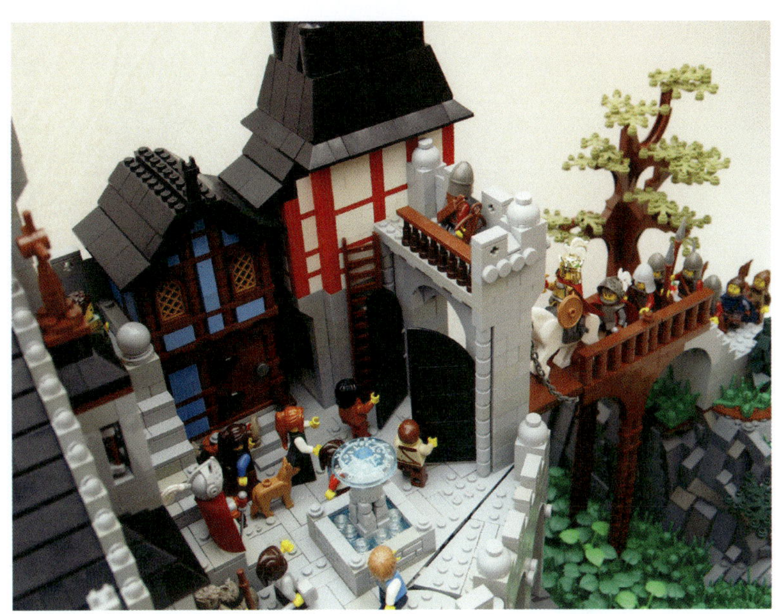

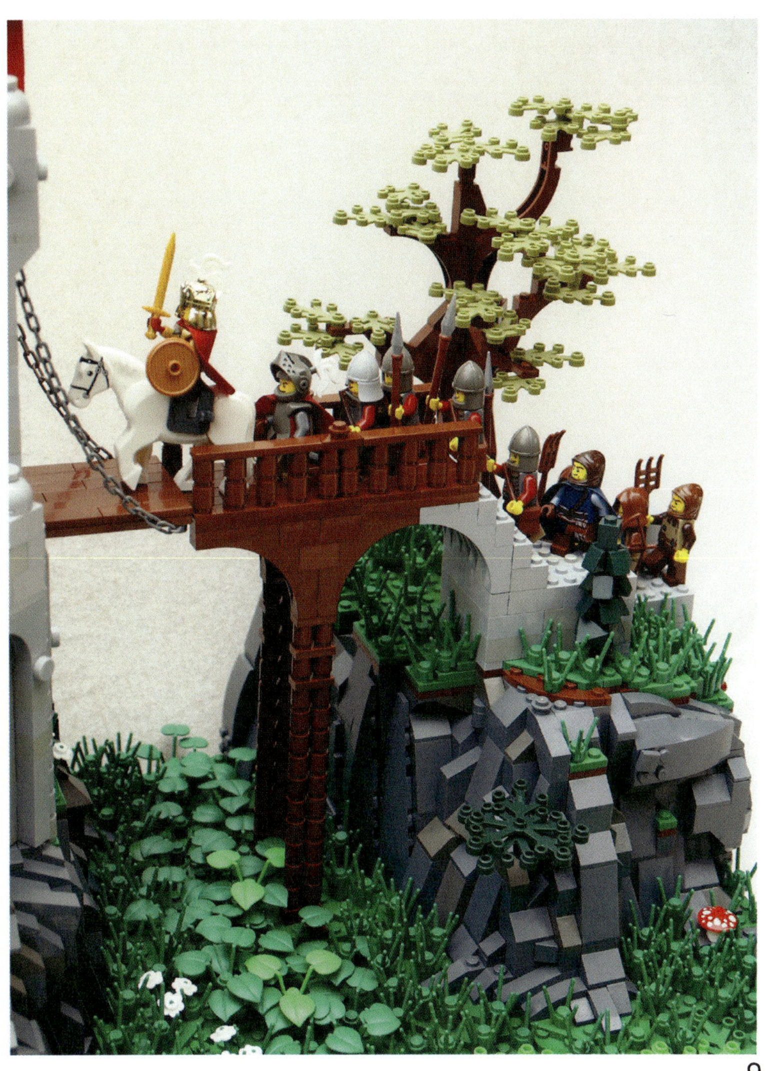

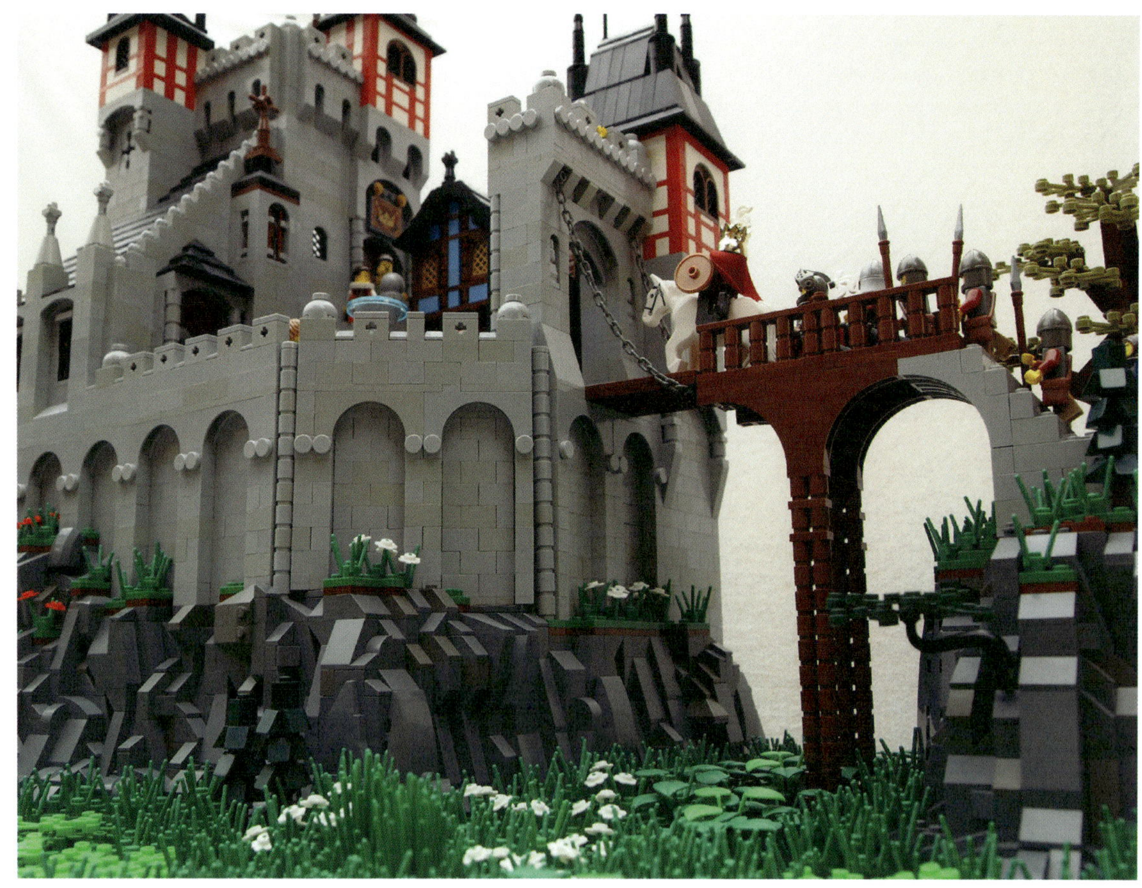

A fun way to make the castle look even larger is to use smaller trees, like the microscale evergreens at the base of these craggy rocks and the side of the castle.

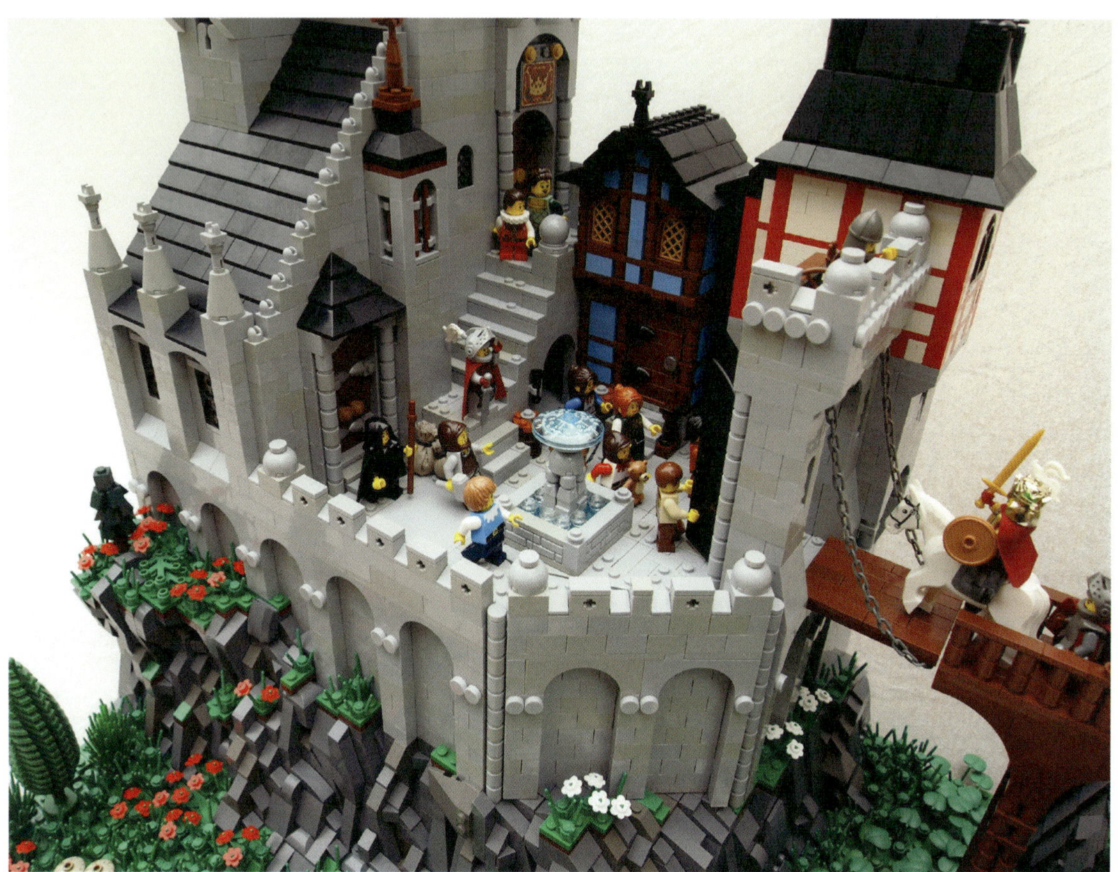

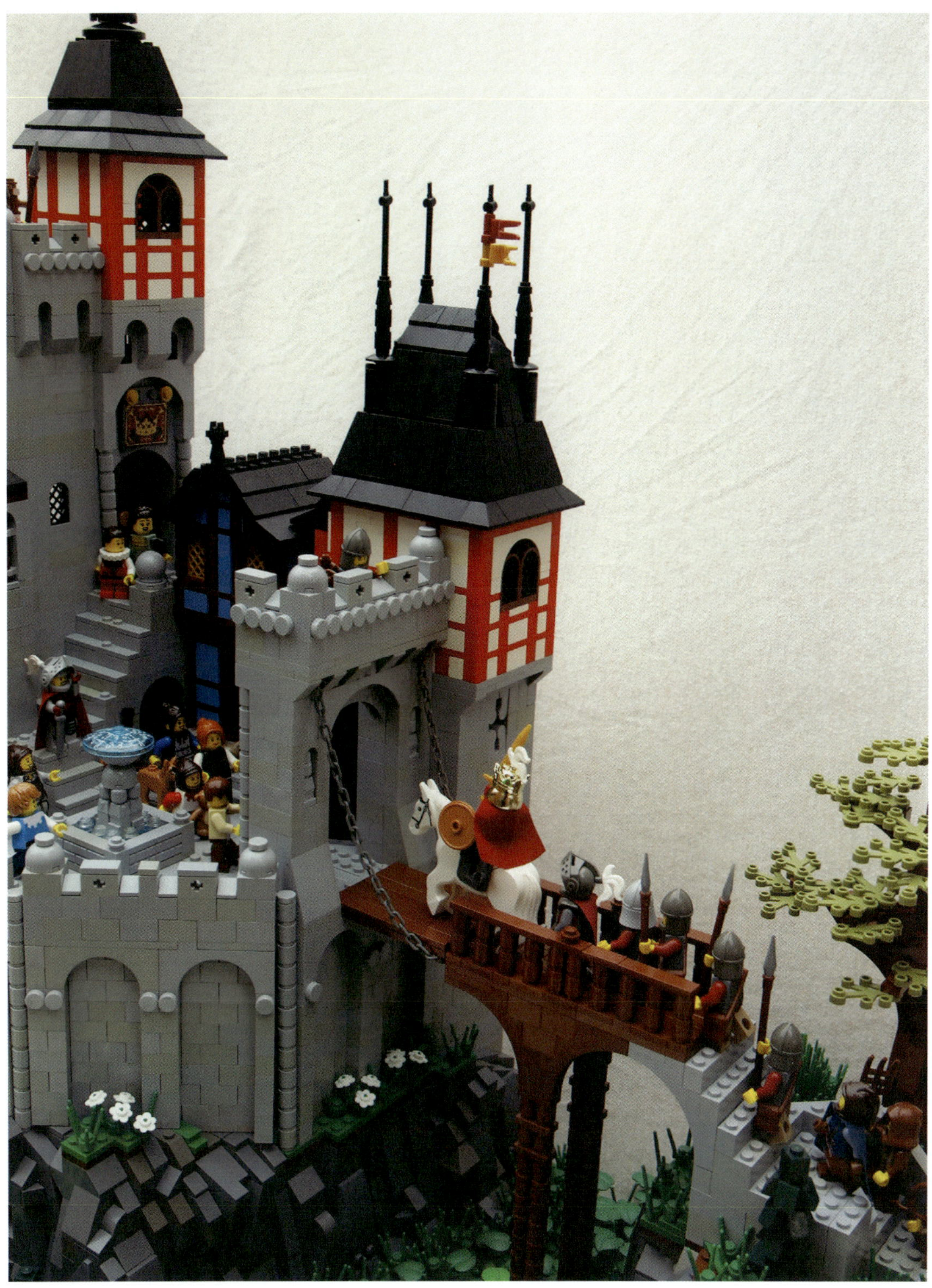

An interesting highlight is the red and white tudor towers. Those colors specifically are inspired by Burg Eltz, a real-life castle in the Rheinland-Pfalz province of Germany. The towers add a unique look to the castle as most tudor structures would typically use brown and black, staying more neutral in color.

This was my first major online contest win for a LEGO® build and it took first place in its category. I was honored, considering it was only my second try at a win.

Rosewood Hall

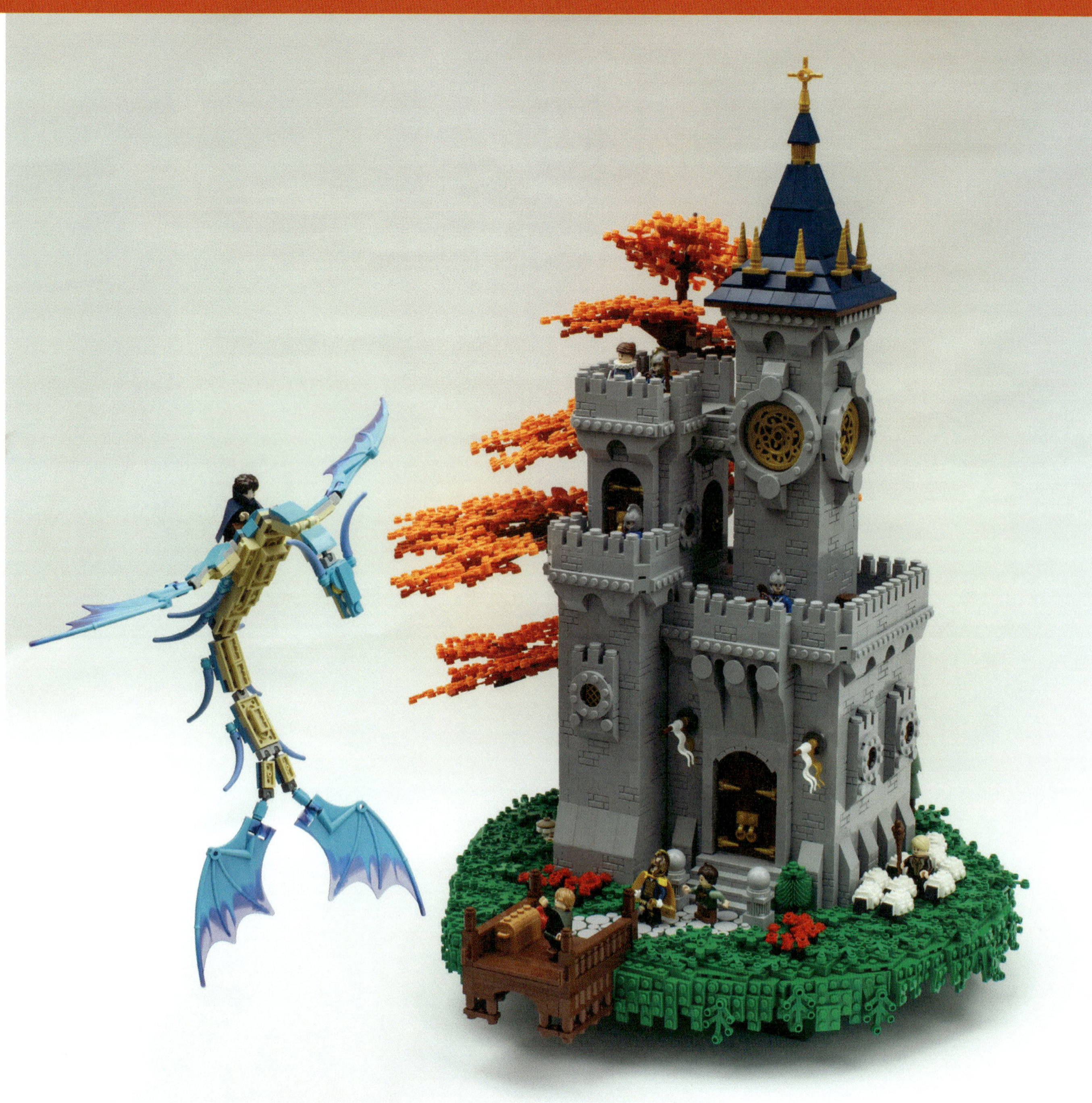

Rosewood Hall takes things up yet another notch! As one of my more recent castles, the fine-tuning on the detail is nearly topped out. In previous creations, there was less emphasis on the extra details like the characters. Here - even on a such a small footprint - I was able to add mushroom gatherers, a flock of fluffy sheep, and a large dragon (more on the dragon later!).

A notable improvement here are the windows, all well-placed and well-defined, with an overarching circular style. To employ a more fantasy-inspired color scheme, I traded out the black color hardware with a gold finish. The sharp roof has been simplified from previous designs, making it strangely more striking with the blue and gold contrast.

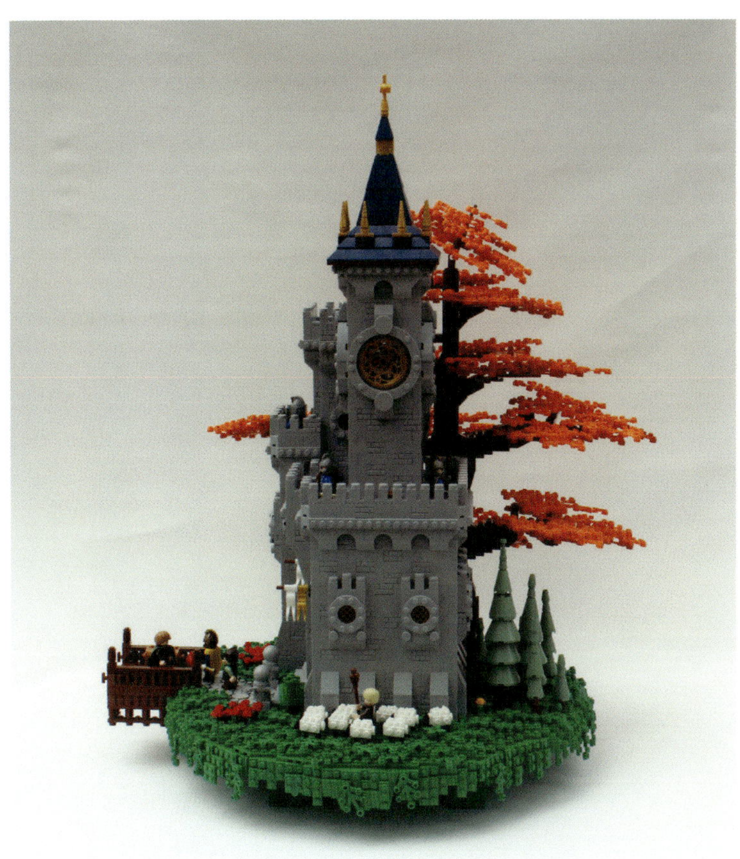

The decorative crenells compliment the castle as well, being pleasantly centered in their spaces on the structure. And of course, all the floors and doorways are sized for a minifig to theoretically reach any point in the castle.

In this castle, I incorporated the original stacked-half-on-top style for the bricks in the walls as I did with the Ald Wickeraus build, only here I've added a new element - the masonry (or profile) bricks, which add a subtle extra layer of detail since they are used sparsely.

As you've most likely noticed, my builds use color as an important feature and this MOC is no exception. The blue roof alongside the orange tree is an excellent contrast, as are the red flowers with the green grass.

Both of these contrasting complementary color pairs are seen here, yet somehow they don't interrupt each other.

By this point, I had done a lot of irregularly shaped baseplates for other creations.

The model here has a circular base lined with overhanging grass, giving the illusion that the island itself is floating - further adding to the fictional/fantasy element.

This surprisingly heavy model is supported by LEGO® DUPLO blocks!

There's a basic trick of perspective in play here using only the tree size. With Ald Wickeraus castle earlier, we had small trees to make the large castle appear even bigger.

Here at Rosewood Hall the gigantic flaming orange maple beside the castle creates the impression that the castle is smaller than it is.

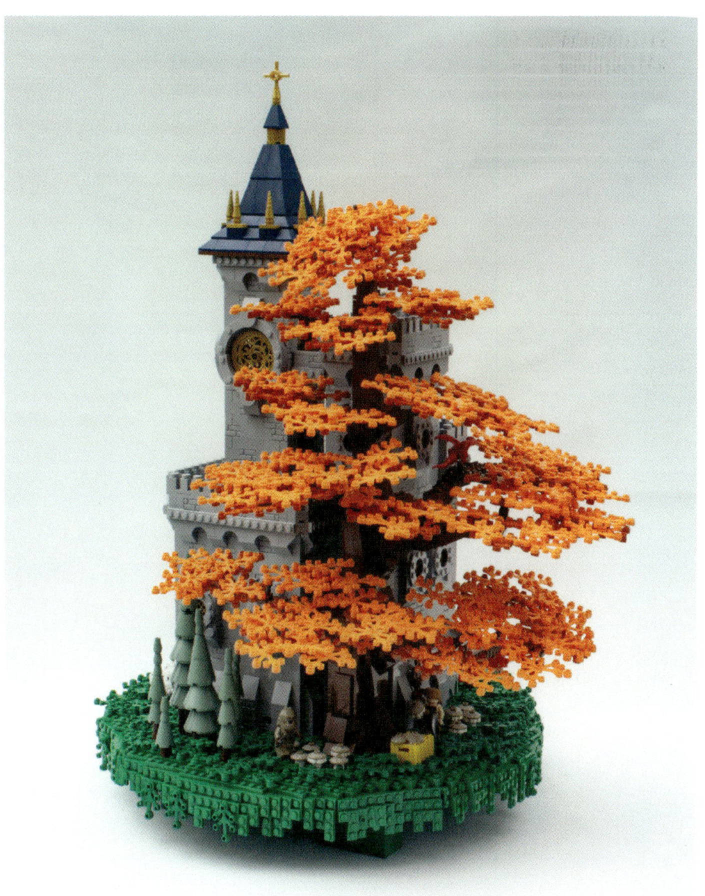

A Lot in a Little

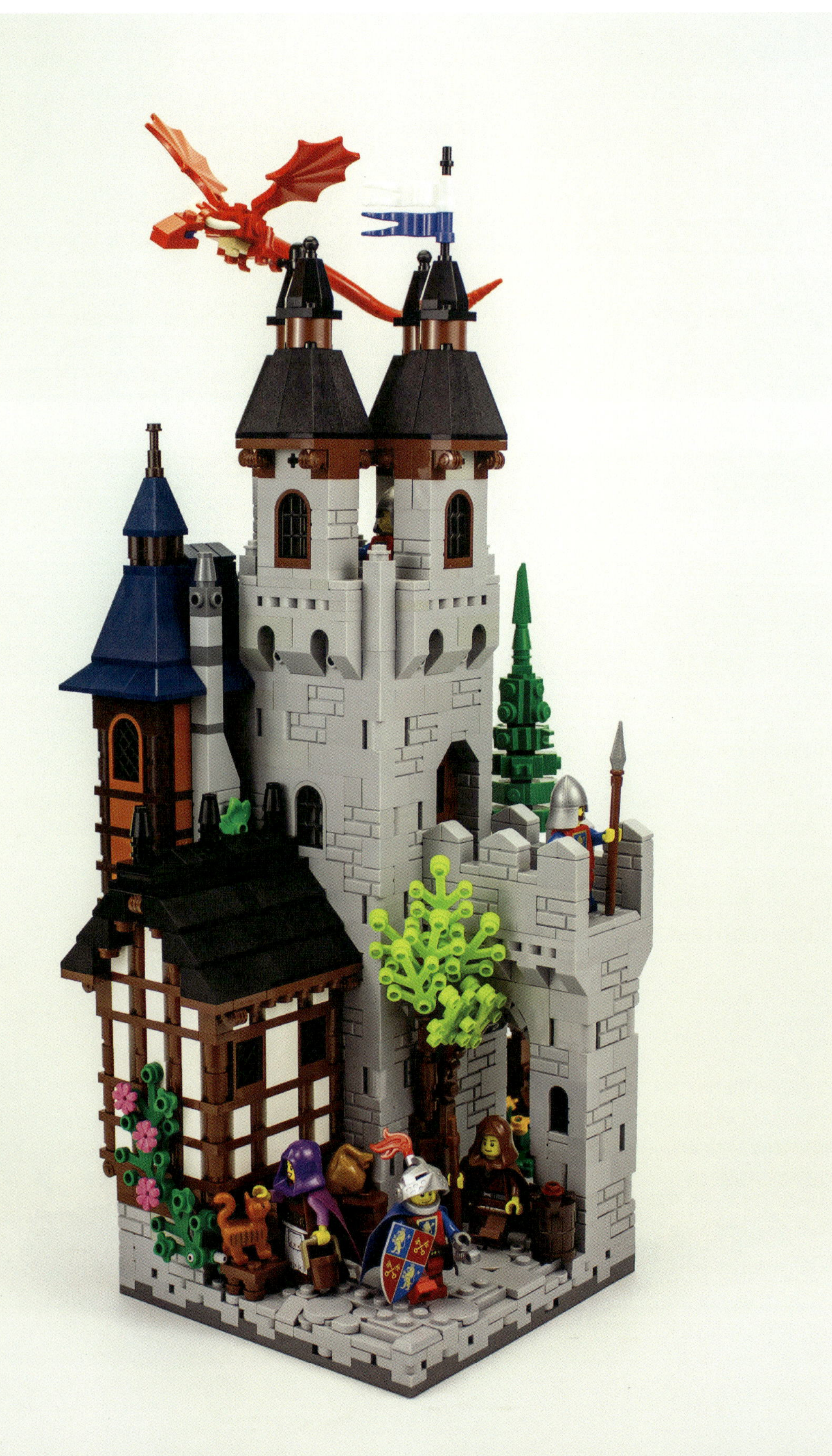

One of my favorite styles of building is to cram in a maximum amount detail and features in as small a space as possible without visually overwhelming the viewer. **Ye Town Square Tower** (left) is a fantastic specimen of this.

The goal here was to build an entire city on a 16x16 stud base. With some clever overhangs, I was able to add a second house along with a fir tree to bookend the center house, the light green tree, and alleyway. They are all resting under a castle tower.

Five interesting minifigs are scattered throughout the build, as well as a dragon and a kitty cat.

The Library of St. Ablasterio

The biggest focus of the library here is its intricate architectural details. The statues embedded in the alcoves give it a religious flavor. Each tower is unique from the other and the wall detail differs from the gate. These differences give as many layers of richness to the design as I could manage.

The checkered floor is given its own level of definition with the extra contrasting colors.

Another splash of color is the white tree, not unlike a cherry tree in full bloom. This adds another layer of color with minimal intrusion since the white recedes gracefully.

The pink blossoms in the flowerbeds add a cheerful note to an overall stoic build.

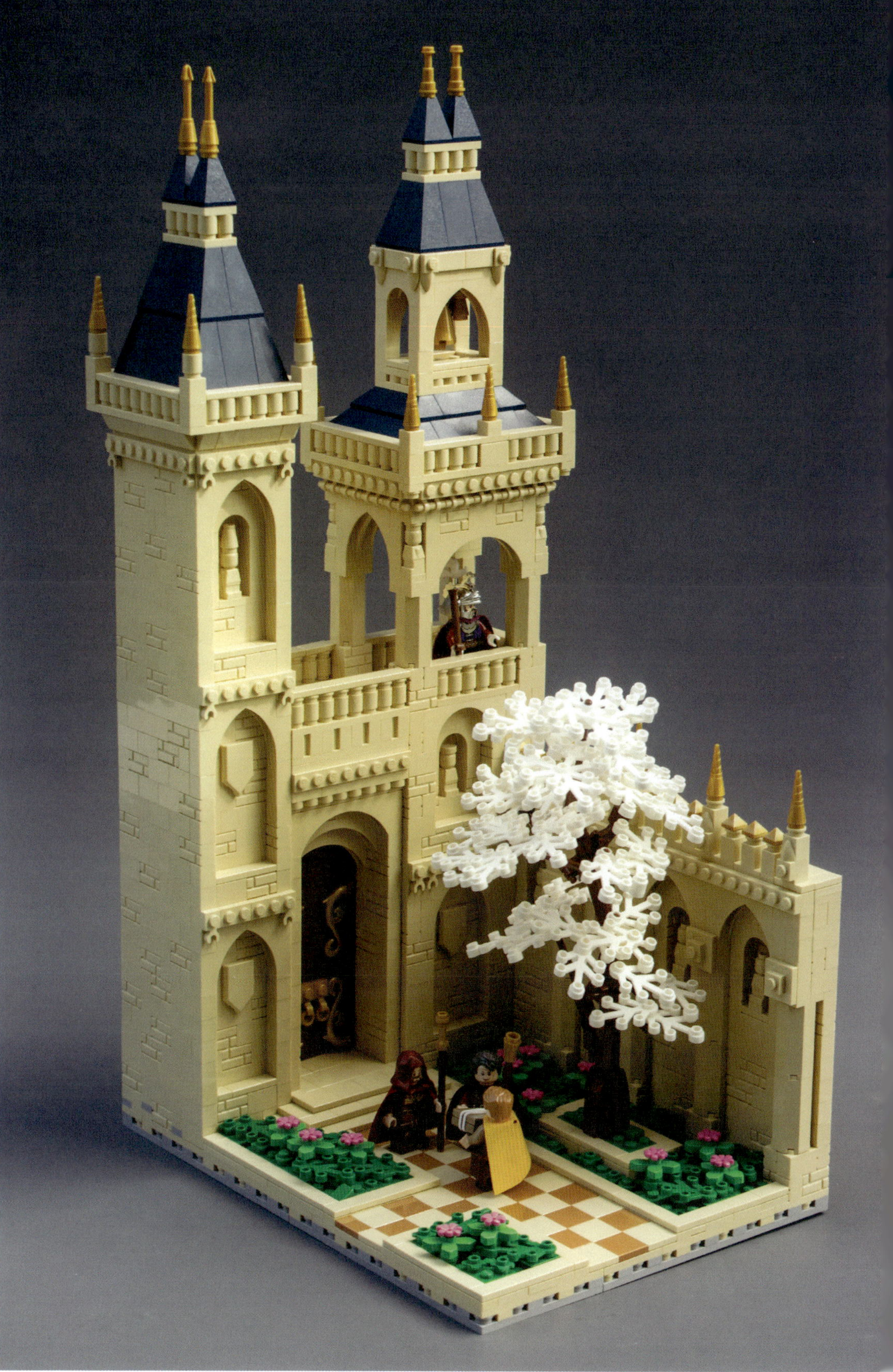

Speaking of stoic, the formal crenells with their gold accents tell a story of wealth and history.

As a note to the photography, the gray background here really highlights the warmer golden tones of the structure. A white background could have easily washed it out.

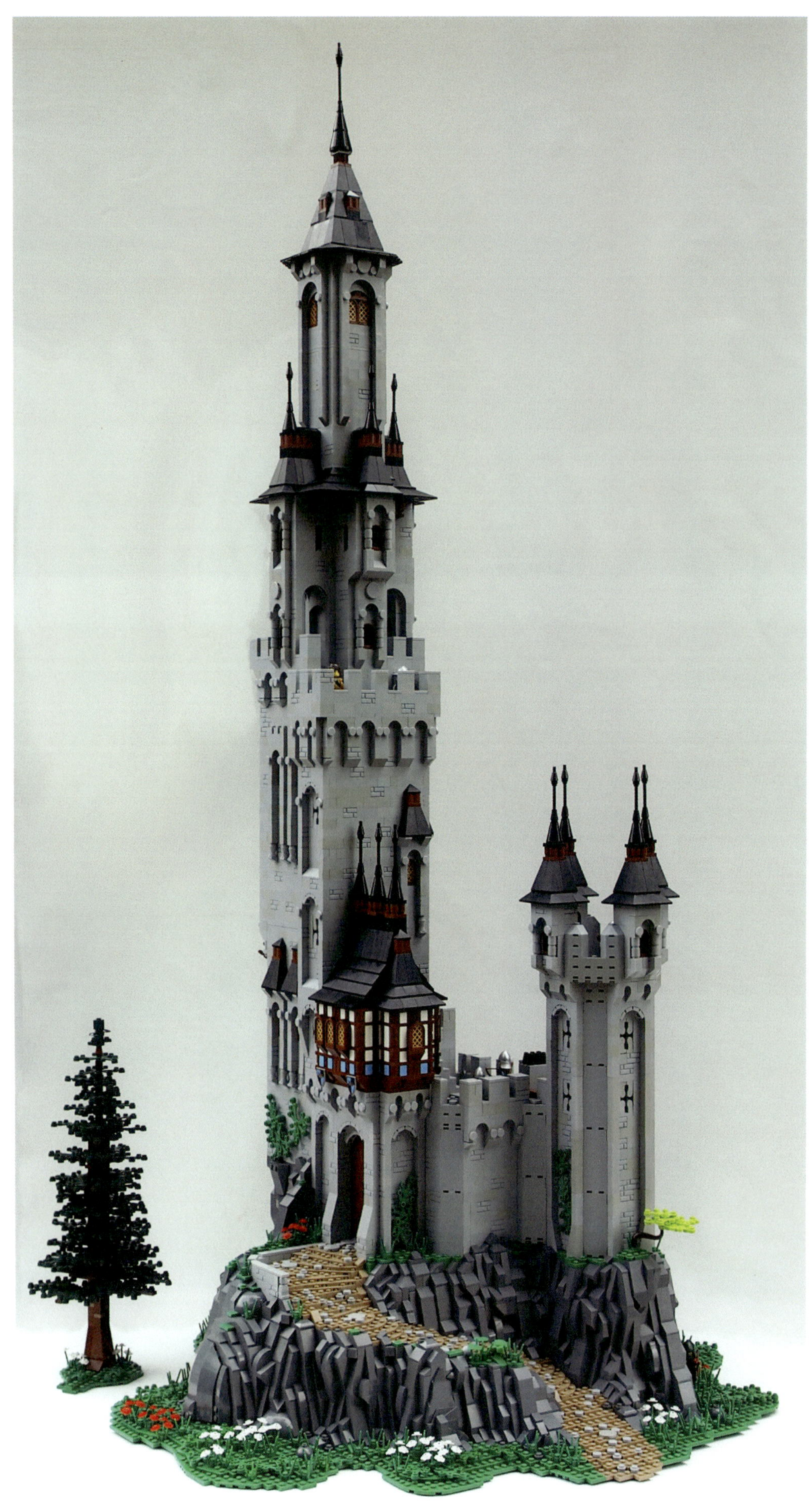

Farwin Castle

Farwin Castle - This creation was made just for fun, not part of any contest, but it was a collaboration build - my first, in fact. Farwin was the centerpiece for a collaboration with my LEGO® users group which was displayed at the Brickfair convention in Washington, DC way back in 2016.

For years, this castle set my personal record for tallest build yet at 4 feet 4 inches high! Because it was so giant, the detail is spread relatively thin, similar to Ald Wickeraus castle.

There's less foliage on this build than usual, but you don't need it here on the irregular base with all the cliffs.

At this time, this amount of gray bricks in both the walls and the cliffs was a major stretch on my collection of LEGO® parts!

The windows have an exaggerated length, giving the appearance that the castle is even taller. My aim here was to create an atmosphere of grandeur - a tall and imposing fortress that towered over all the lands around it.

This castle was by far my most popular creation of all time to date and became an iconic build for me.

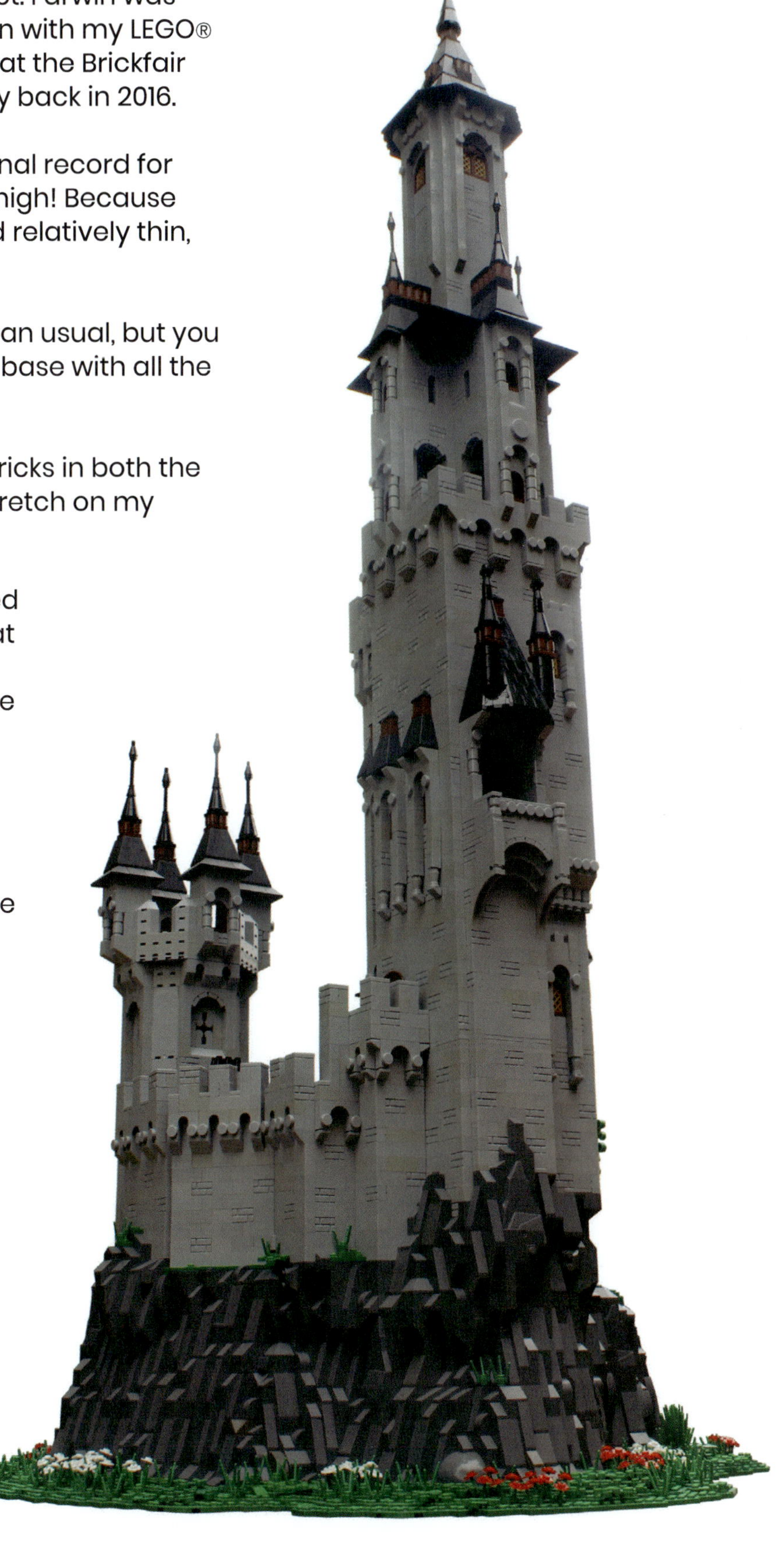

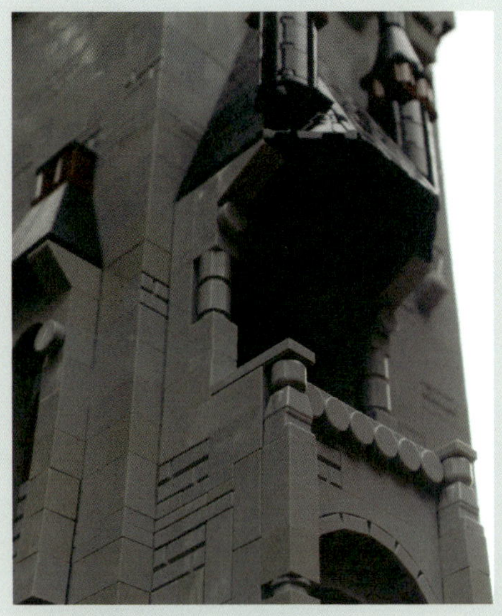

The interior of this castle was surprisingly complex! If you were the exact size of a LEGO® minifigure, you would be able to travel from the very bottom floor to the very top level of the castle through various entry points, staircases, and ladders.

A fun secret about the cross-shaped window slits is that they are actually minifig leg pieces! This is a very old medieval arrow slit building technique but one that is still effective and holds relevance today.

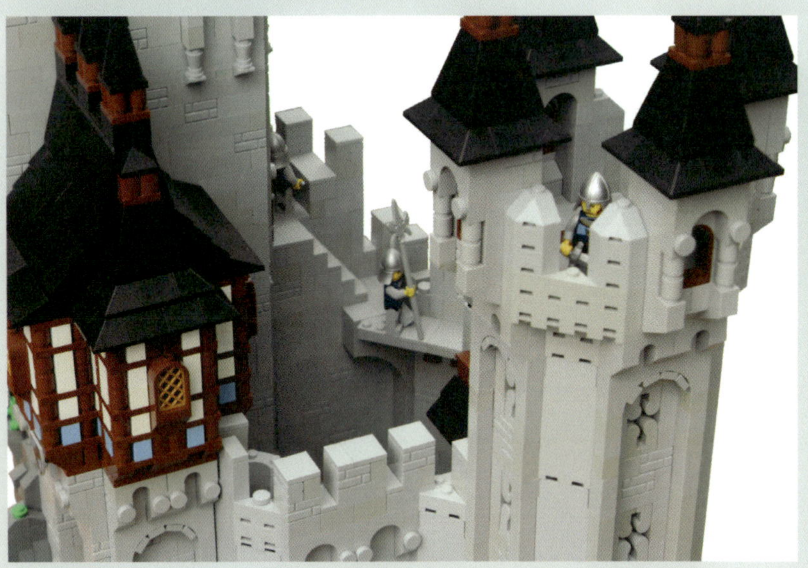

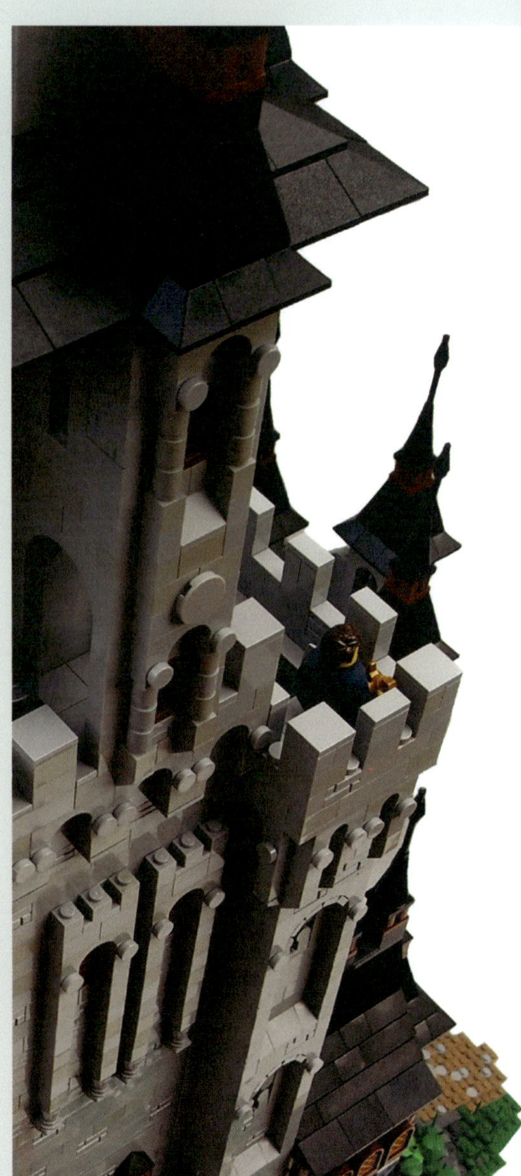

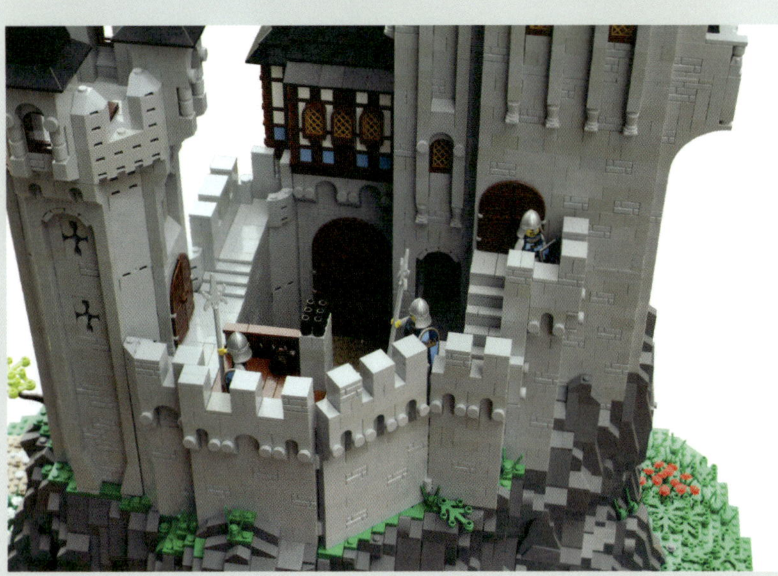

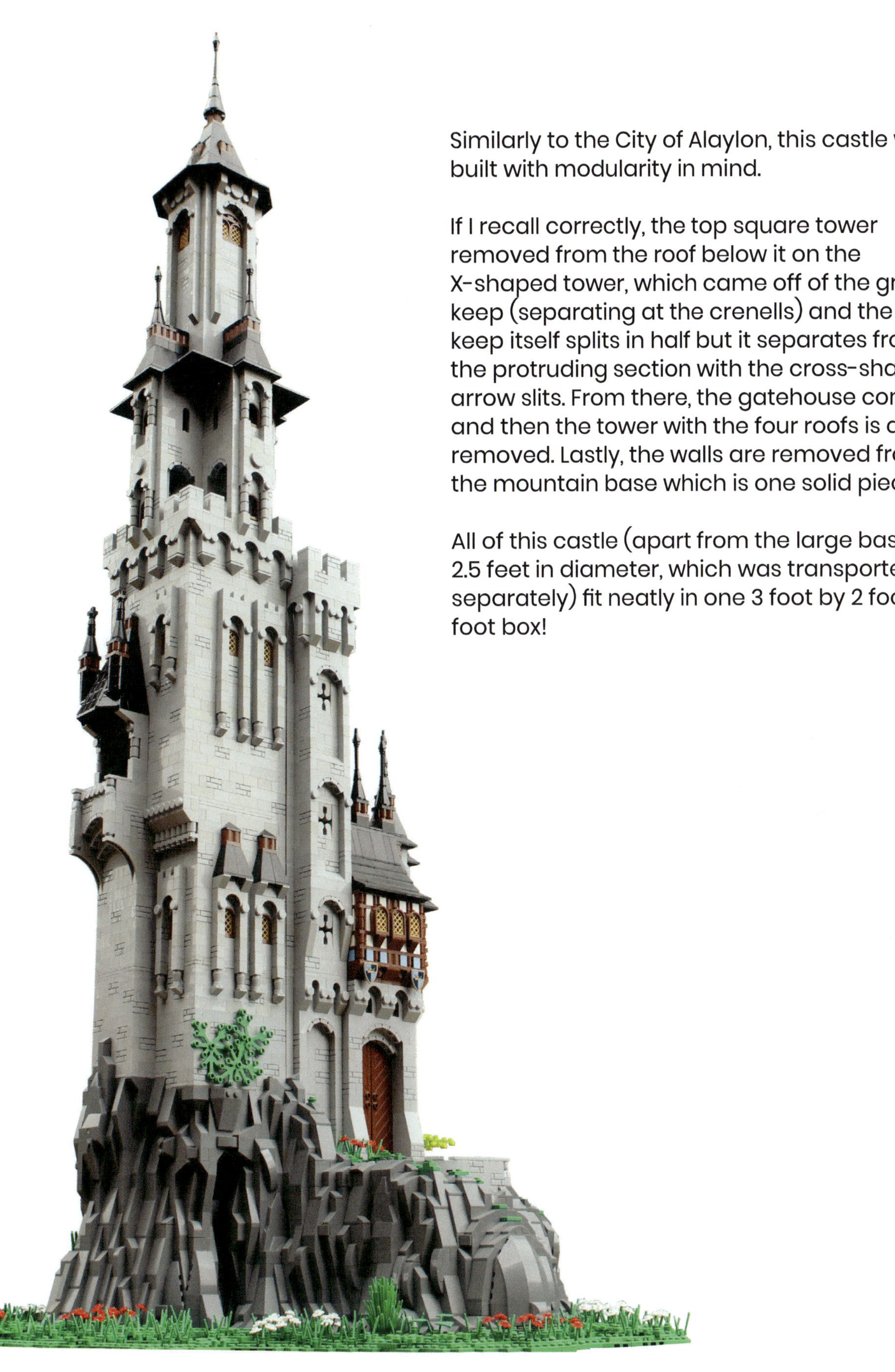

Similarly to the City of Alaylon, this castle was built with modularity in mind.

If I recall correctly, the top square tower removed from the roof below it on the X-shaped tower, which came off of the great keep (separating at the crenells) and the keep itself splits in half but it separates from the protruding section with the cross-shaped arrow slits. From there, the gatehouse come off and then the tower with the four roofs is also removed. Lastly, the walls are removed from the mountain base which is one solid piece.

All of this castle (apart from the large base, 2.5 feet in diameter, which was transported separately) fit neatly in one 3 foot by 2 foot by 2 foot box!

Floating Castles

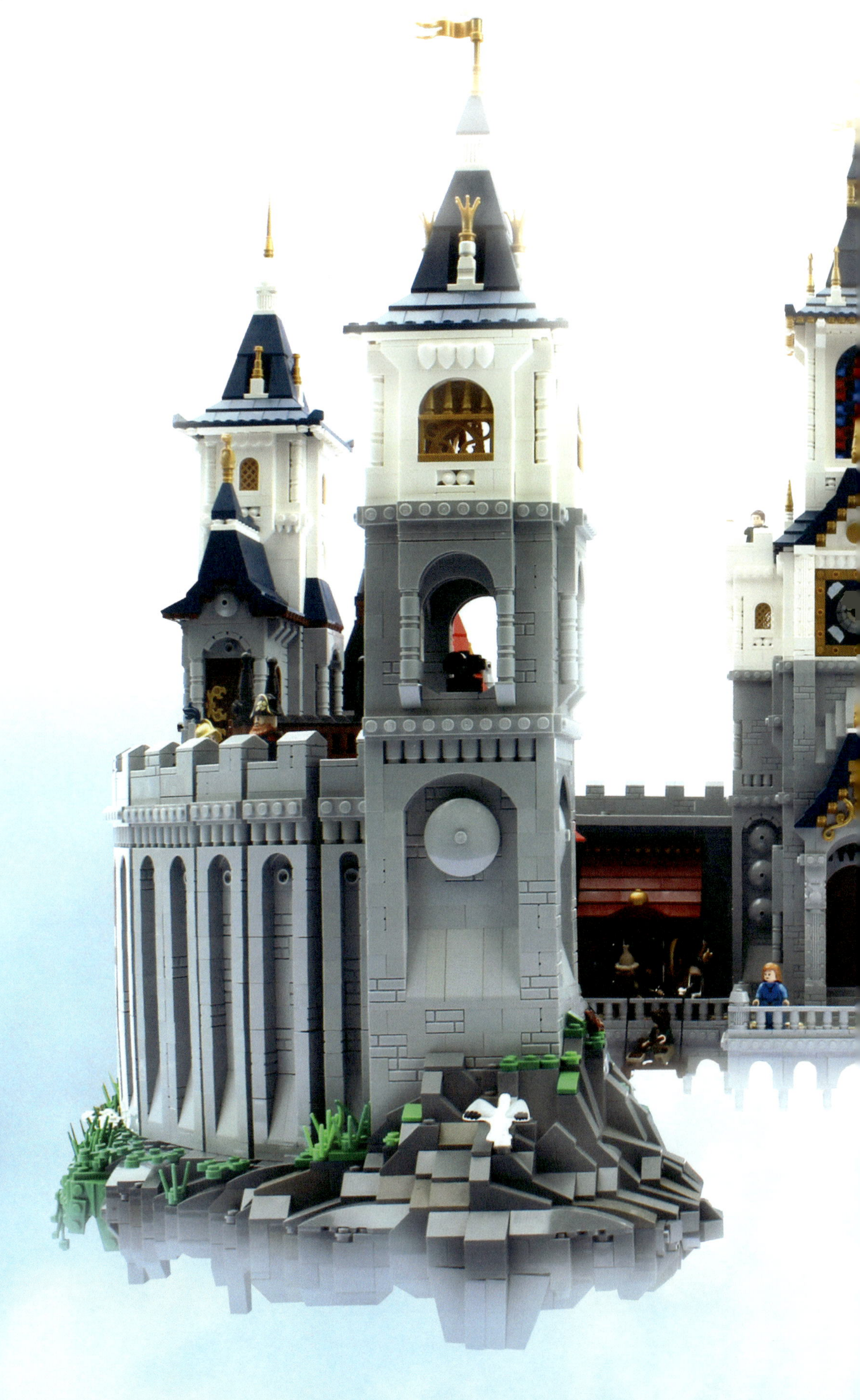

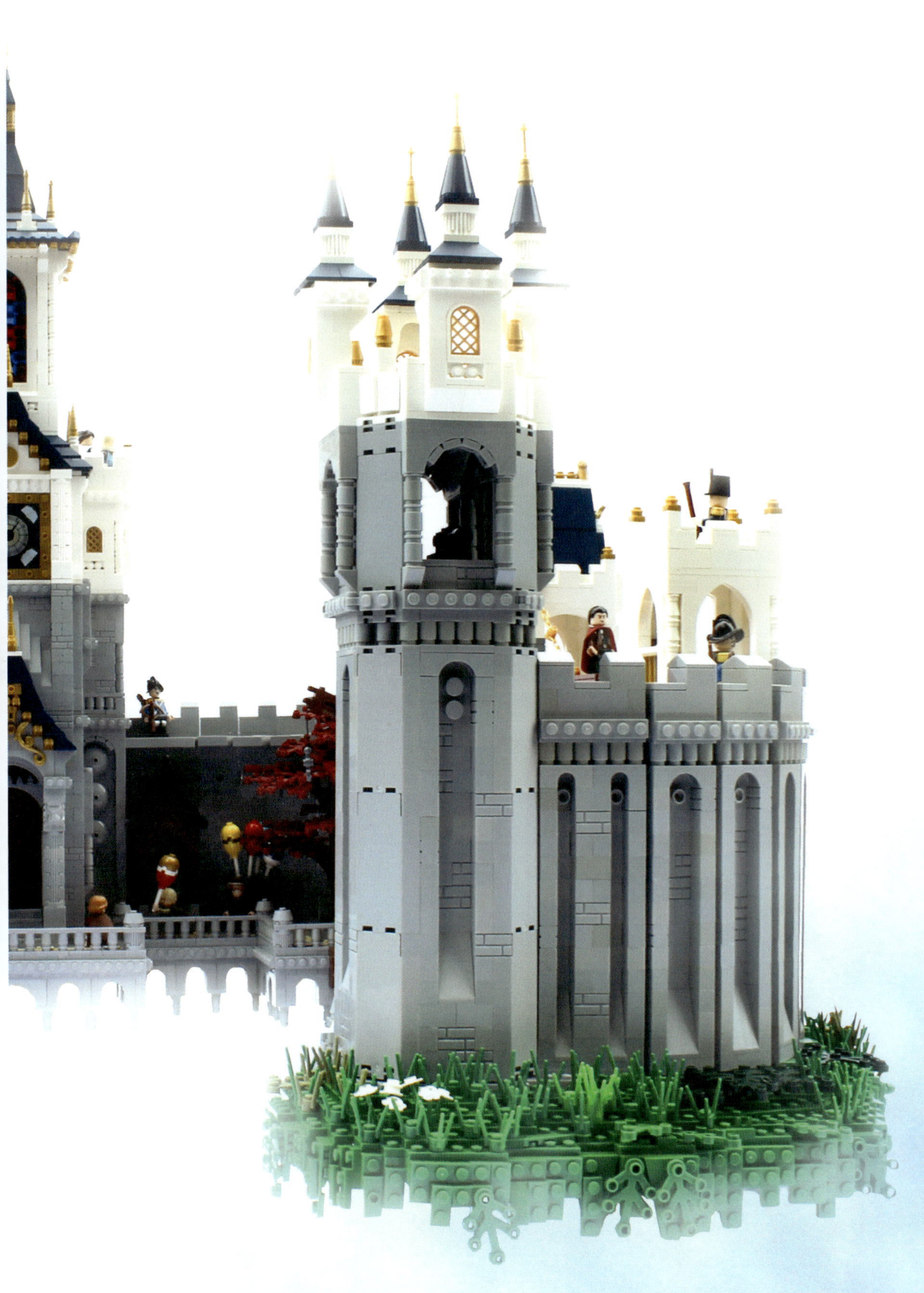

The City of Alaylon

Here's where things really get crazy! **The City of Alaylon** -It's as large as it looks, at about 4 feet by 4 feet and around 3 feet tall! It took around 3 months to complete and was built specifically for a collaboration project with my LEGO® users group (LUG).

Nearly every architectural detail I've ever concocted in a previous creation was added to the mix here and put on full display. The general look was "Strength, Wealth & Fantasy" as Alaylon represents a city with military readiness but was constructed as an artistic masterpiece. The top sections are a pure, clean white to emphasize this extreme wealth, but the lower parts of the walls are more heavy-duty and are stronger to defend the treasures within.

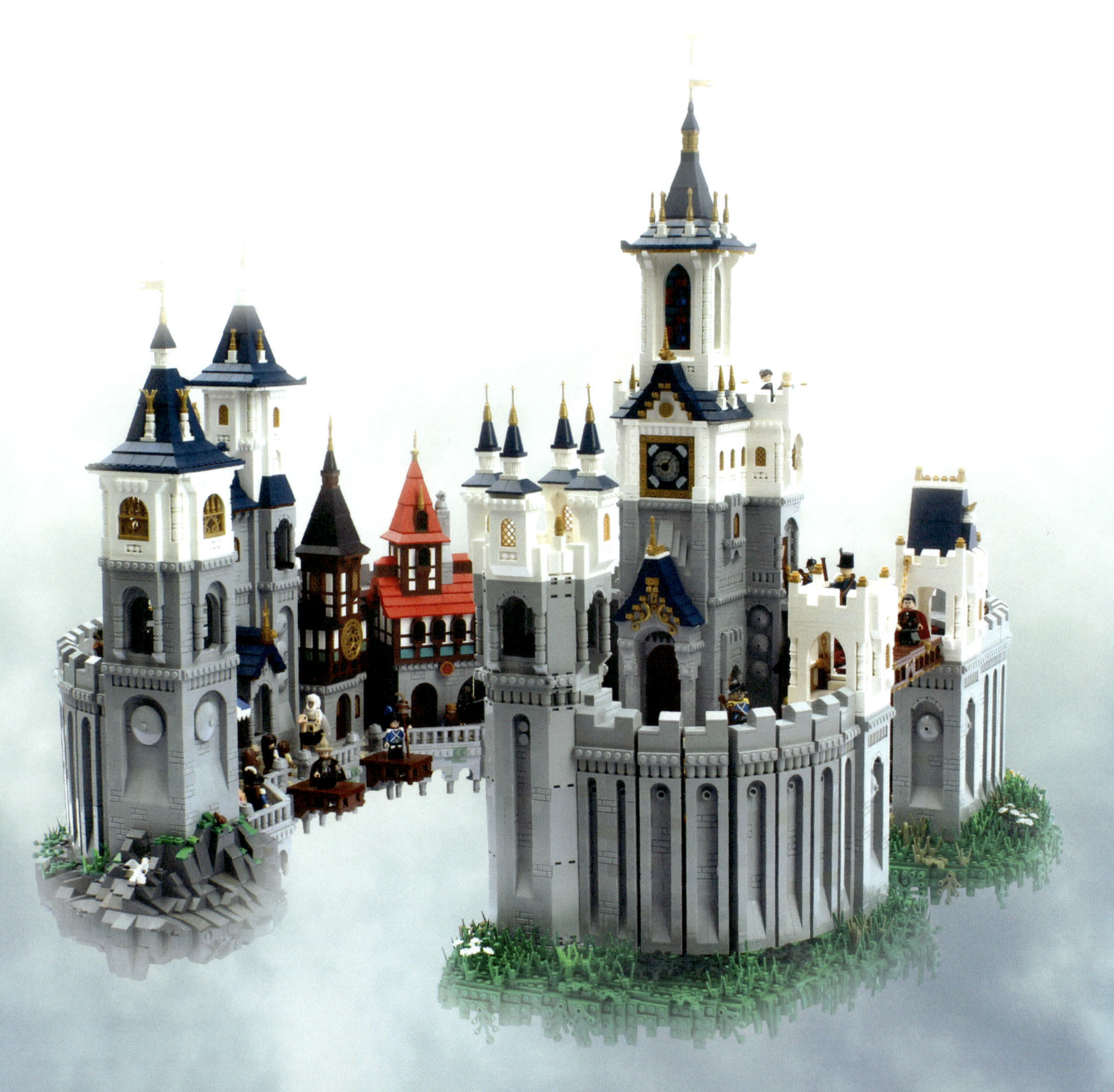

The City of Alaylon

But it's not all about the walls and towers. Alaylon was built with many features inside, including a blacksmith forge, a market center, an orchard, a tavern, and docks for harboring airships. When this creation was on display in Chicago in 2018, one of the most popular questions I was asked was "How did you transport this thing?!" The answer applies to most of my larger builds and it's a simple technique - modularity.

The large clock tower could come apart into 4 separate pieces, the walls could be removed from the landscape, and most of the towers were built in 2 sections, making the whole thing much more managable for transport.

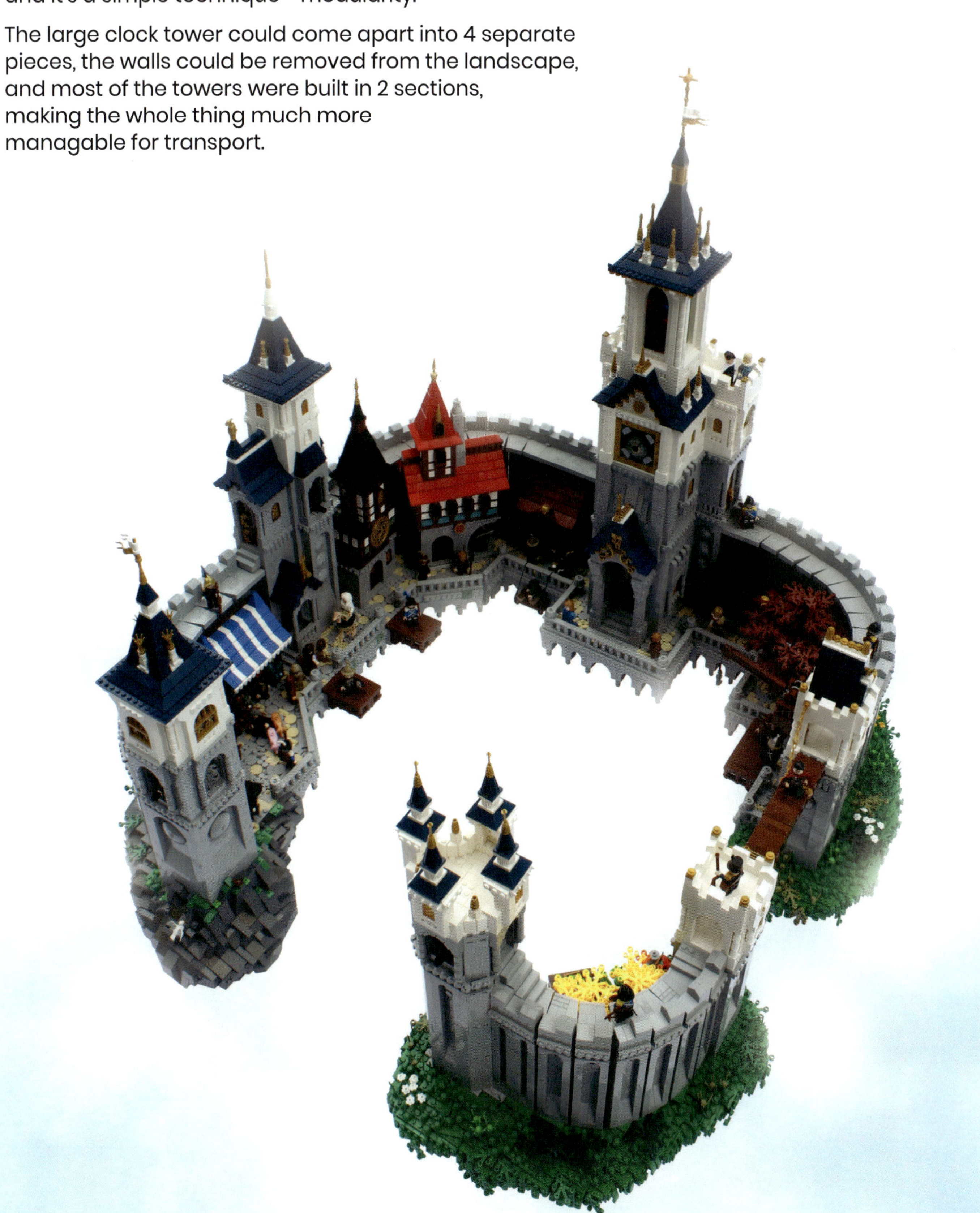

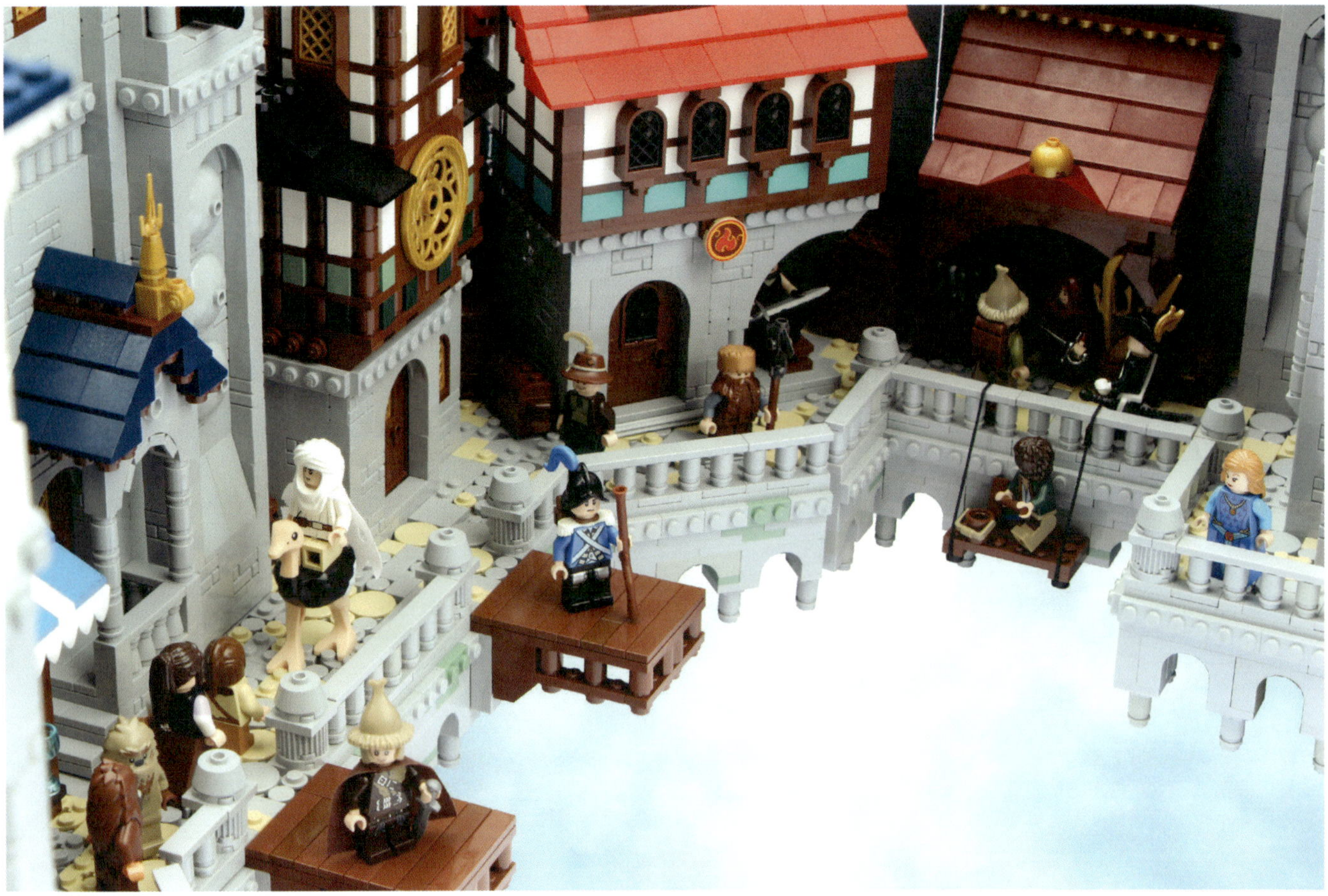

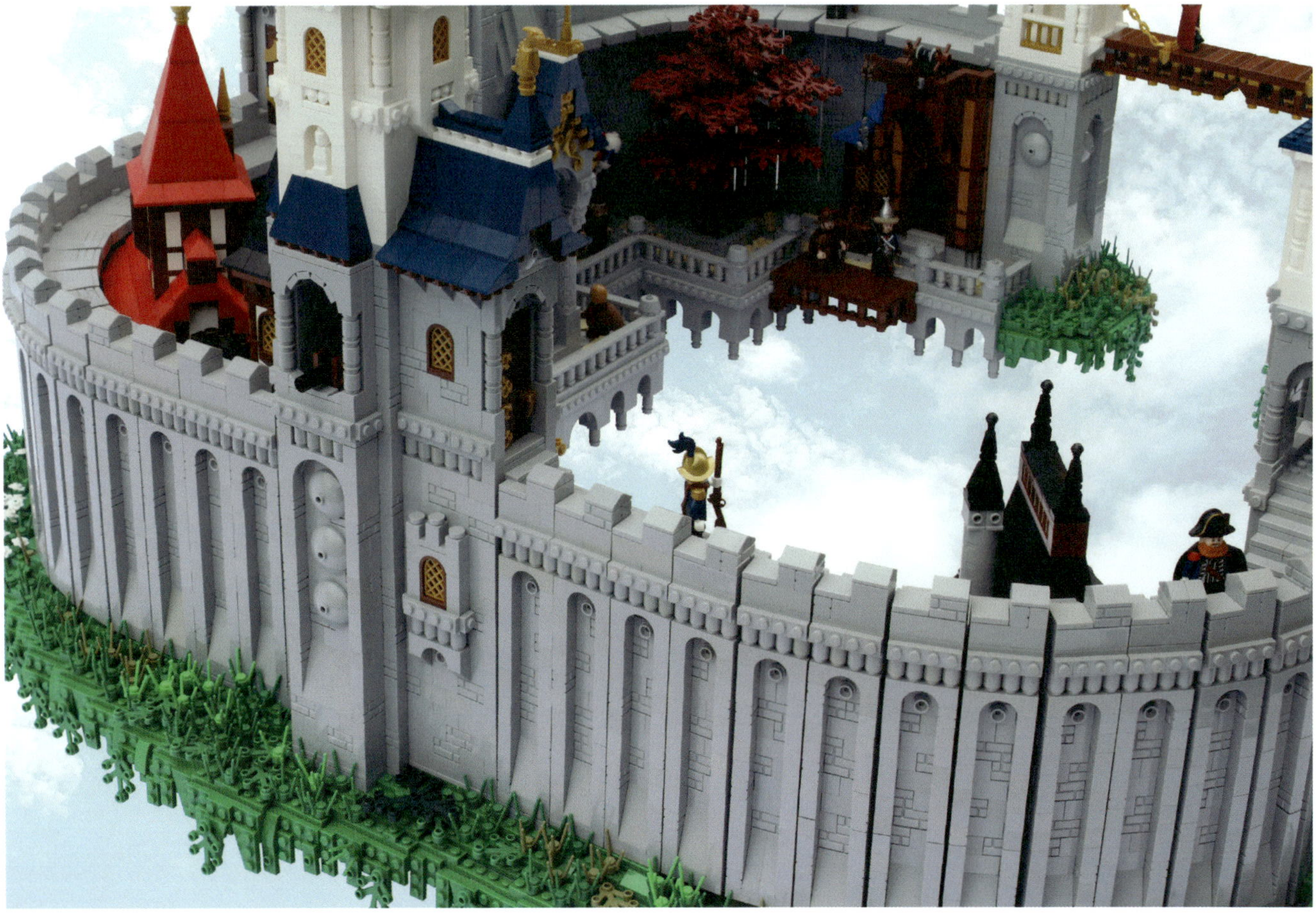

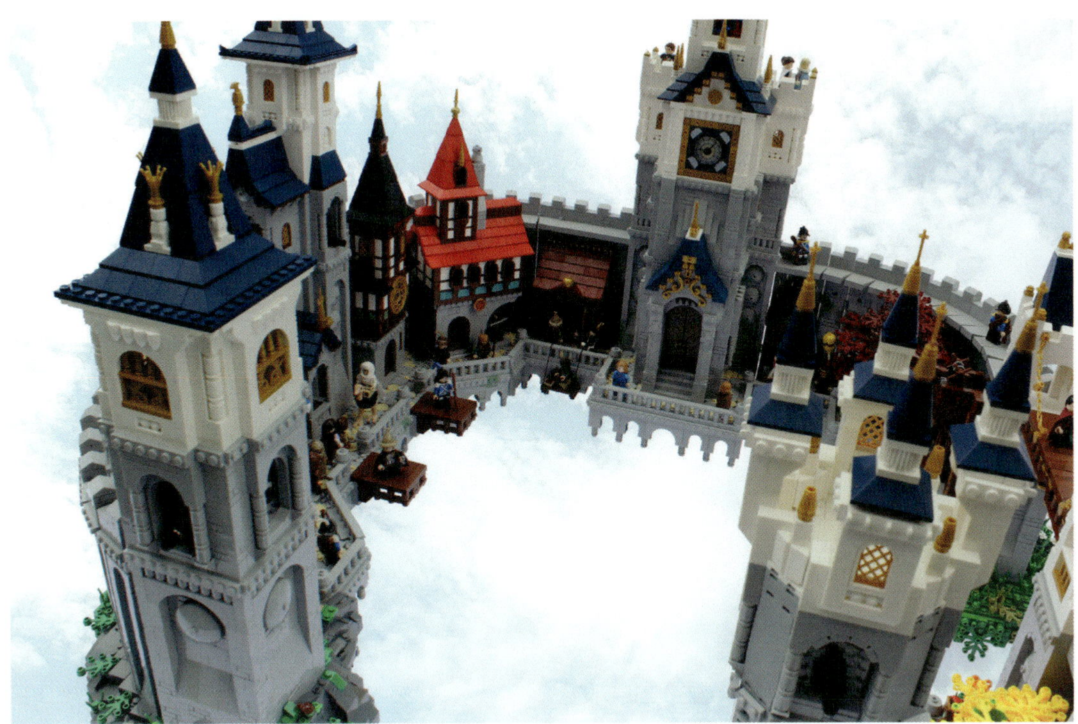

So, a fun fact about the city of Alaylon is the name itself, which comes from ancient Greek and means "one another". I found this appropriate considering that this castle was the centerpiece for our largest collaboration yet.

One of the things I enjoy most about this MOC is the unique Floating Islands theme - something that the members of my LUG and I called the Isles of Aura - a combination of castle and steampunk employing the best elements of both. It uses the general structural styles of castle like Tudor and crenellation with some exotic elements like fanciful beasts but adds gunpowder and flying ships from the steampunk genre.

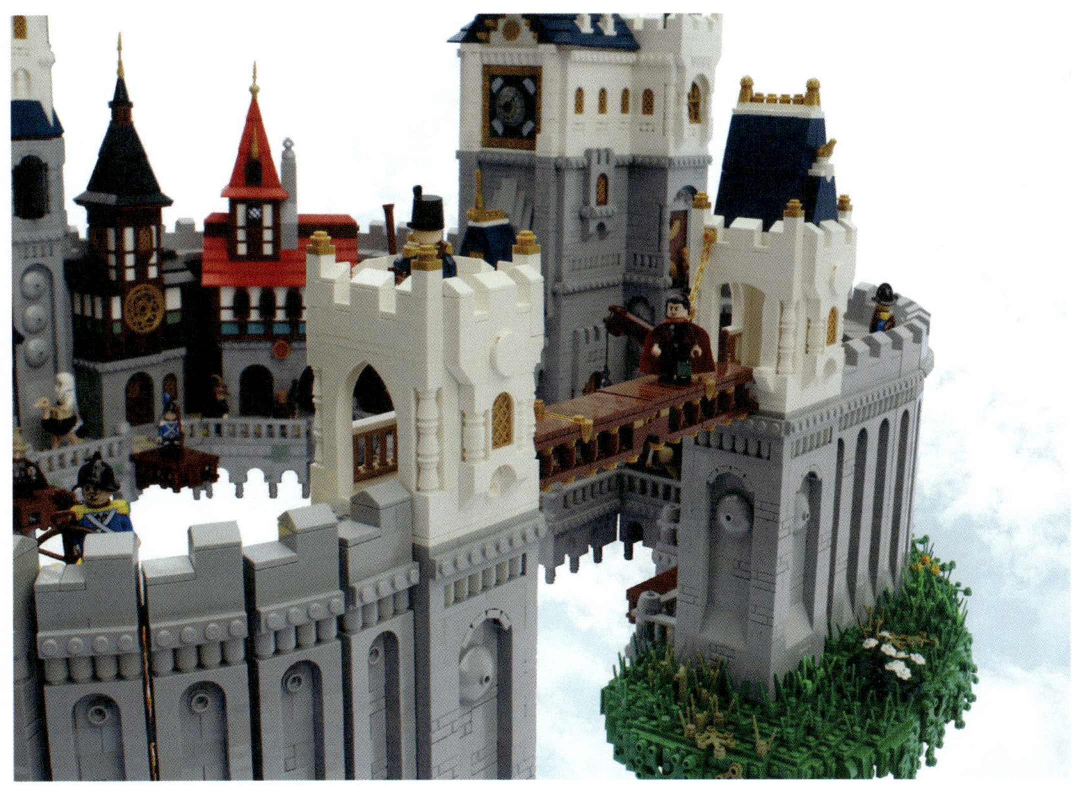

A brief note: when I first uploaded this creation on Flickr, people absolutely loved the description so I thought I should include it here for your reading pleasure (see right).

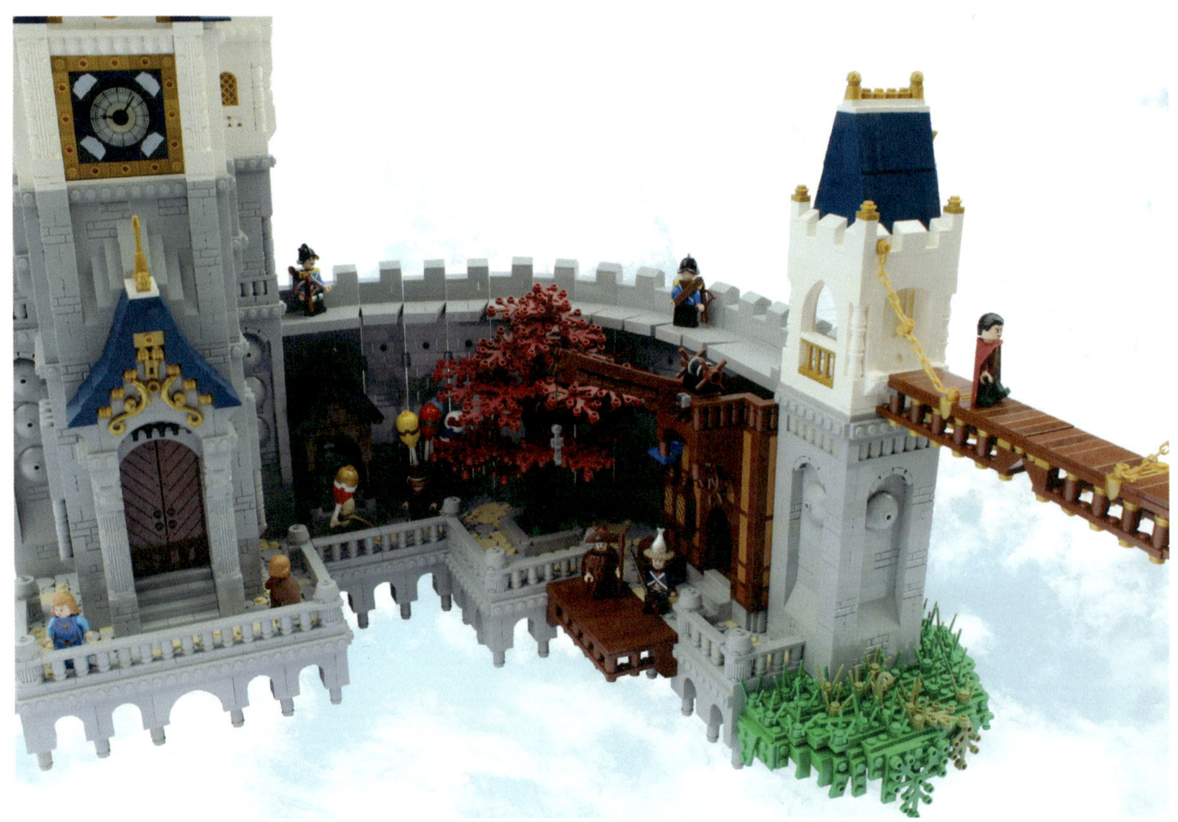

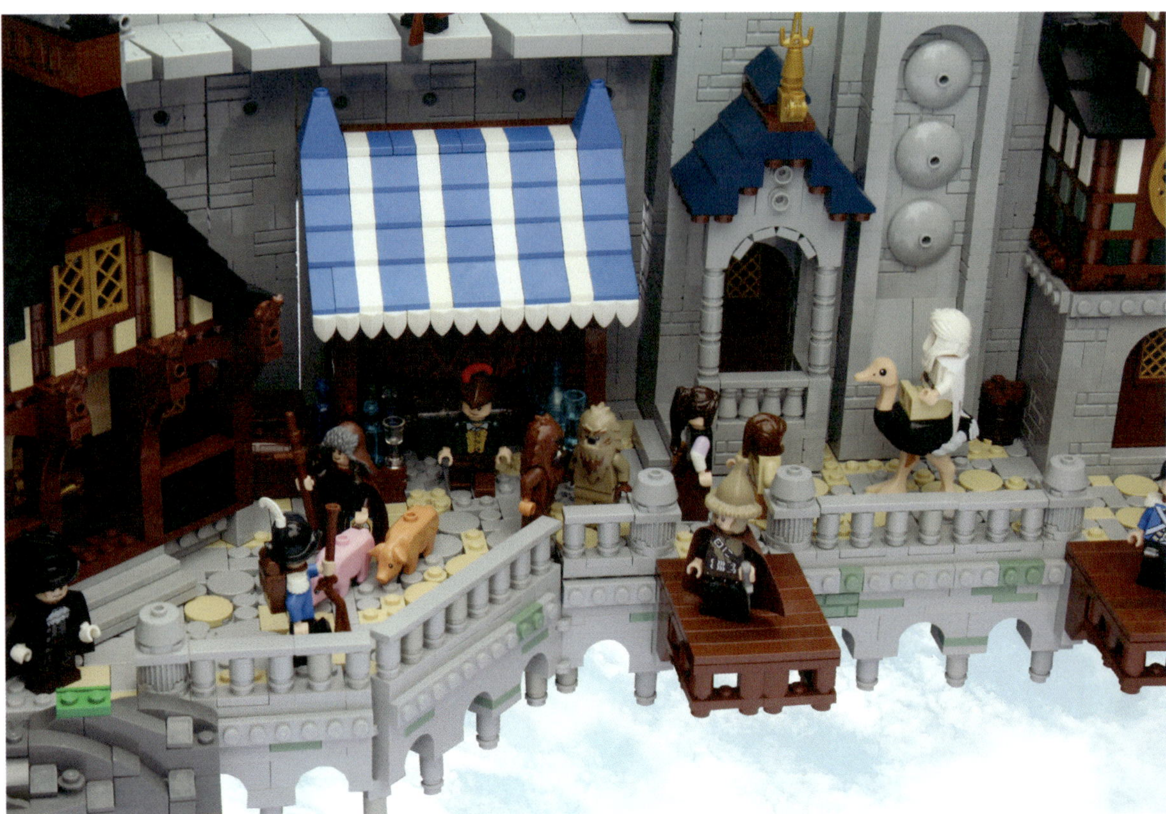

The century-old merchant city of Alaylon is a beacon of prosperity and power for the Cerulean kingdom. It is also known as "The Crown of Cerulea" resting upon the brow of the heavens. Its signature shape is as much art as function.

The city is nearly impossible for large ships to attack for the shape of the walls creates a steady spiraled vortex inside the city which keeps invading ships from coming up or down upon it. This current also keeps the city upright like a spinning plate. Alaylon has an annual cycle - it drifts along a massive jetstream that loops along the interior of the Cerulean border in a circuitous route.

No one is really sure how such a heavy structure floats so effortlessly, even with the assisting winds, because the legendary architect who built it - Sir Alberto Mauriccio - wrote all the plans and layouts in his own invented language so no one could copy his precious life's work.

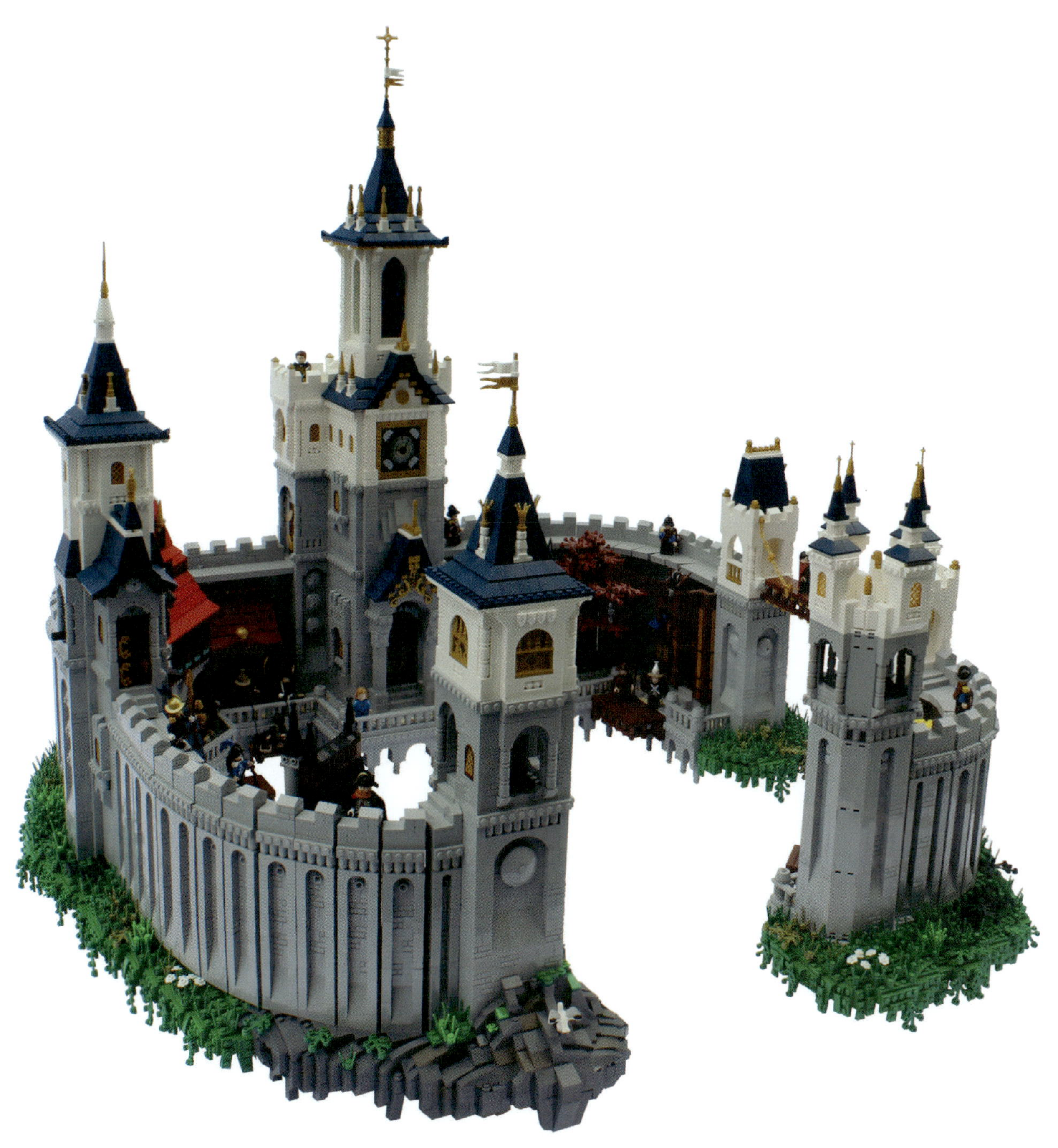

The Isle of Dalkaria

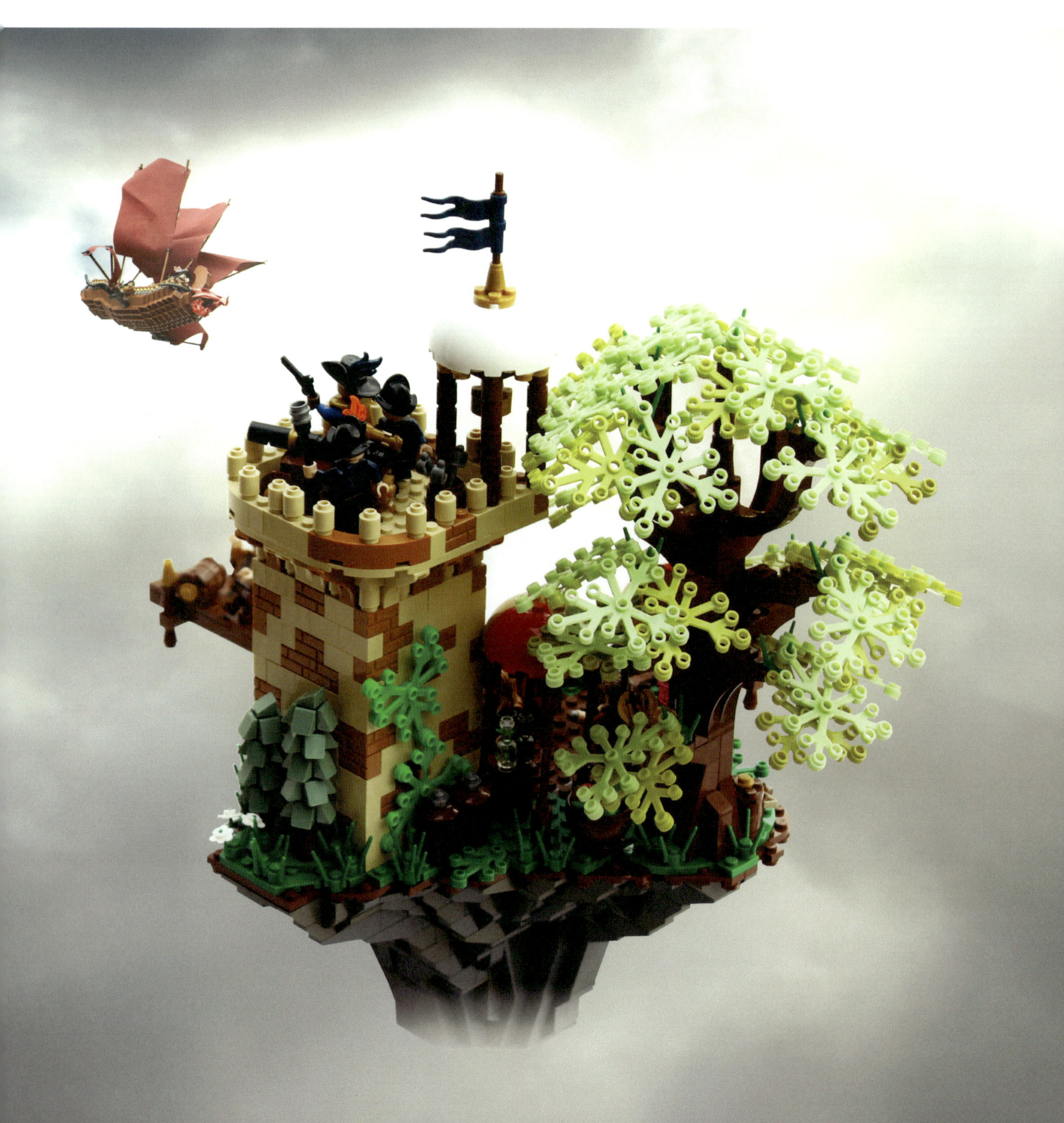

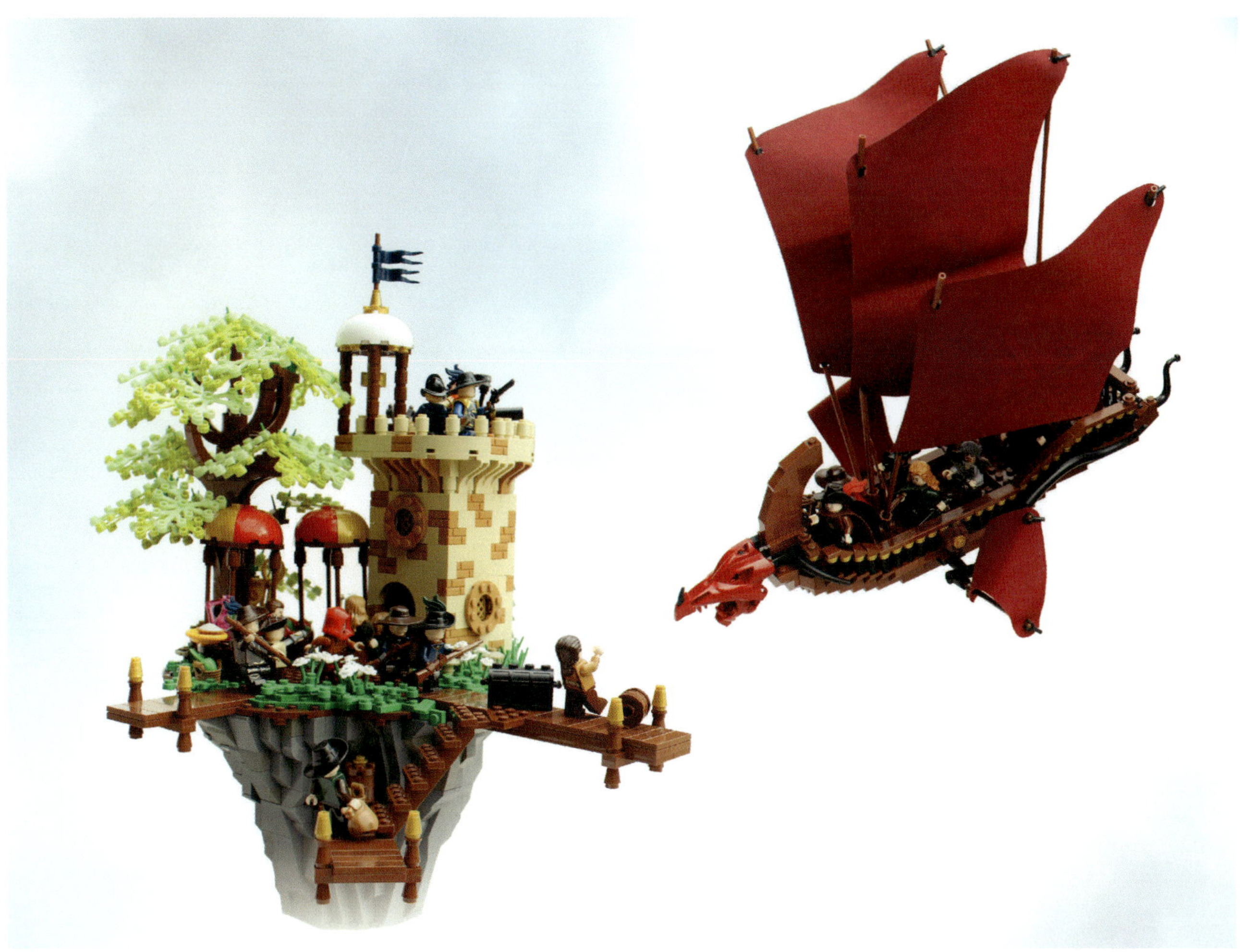

In the earlier days of the Isles of Aura subgenre, which was informally known as "The World of Wind", I was experimenting with some new techniques, specifically the upside-down rockwork on the bottom of this island!

Basically, all you have to do is build a rockwork structure, turn it upside down, and then build another MOC on top of it, connecting the two with some LEGO® 'technic' elements. The reason for this technique is the fact that there is far more variety in LEGO® elements sloping downward rather than upward, which helps give the mountain more detail.

Airships are a bit different than normal ships! For the pirate Airship design, I actually incorporated more elements that I use for animal building rather than boat building in a typical ship to give it more of a body of a creature rather than a vessel.

An advantage for me personally building these floating islands is - I got to employ my favorite concept, a lot in a little! (cramming in lots of detail without overwhelming the creation) For example, there are 13 minifigures on the island alone, along with a small produce market and a tower! There was even some room for foliage, a larger oak, and some smaller evergreens.

One thing that should be mentioned was the use of third-party LEGO® lookalike elements used on the oak tree. These leaf colors are not available currently in LEGO® parts.

MINIFIGS

Sometimes a lone character can be just as interesting as an entire LEGO® MOC.

The only thing I carry over from building a whole creation as opposed to just a minifig is color consistency. You definitely want the details consistent as well but it's not the same as a larger build.

Also in this section you'll see vignettes, tiny scenes that are of equal relevance to the minifigs they showcase. Neither the scene or the minifig are the main focus but complement each other beautifully.

In this section, we'll showcase some examples of LEGO®'s huge variety of LEGO® parts and elements, but I'd also like to mention that there are plenty of elements in here that are not LEGO® or have been heavily modified and customized.

For minifigs, you have great opportunities for dramatic and in-depth photography like macro (zoomed-in) shots, and more emphasis on lighting and backgrounds. A normal creation is focused on clarity and presentation of the overall image.

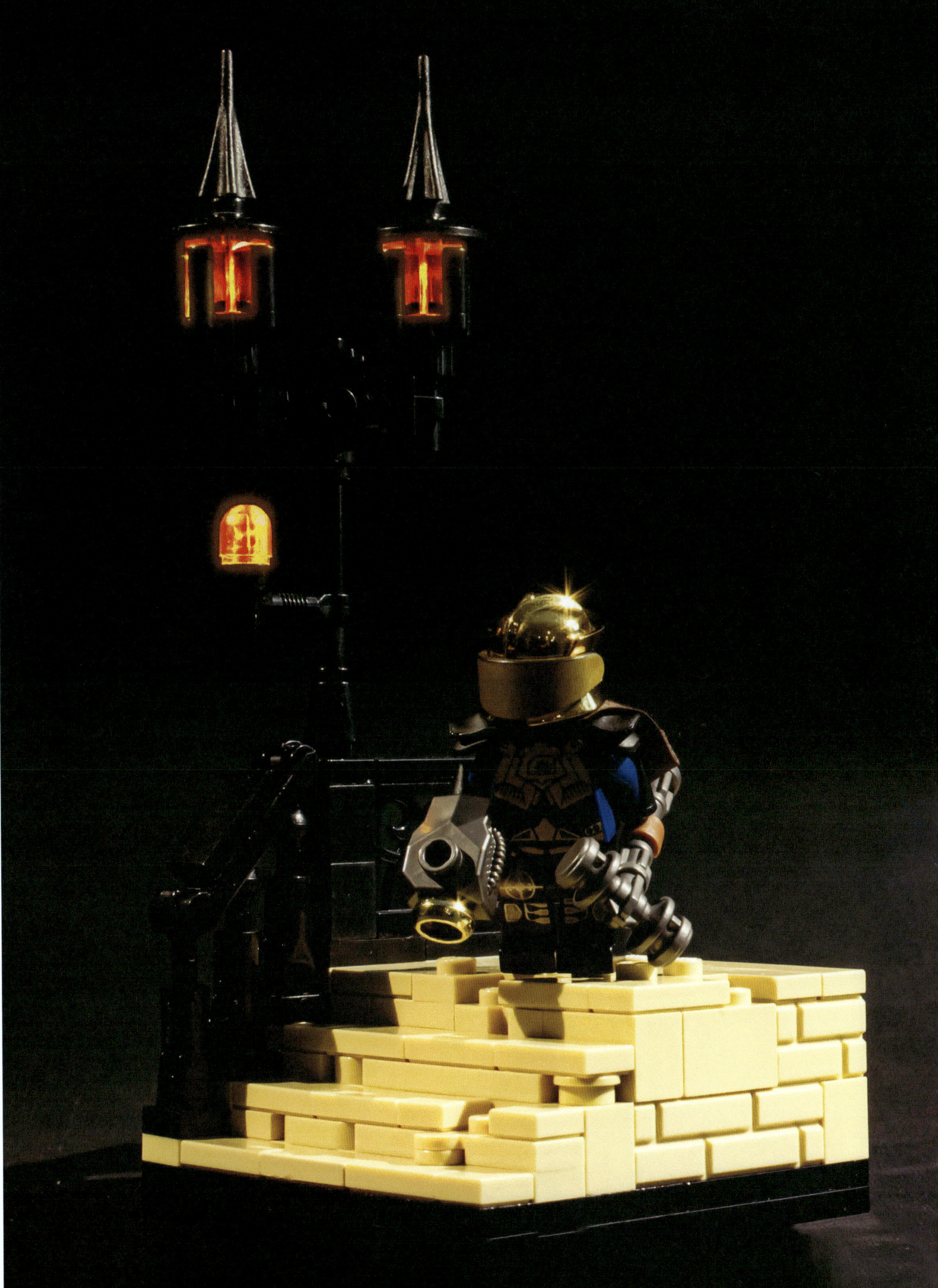

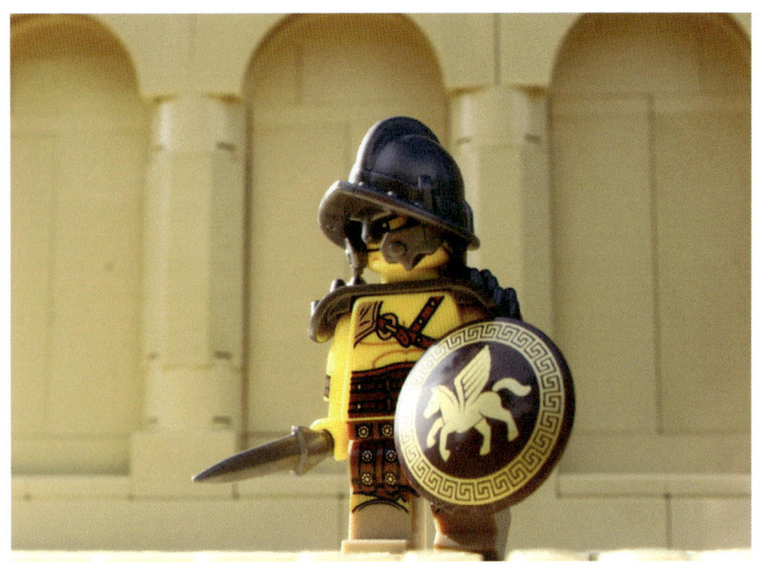

A lot of these minifigs (but not all) were created for something we called the "Bro Fig Brawls", an online contest between me and my older brother, Mark.

Both of us would upload a character or group of characters of similar genres and then have people comment and vote on which was their favorite.

Interestingly, we had an equal amount of wins and losses! Everything pictured here in this book are ones that I built and uploaded.

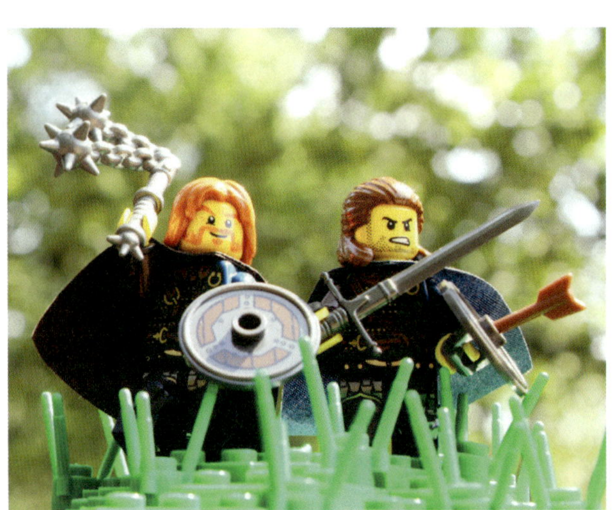

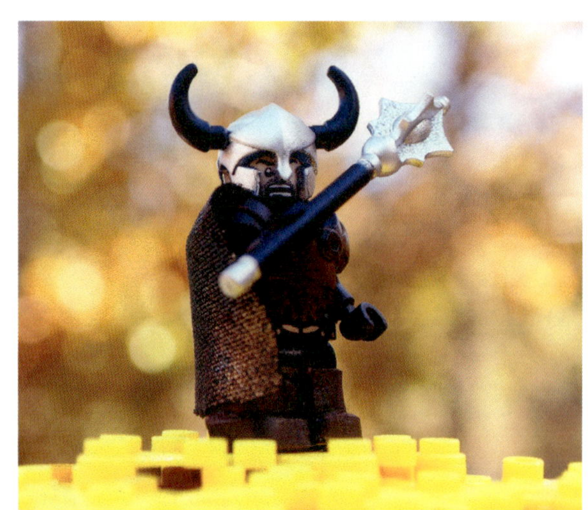

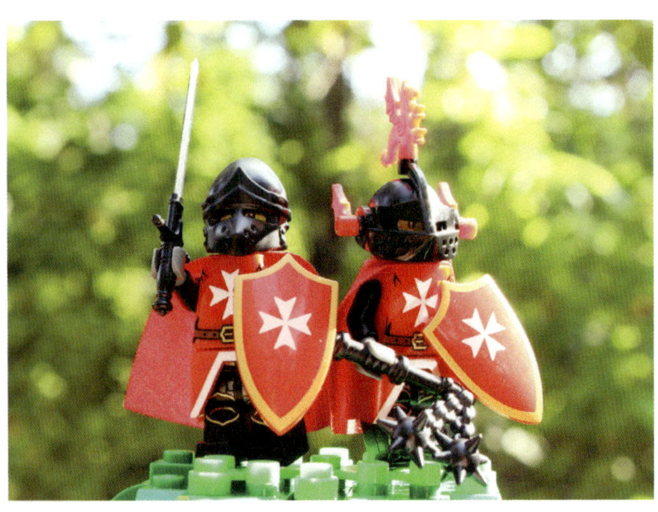

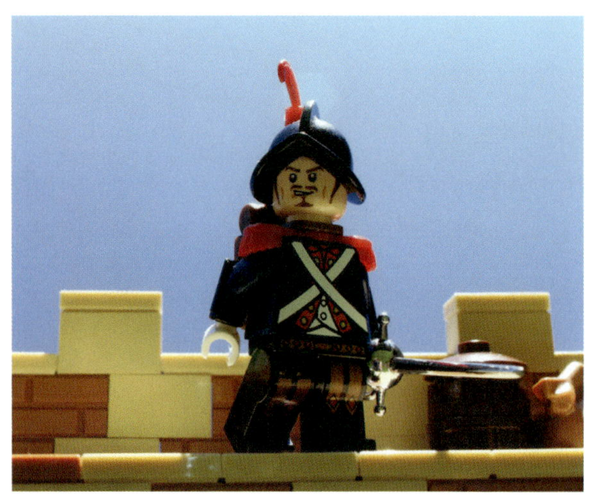

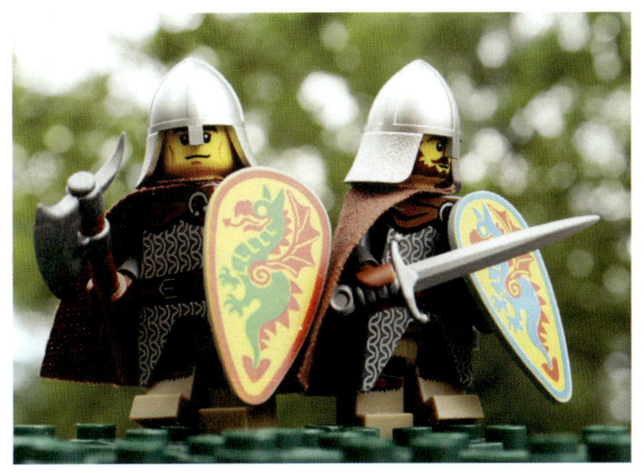

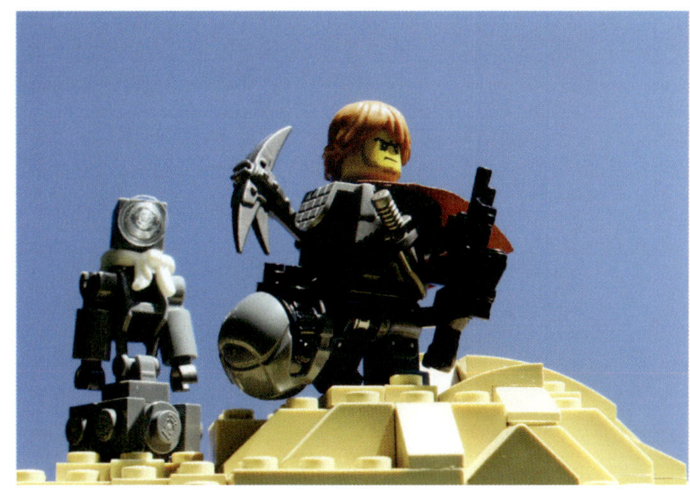

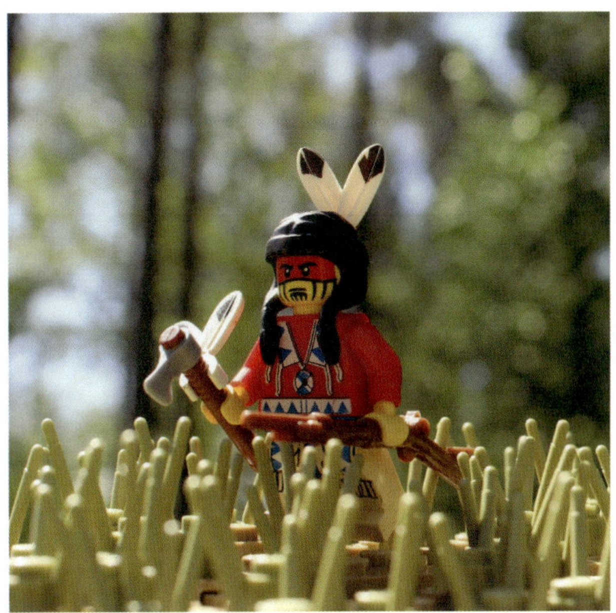

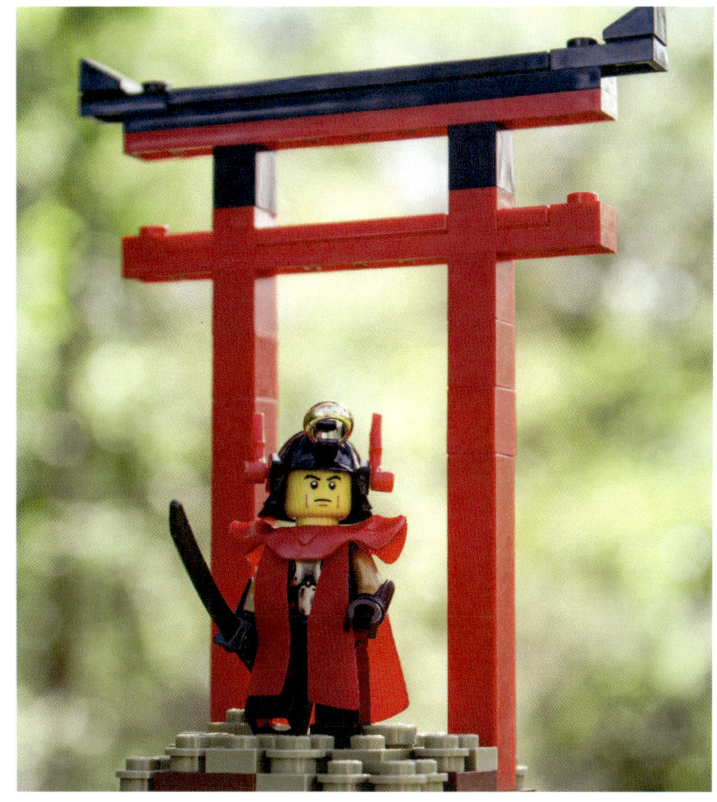

Another event that inspired the creation of these figures was the Colossal Castle Contest. Every year, this contest would have a variety of challenge categories in different medieval-themed categories. One of the most consistent themes was "Custom Minifigures". Some of these characters, including the viking on the opposite page with the hot-glued leather boots, were in this contest.

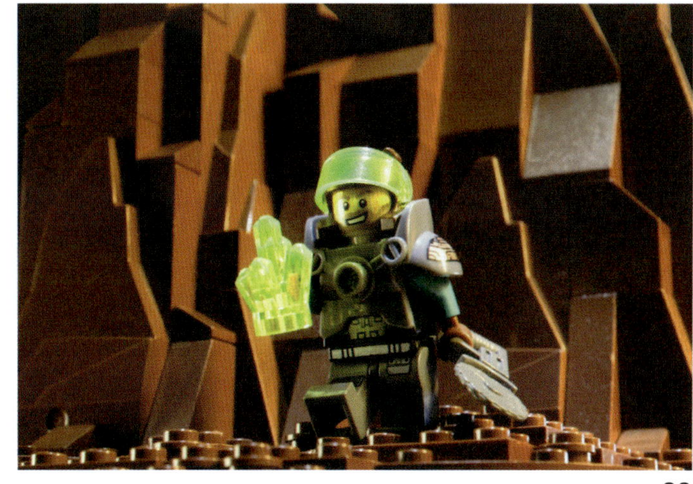

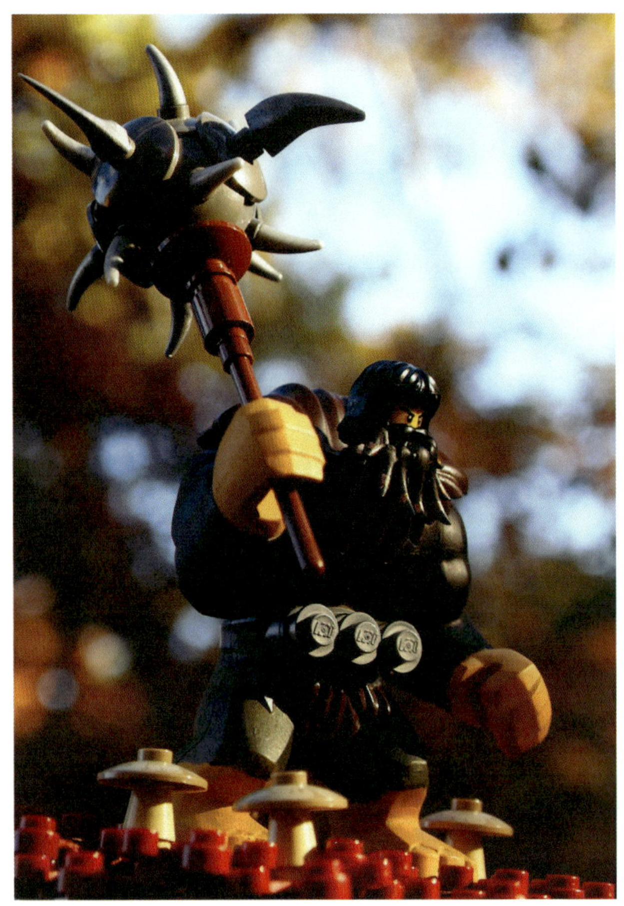

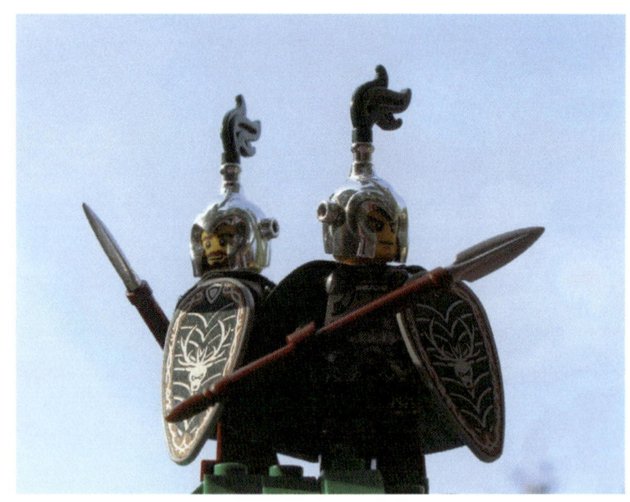

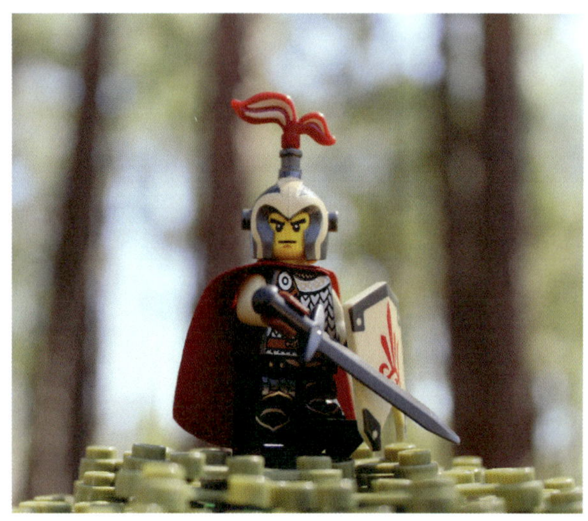

One character I'd like to highlight is **Groz the Giant**. He used to be a wooly mammoth maxifig from the LEGO® "Chima" line, but was given a custom paint job! He has a standard size minifig head with a custom beard formed from hot glue and then painted! Although I love the character, I would not recommend this level of customization unless it's for a very special occasion.

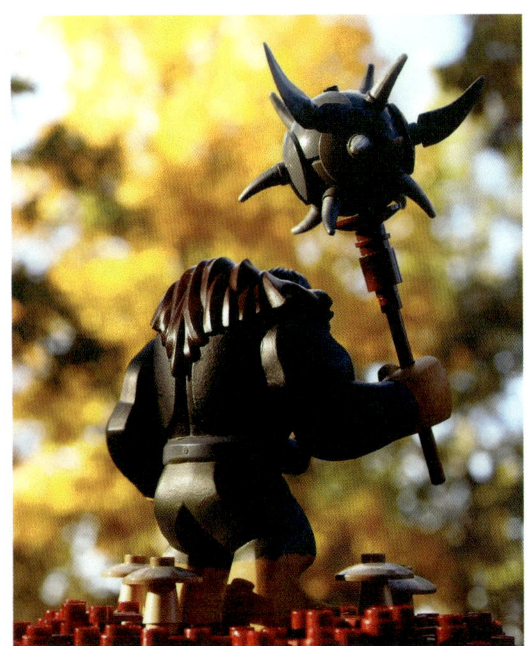

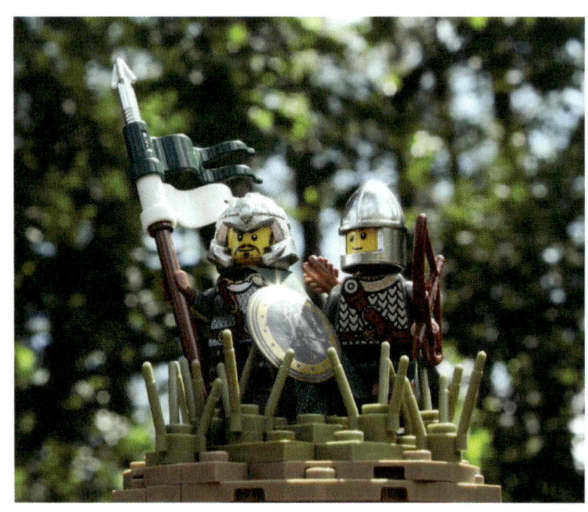

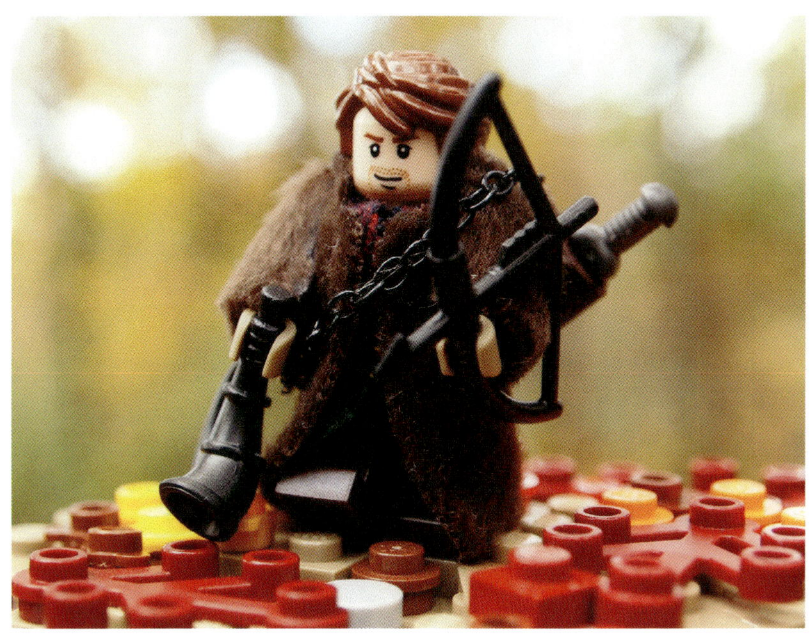

The Elk Hunter (see right) has another custom accessory - his heavy fur coat is in three pieces, the vest slips on over the body but sleeves are glued to the arms. He also has a custom leather sword sheath which has a chain glued to either end.

The Elk Hunter and Groz the Giant were made for the Colossal Castle Contest (the Elk Hunter nabbed an Honorable Mention).

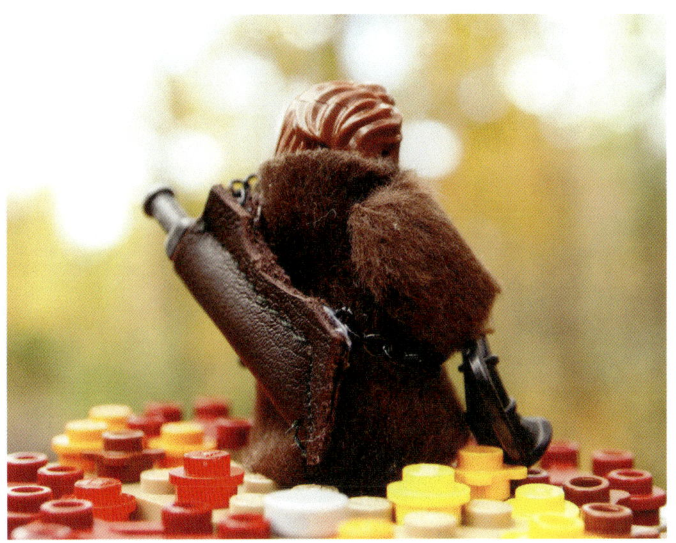

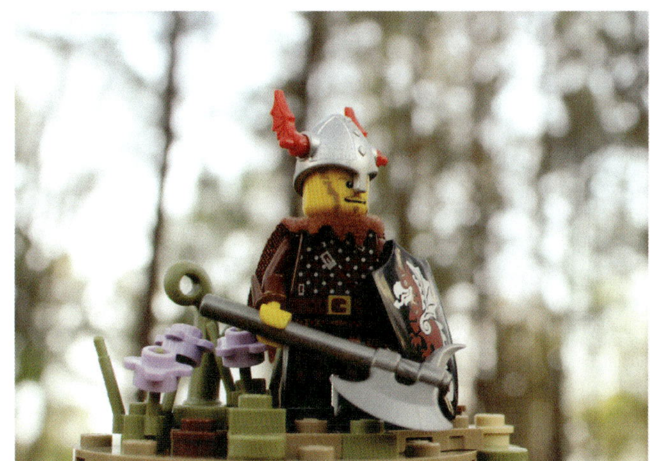

I'm proud of all the characters here, but for some reason the ones that really stood out in a big way are the the **Fungi Freedom Fighters** (right). These guys completely stole the show for their Bro Fig Brawl round, and I just love them. Who knows, I may do more in the future!

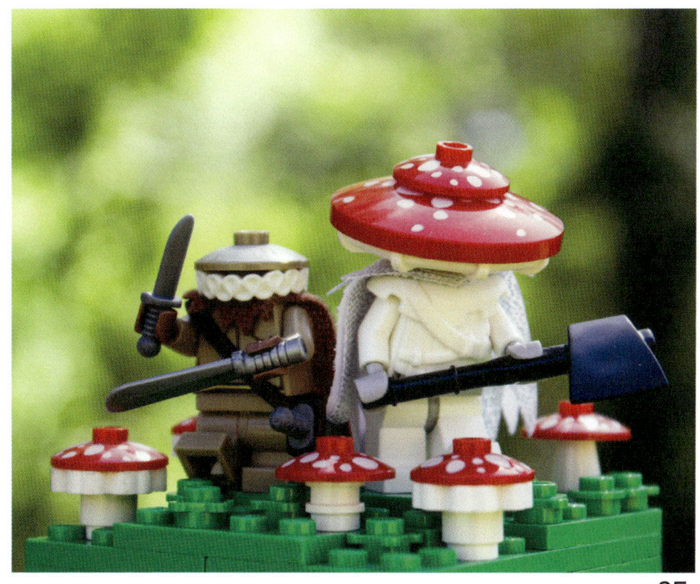

Vignettes

Vignettes are a highlighted minifigure and a creation combined in one small, but delightful, scene.

Most of these are a lot in a little, pushed to the absolute max! Some are a tad larger but nearly all of these are 8x8 studs or less in size.

The vignette on the right, **Bee Keeping**, was for the Colossal Castle Contest (CCC) as well and represents medieval beekeeping.

The trio below, **The Seasonal Coats of the Yetis of Aura** was built for the Isles of Aura and represents the transitioning seasonal pelts of the infamous Yeti. I've always loved the Yeti LEGO® series minifigure, and both him and the Bigfoot are recurring characters in the Isles of Aura. (You may spot them in previous and future Isles of Aura creations in this book!)

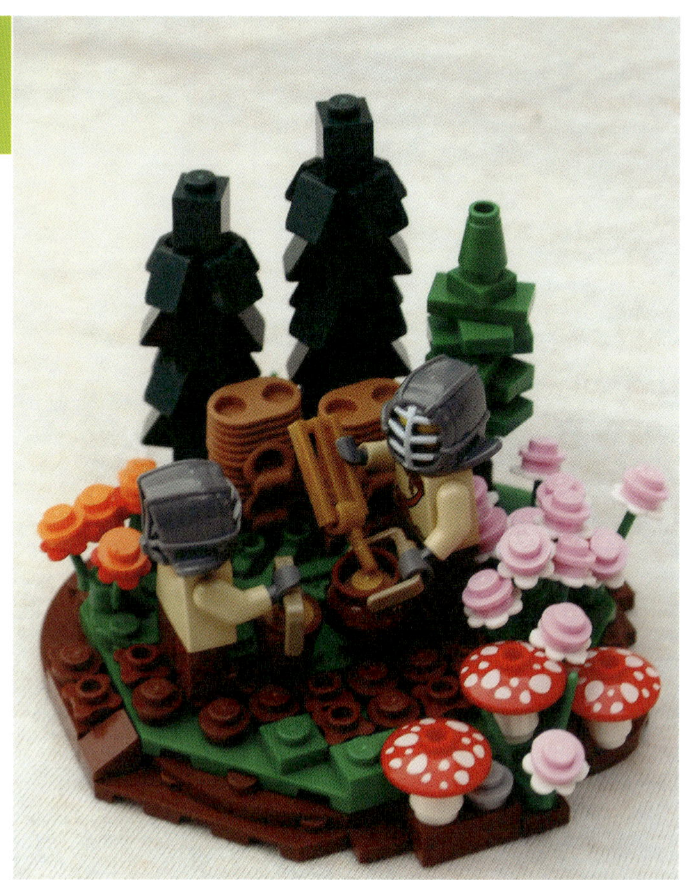

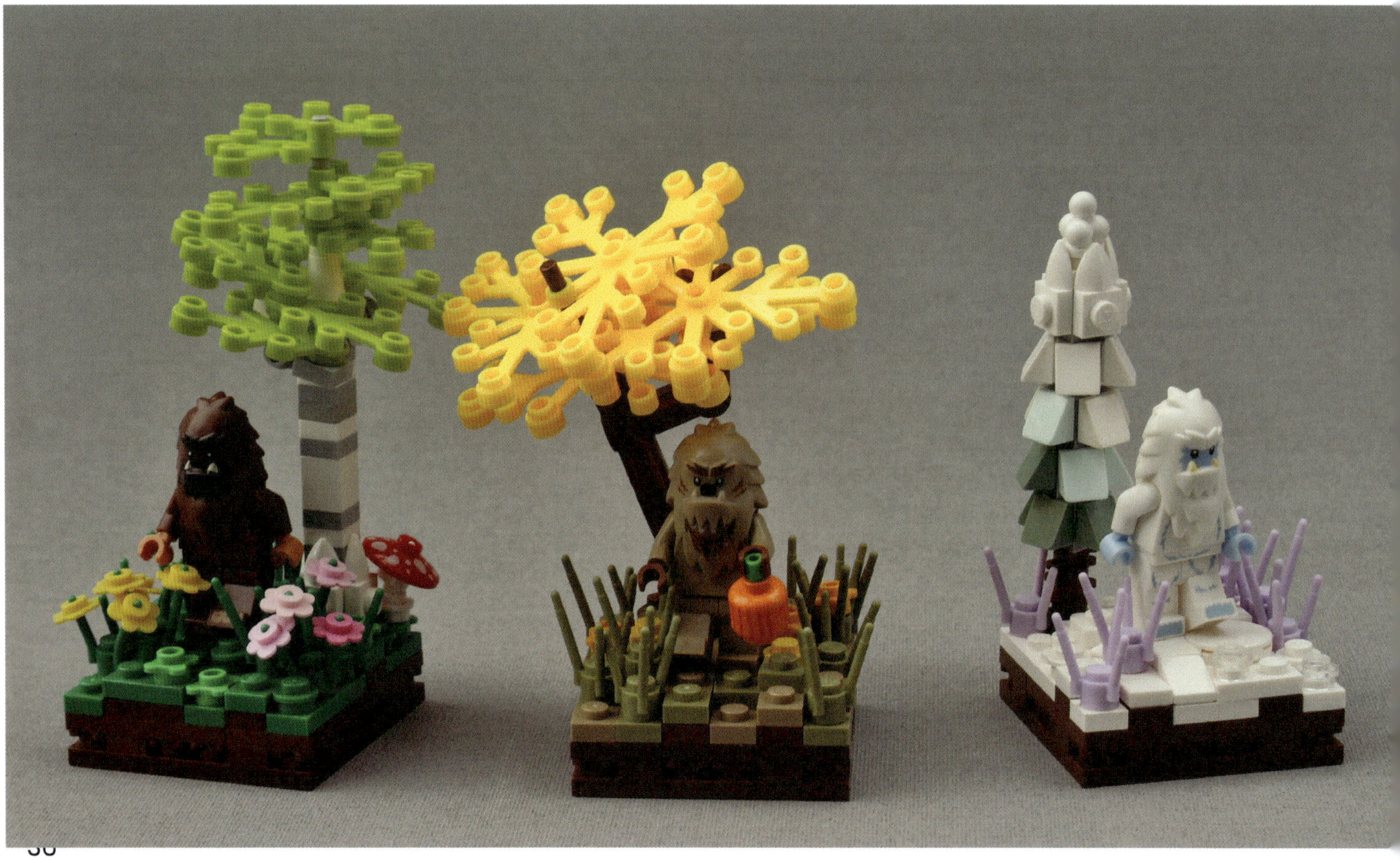

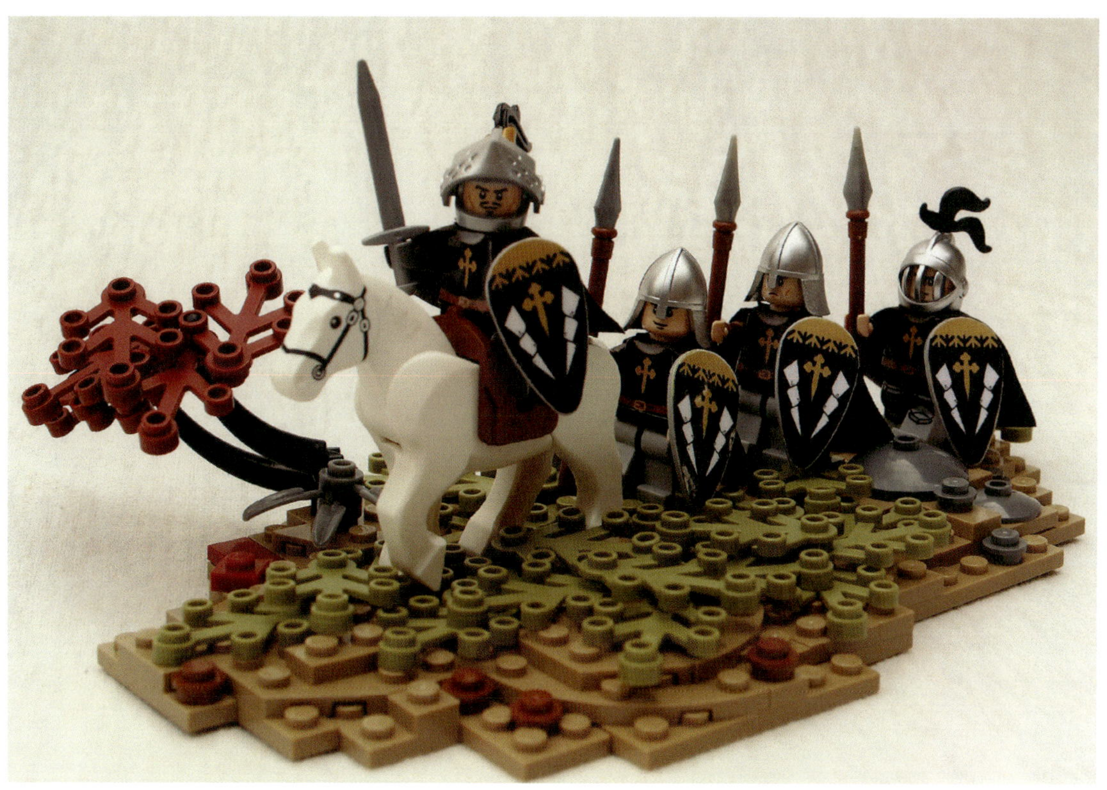

For the **Warriors of Finland**, a Finnish army above, I used custom printed stickers on their shields and torso assemblies. The top edge gold to black transition pattern represents a forest, and the white spirals symbolize birch bark trumpets. Imagery and symbolism were extremely important for medieval heraldry. This build was also built for the CCC.

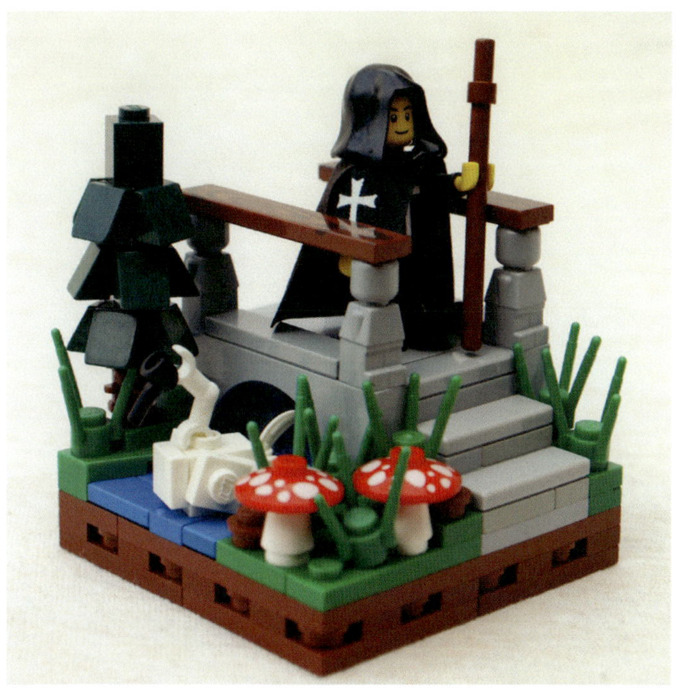

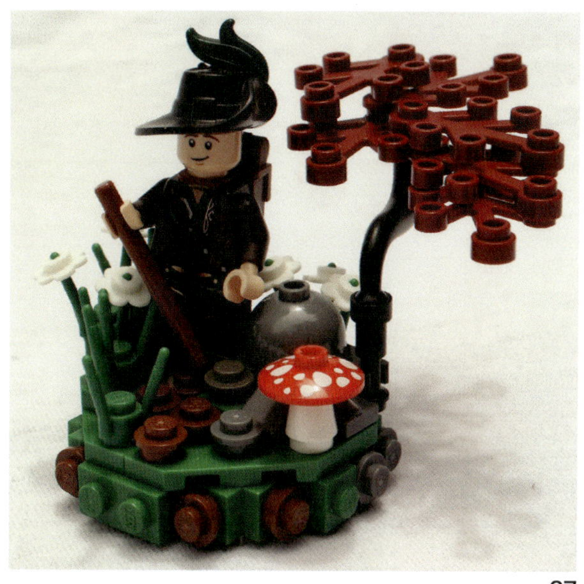

Two figures very iconic for me appear here, right is **Zenas Abbington**, an adventurer in the Isles of Aura, who acts as a narrator for the builds I create in that genre. **Brother Steven** (above) is my own signature avatar figure and one of my oldest characters. (It's no coincidence that Brother Steven is also my Flickr username.)

Fig Barfs

What's a fig barf, you ask? It's a compilation of similarly themed minifigures all posted together in a group shot. It's been a 'thing' for a long time and one of my favorite themes to fig barf is the Isles of Aura.

Below we have some examples - farmers, pirates, and explorers. In the bottom shot, we've also got a dwarf, a dragon tamer, a yeti chief (with husky dog) and a desert explorer.

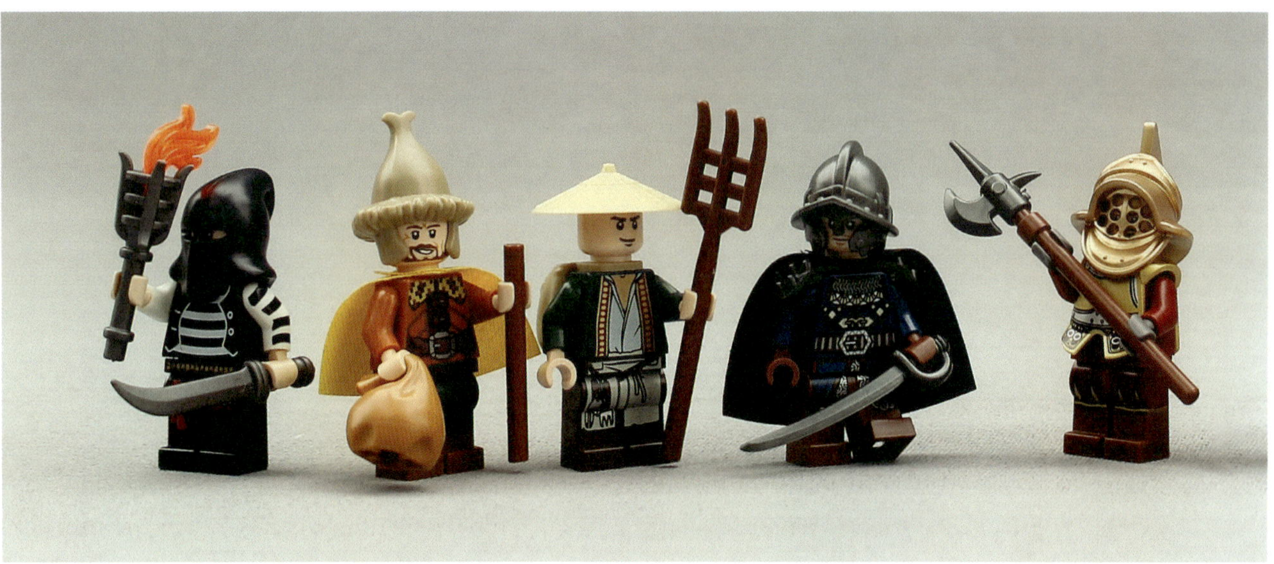

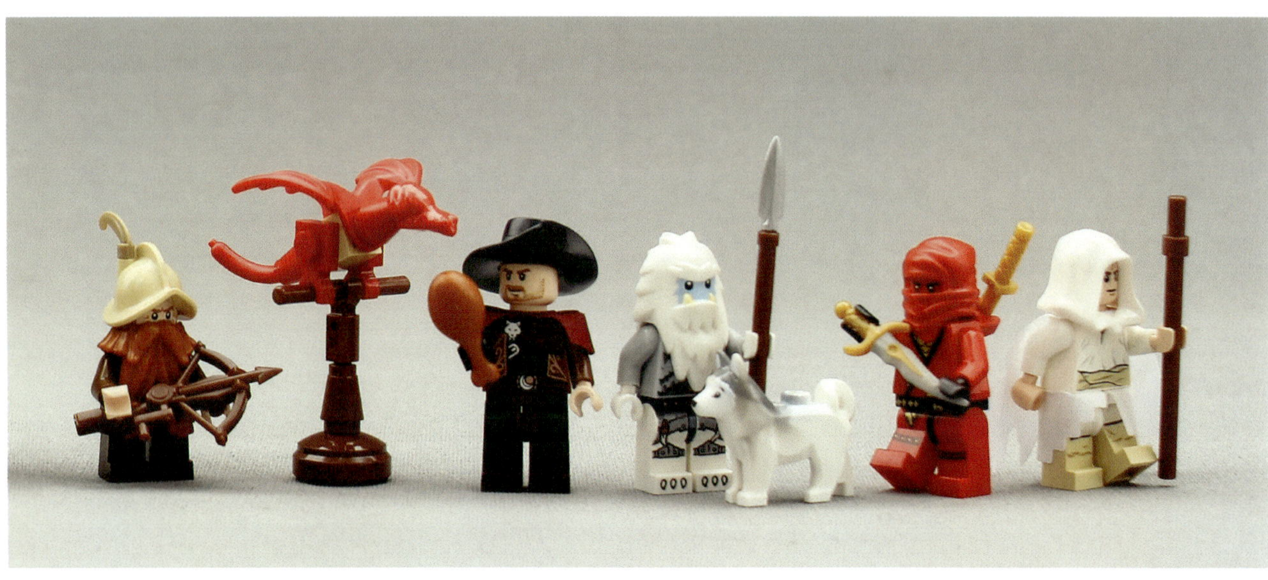

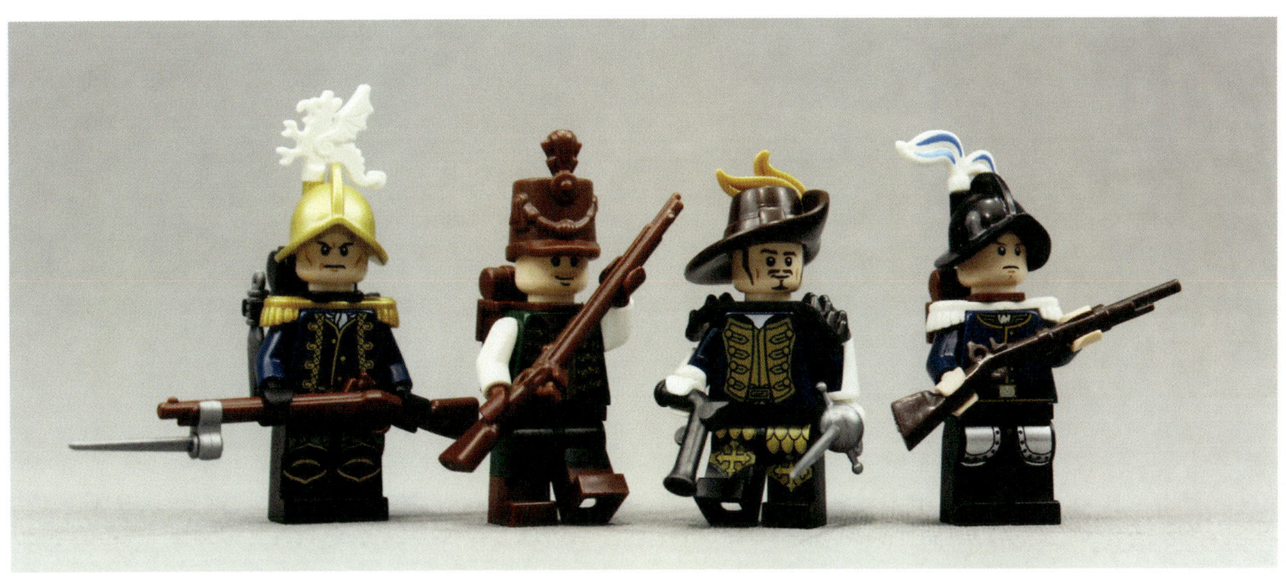

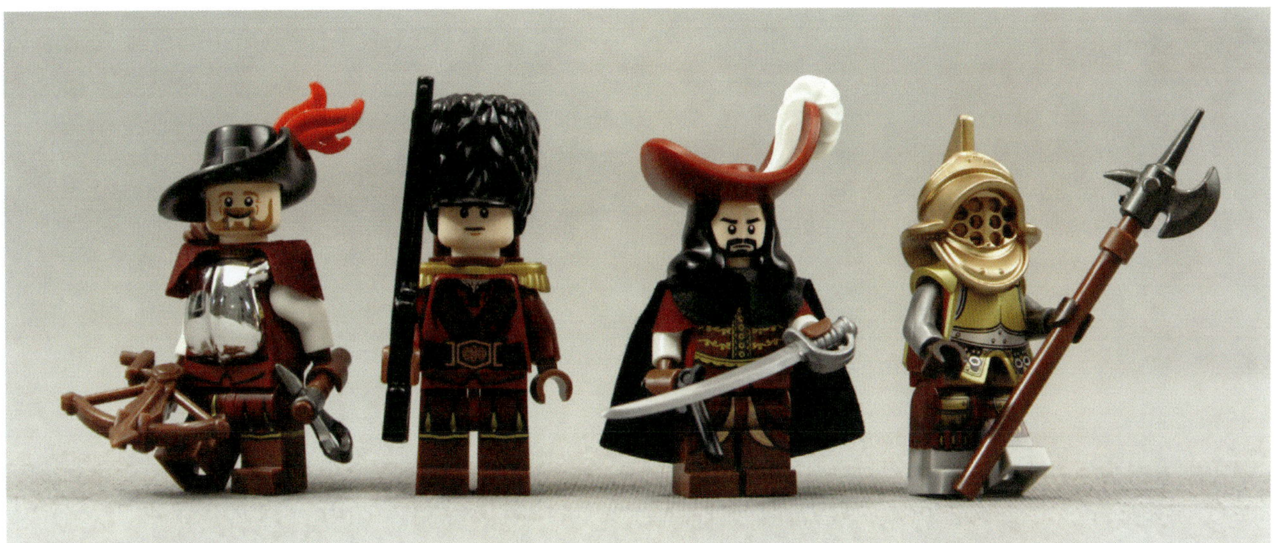

Above, we have two main empires of the Isles of Aura.

(Top) We have the **Cerulean Empire** here in the top photo, who are loosely inspired from late Renaissance-era Spain and Switzerland.

(Bottom) Next, we have the **Vermillion Empire.** These guys are based on late Renaissance-era England and Germany. Basically, these are all from emperial age Europe, sort of going for a fantasy mashup of Pirate and Castle themes, both using gunpowder.

There are many third-party elements here, including the the rifles, swords, crossbow, axes, and bayonets, as well as the musketeer's brown hat in the top photo.

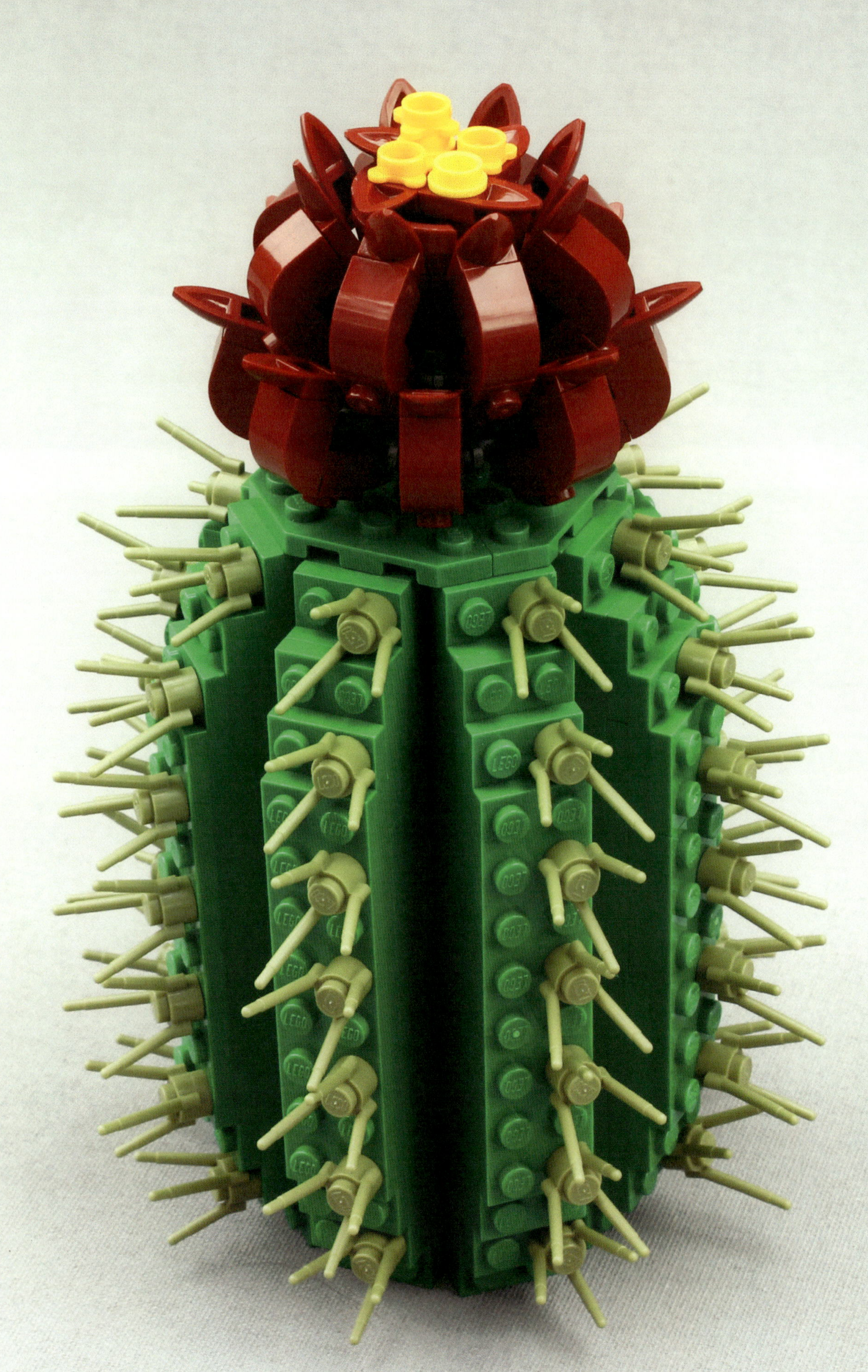

SEED PART

One of the more unique contests of the LEGO® community is something known as the Seed Part Challenge. There's really only one rule: whoever incorporates the specific "seed part" in the most creative way in each of their builds (however many) is the winner. Each build must include this specific piece, however, this shouldn't be confused with only using ONE single style of piece for the creation. It just has to appear in the creation and must be an integral part of the design.

In this section, there are three different Seed Part Contests shown, the two ABS builder challenges, and the infamous Iron Builder Contest (which actually got us featured in the LEGO® Club Magazine!).

The ABS builder challenges were more relaxed and often used teammates to help spread out the number of builds per person and only lasted about 2 weeks each. The Iron Builder, by contrast, is one of the most ferocious and competitive contests in the online LEGO® community and is a solid month of nonstop building usually paired with one single worthy opponent! In our case, it was unique since we had teams of two, going head to head.

Not all our Iron Builder creations are featured in this book, since some of them were built by my brother and teammate Mark. The ones here are just my own and my favorites that were featured on my social media accounts.

Iron Builder Contest - Green Spike

On a technical level, the green spike was a pretty serious challenge, since not only did it have an inescapable green color, it only has one single connection point! This may seem inconsequential, but it limits the usage significantly. Thankfully, we were able to work around this rather well and found ways to make it a highlight of our creations.

Although we ended up losing this Iron Builder Round, we went on to set a record at the time for the amount of builds produced in the contest - 32 in just one month!

One other note is that you get bonus points for incorporating other colored seed part pieces, for example the spike could also be used in red or gray alongside the green. (As seen in the bottom right in the splotch of ketchup, which is actual LEGO®!)

Below we've got two intrepid space explorers (representing me and my brother!) fending off a beastly green-toothed alien! This MOC was inspired by Bill Watterson's classic 'Spaceman Spiff' from Calvin and Hobbes.

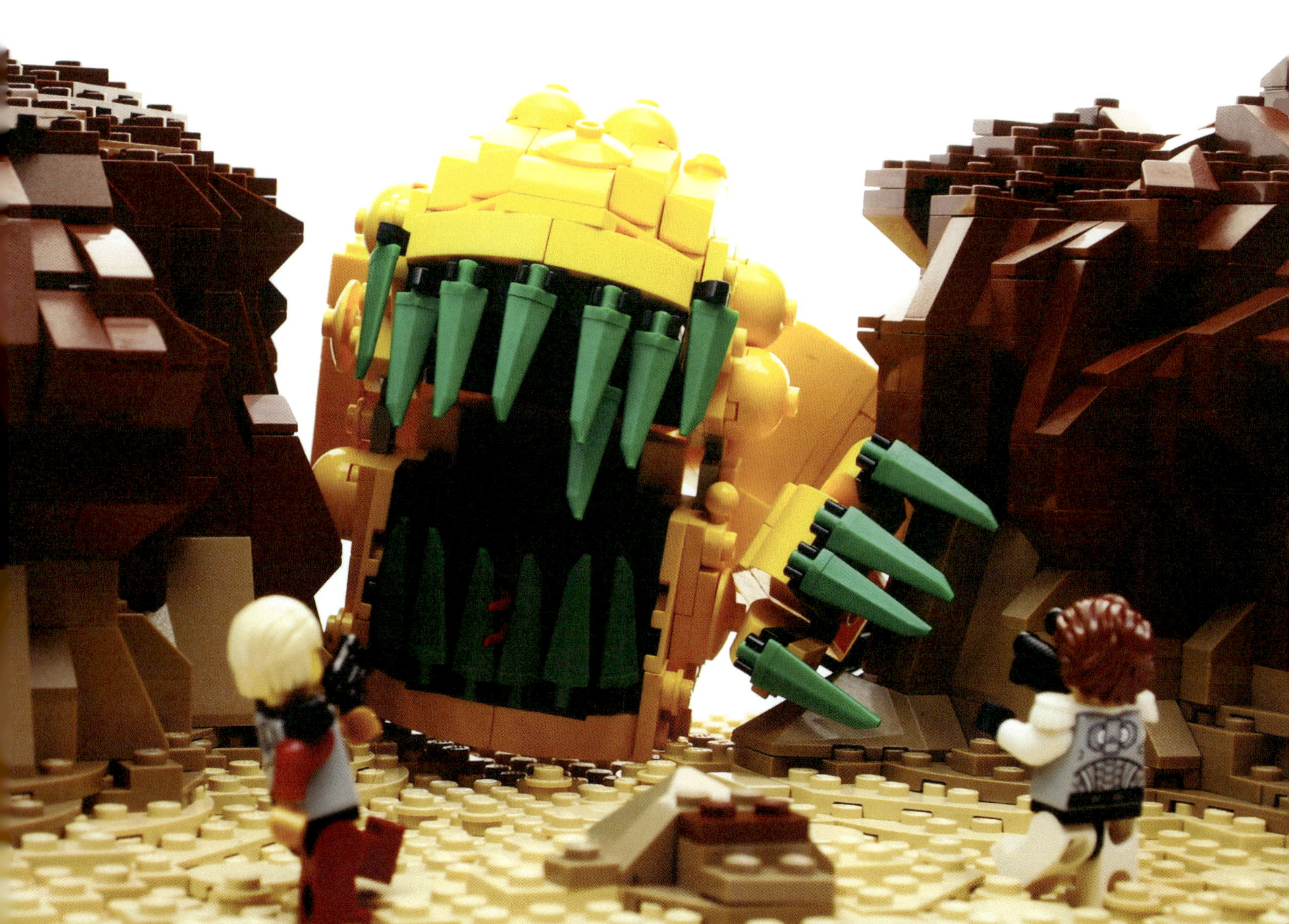

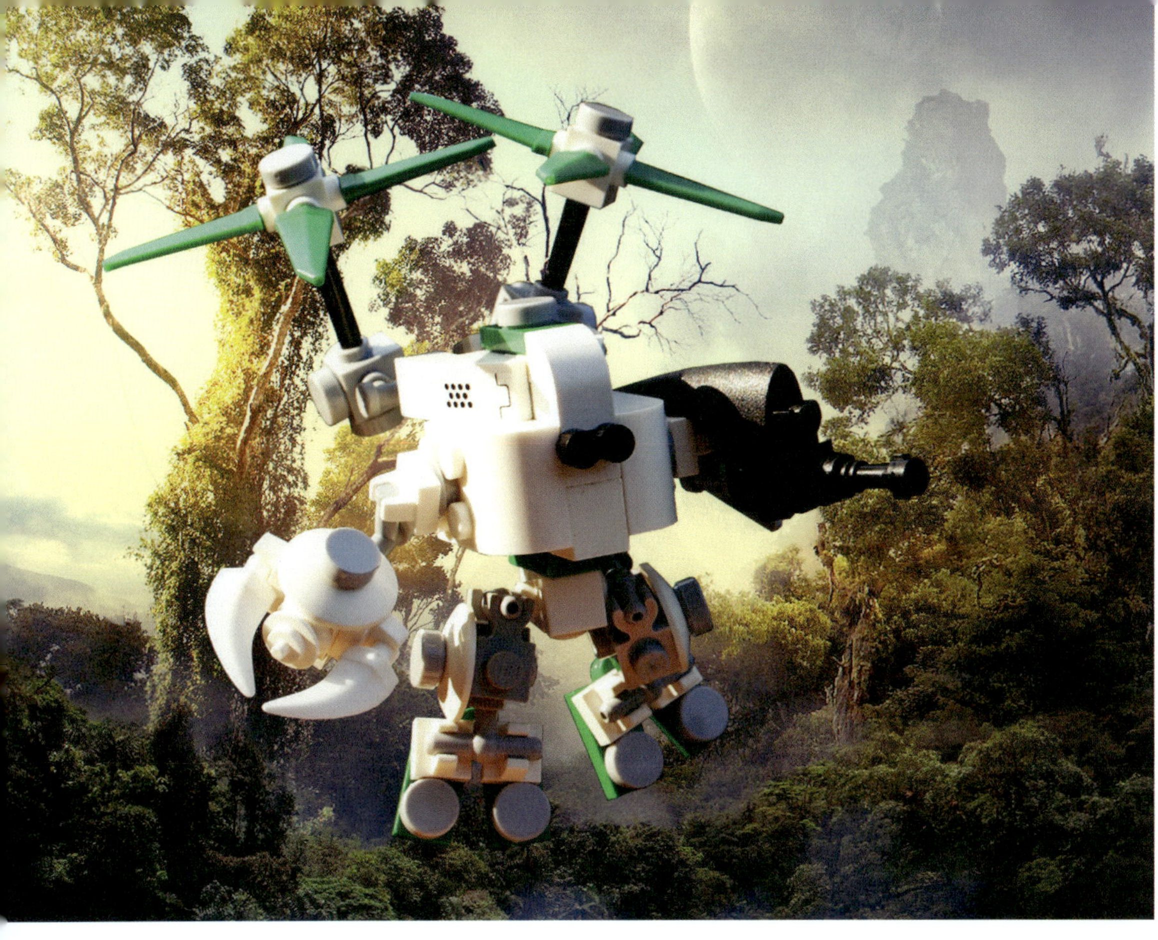

(Left) Meet **CHARL-Z** -whose name is an acronym for:

Conventional Hovering Artificial Reconnaissance Liason: Z-class.

Gourmet Building: Iron Builder Burger (Hold the Mayo!)

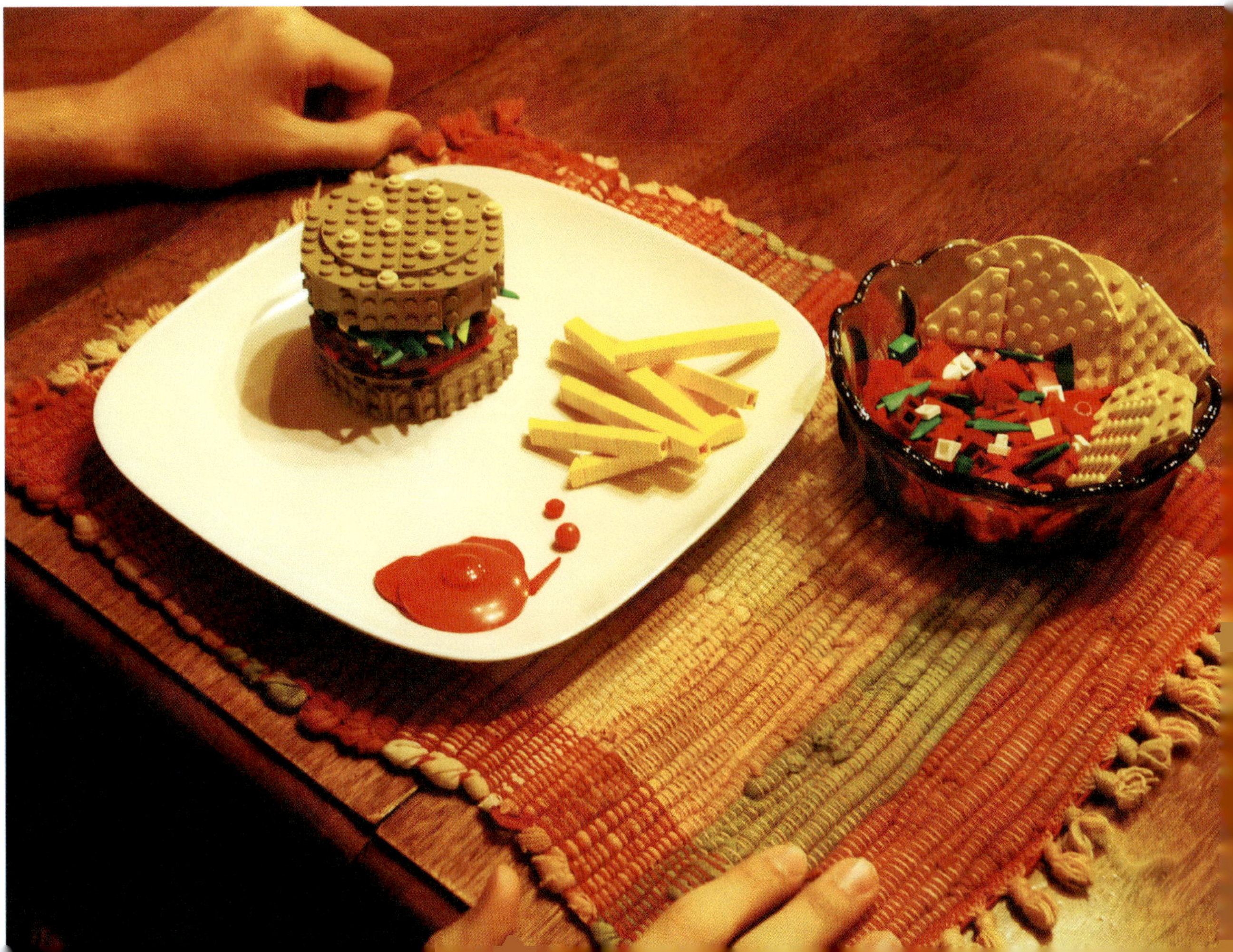

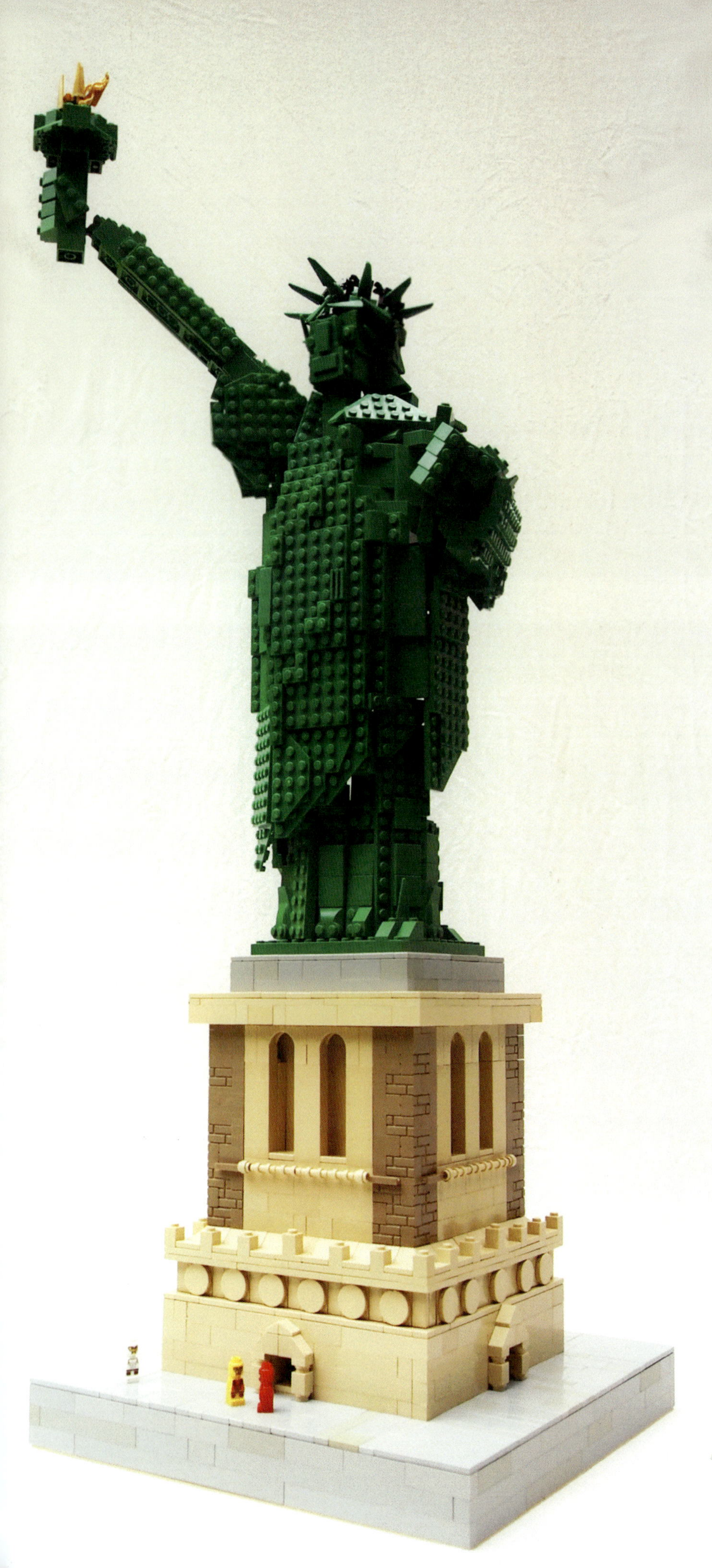

We had the privilege of seeing the **Statue of Liberty** in person just a few weeks before the contest and when we found out what the seed part was, we realized it was PERFECT for Lady Liberty's crown.

This is one of the first big statues I had ever made, with an assist from my brother on the tan and gray base. There are a few issues with the statue design. The arm is a bit too long and the wrist is too thin, and the face certainly isn't feminine. Not to mention the shade of green is a bit dark!

However, it was built under extreme time constraints and I think, all things considered, it gets the point across very well.

She was our largest entry yet in the contest, standing over 104 studs tall and weighing roughly 5 pounds!

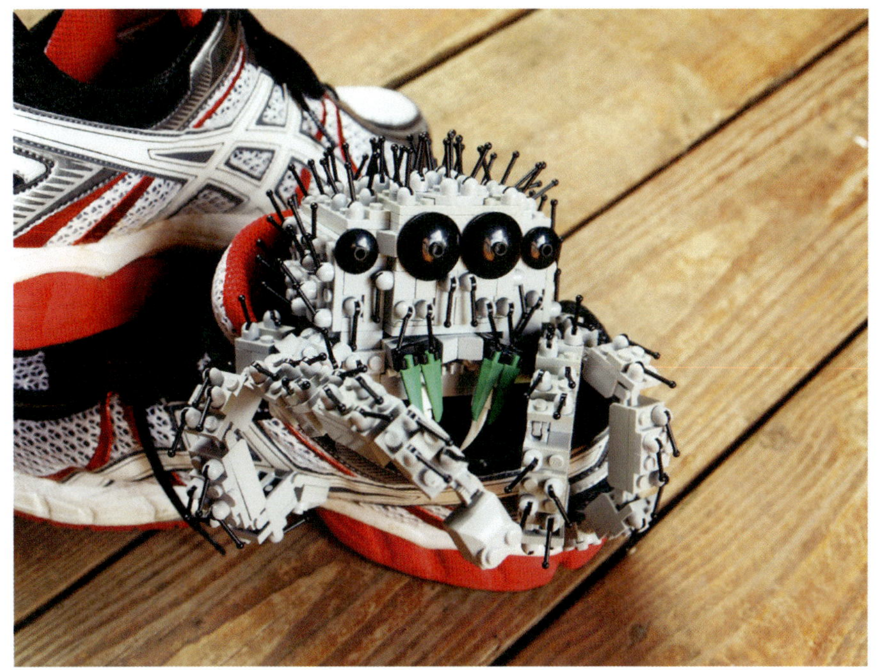

This was a personal favorite of mine for this entire contest. It's adorable yet terrifying.

It's actually a really simple build but has a crazy and detailed look because of the use of LEGO® levers to give it a frighteningly fuzzy appearance!

The little space ship, **The USS Cayman 9r** (center left) used the green spike to smoothly fit on top of the thrusters.

The darts (bottom left) utilize the spikes for the feathered ends.

The Sword of the Brotherhood (bottom right) has green spike detailing on the hilt and the crossguard. It was surprisingly sturdy!

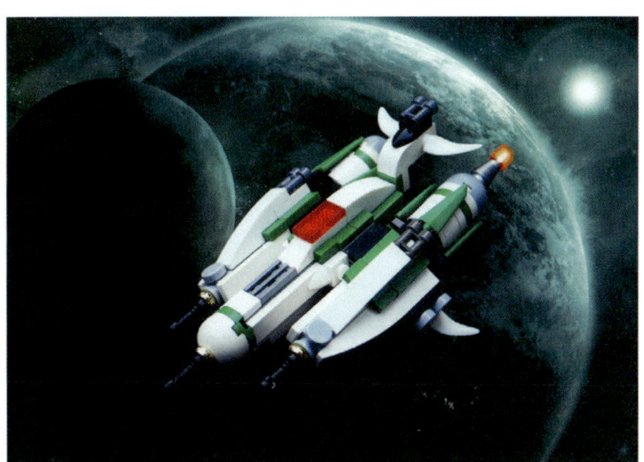

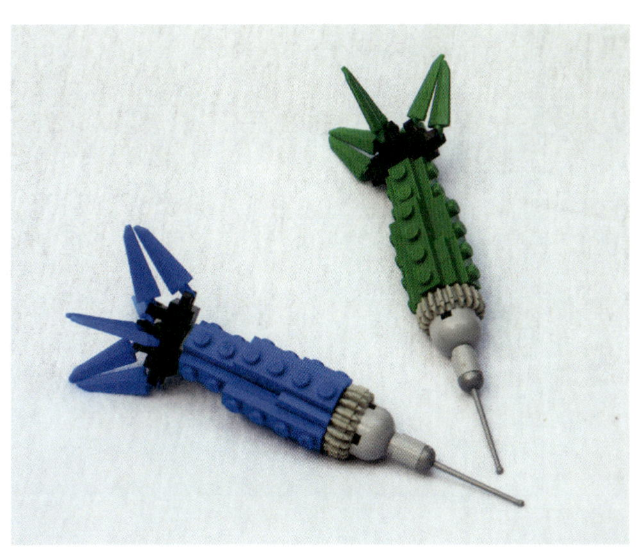

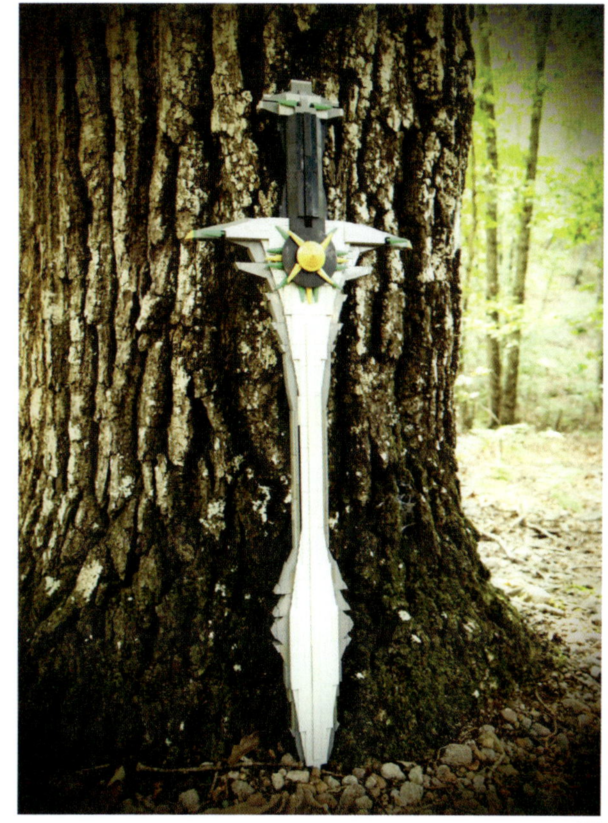

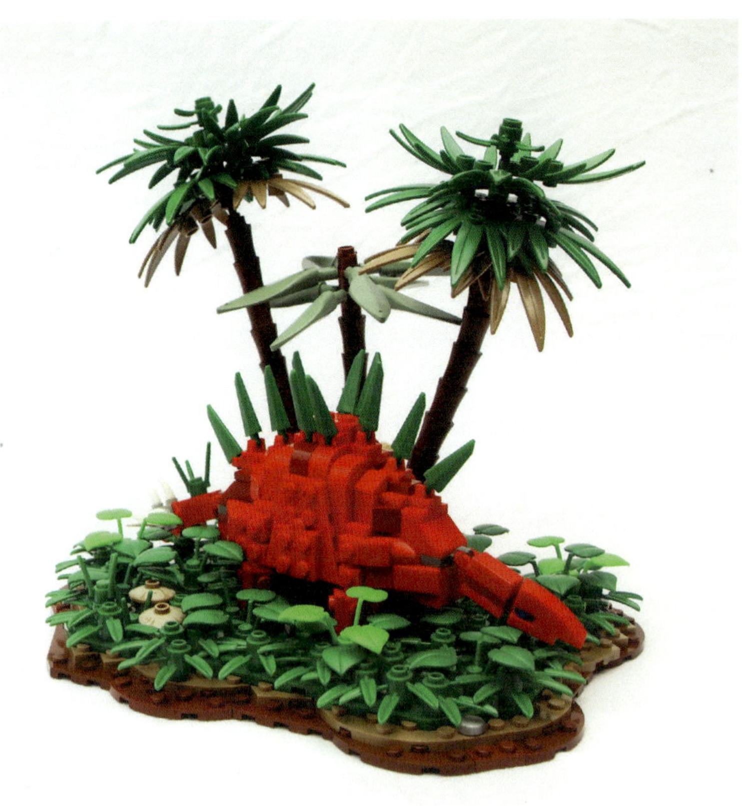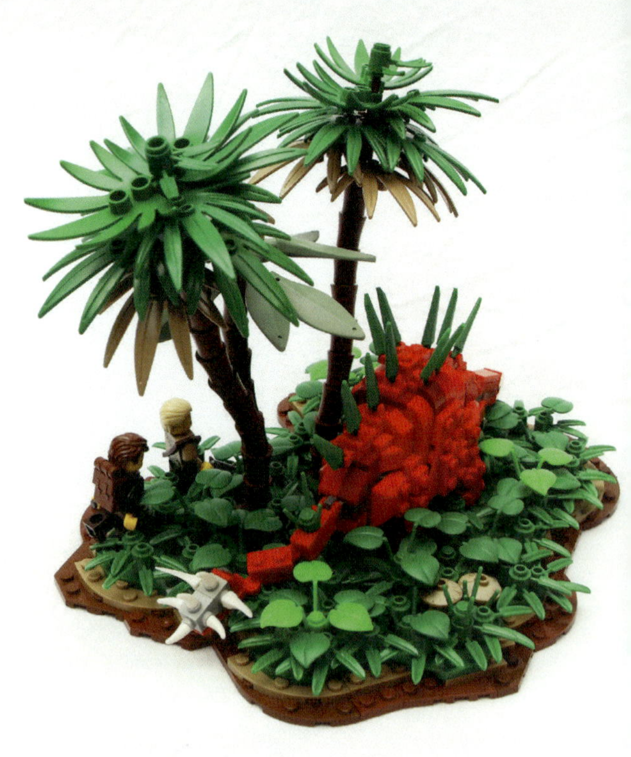

Stegosaurus – Dinosaurs were a huge part of our childhood, and the LEGO® Dinosaur line was one of our favorites. The green spike worked perfectly for this red stegosaur's armored plates (above).

Some of our builds included multiple uses for the seed part. In **The Adirondack Express** (left), the green spike is used in the bridge railing and the foliage on the mountain peaks.

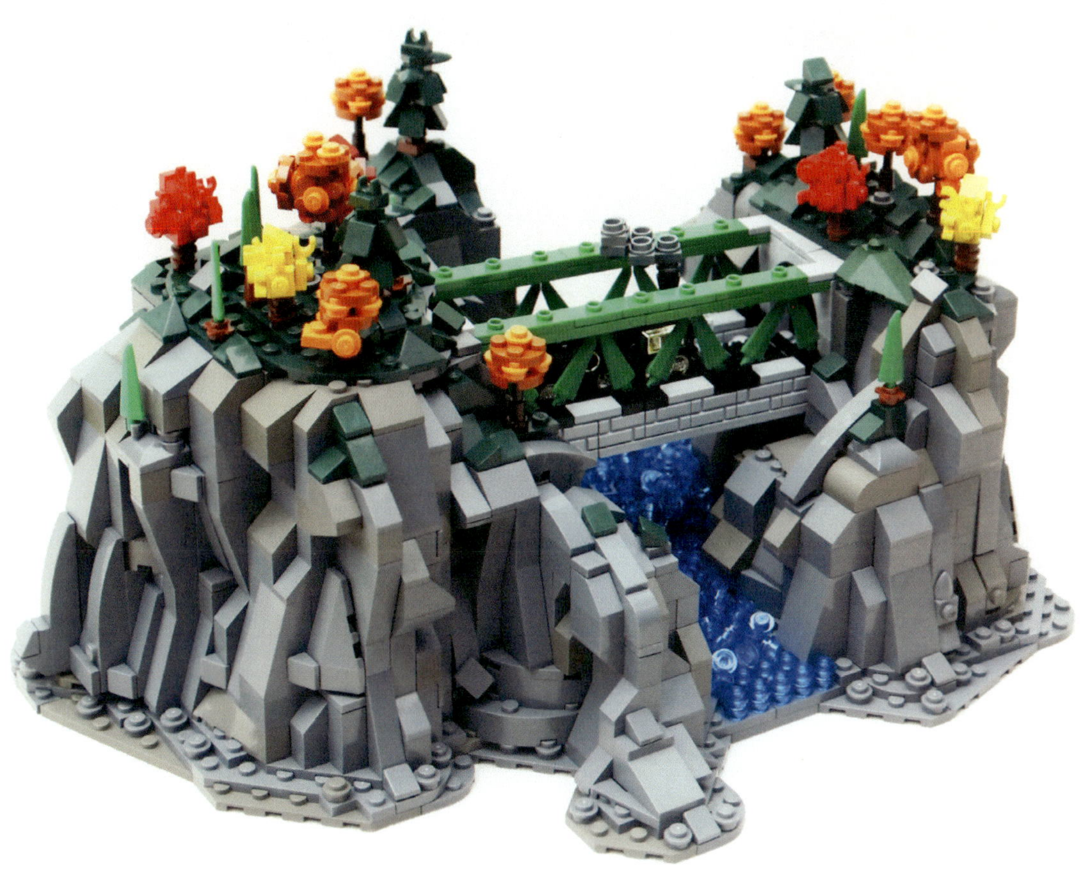

This is the first "Micro-scale" creation featured in this book. Micro-scale is so small that minifigs or any characters would simply not be feasible. This size is usually delegated to cities, vehicles, and landscapes.

This charming diorama was inspired by the Adirondack and Smoky mountains, along with the rich history of railroads found across the areas.

One of the things I liked best about this tiny train was the gold coins used as wheels, which fit nicely into the grill tiles on the railroad which are turned parallel in a strategic arrangement.

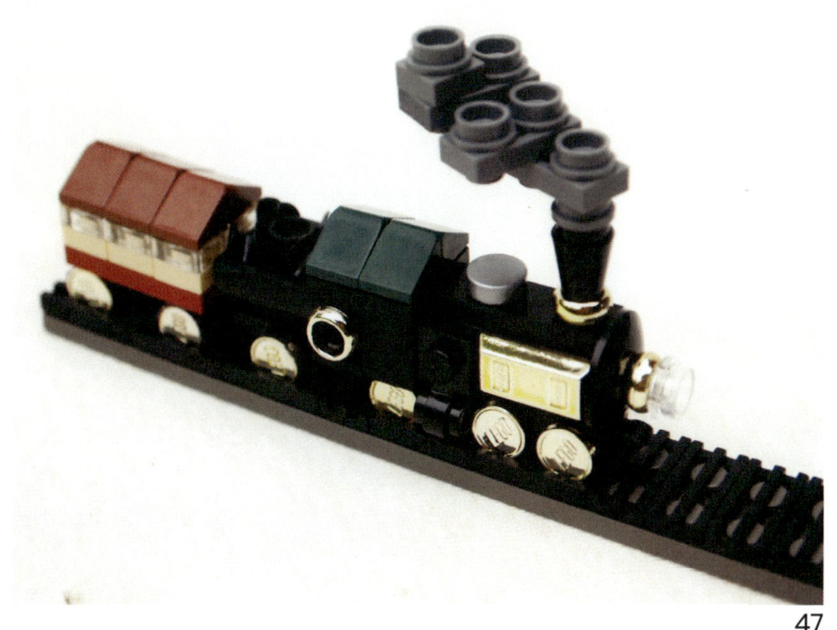

The Art of illusion

For this Iron Builder
entry, I was trying
to bring something
new to a relatively
small creation. Trick
photography!
I could easily have
cut and pasted
the rose with
photoshop, but
instead I built two of
them and shot the
photo at an angle
to where it seemed
that the second
rose was appearing
on the canvas.

The green spike
was used as the
paintbrush tip. In
order to keep the
illusion, I built the
secondary table
with mostly white
bricks to subtly
disappear in the
background.

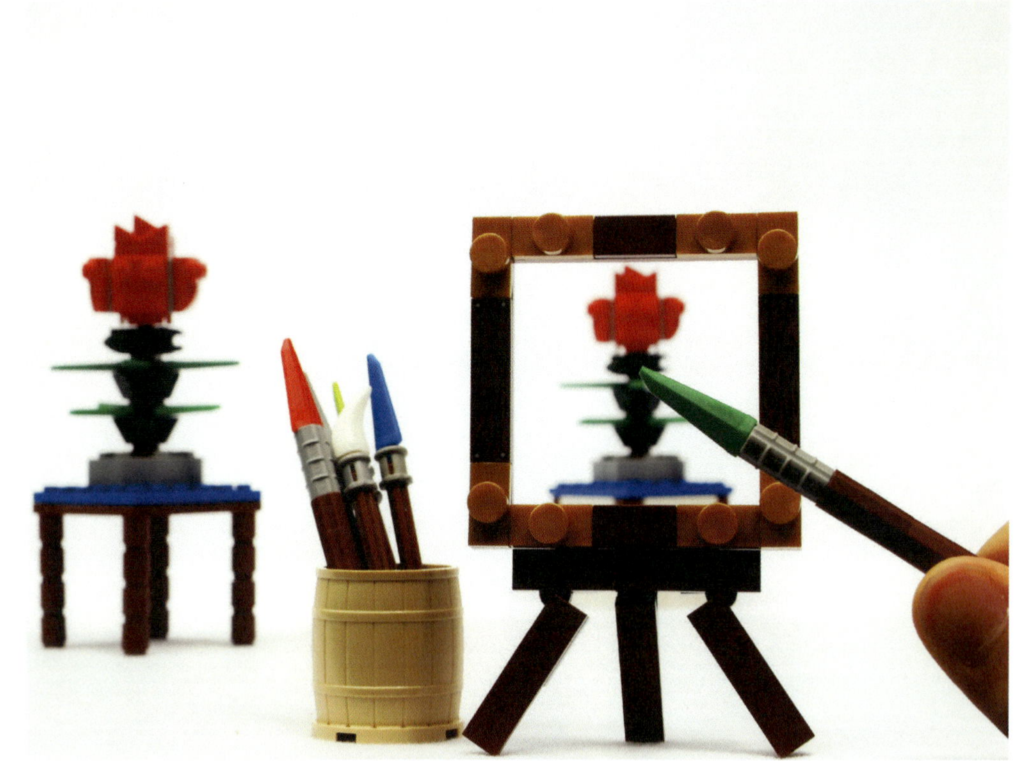

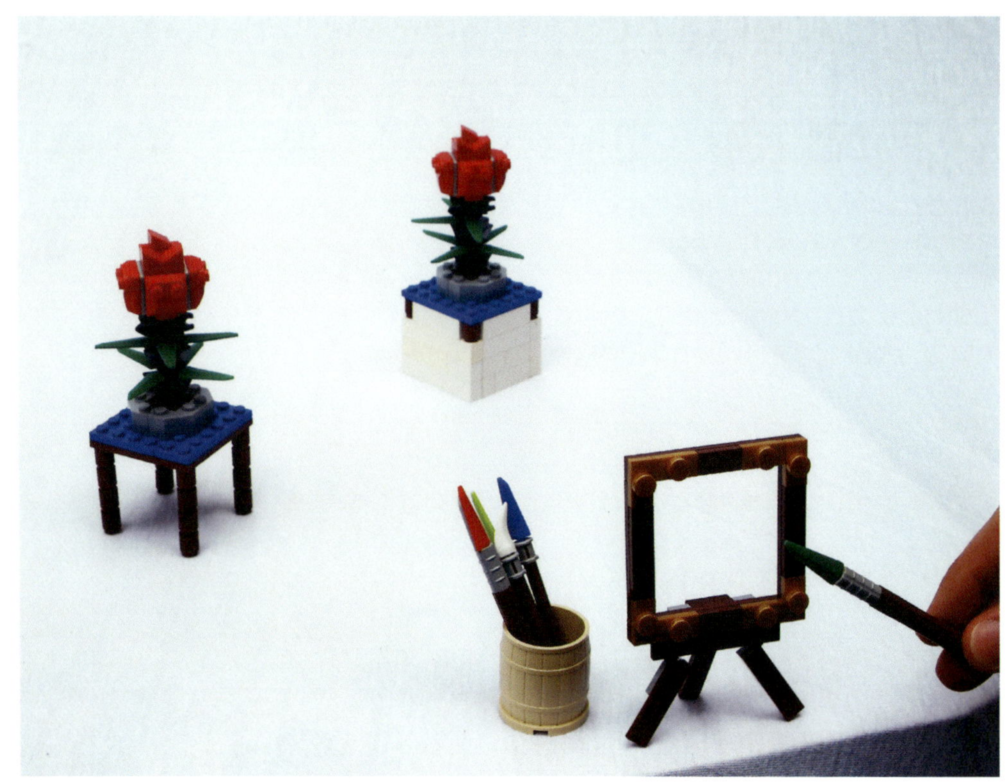

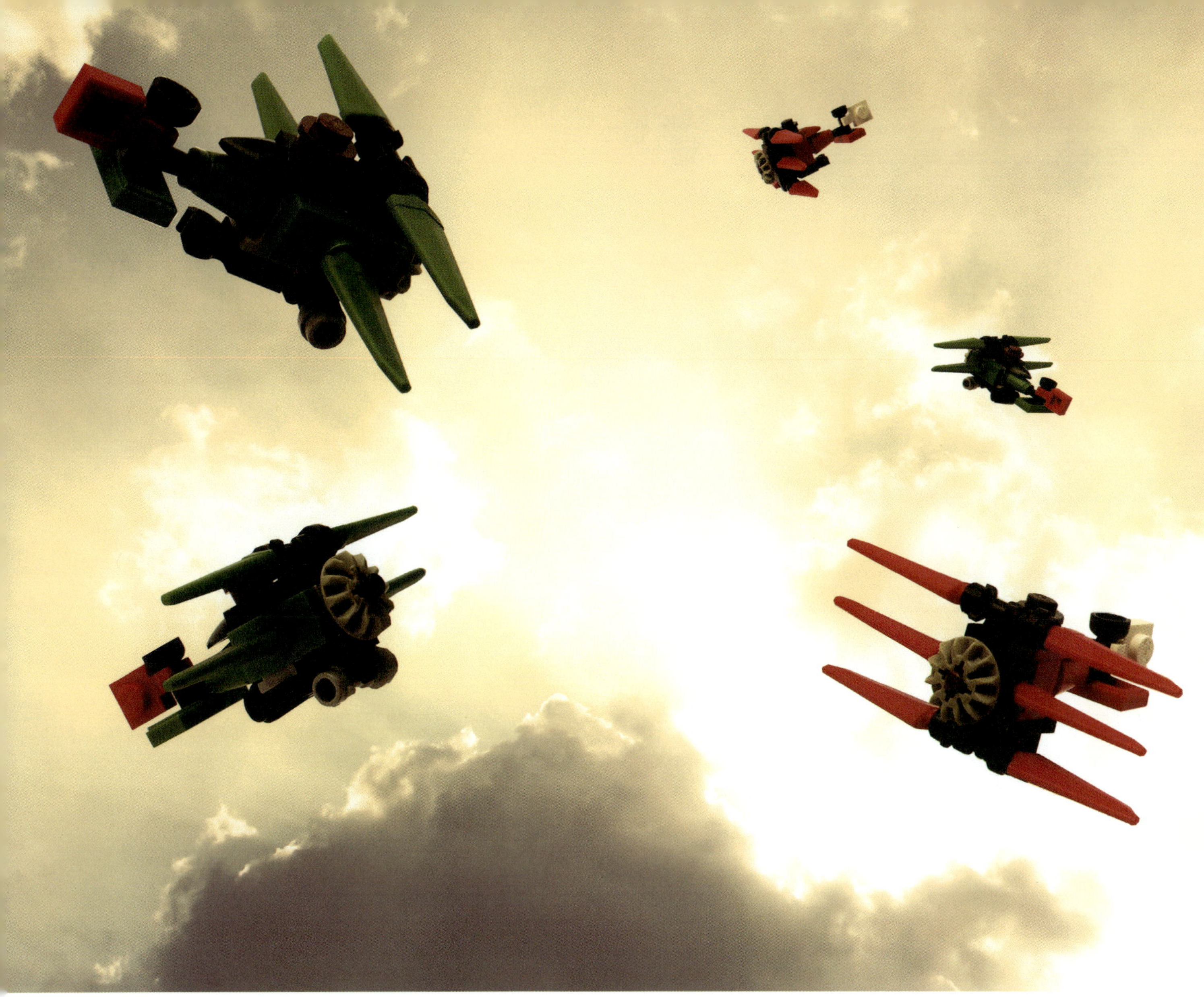

Battle for the Skies! At this point, my teammate (and brother), Mark and I wanted to overwhelm our competition with as many builds as we could. So there appeared a number of smaller builds with a high level of creativity and detail with excellent presentation. From among these builds, the little bi-planes and tri-planes were some of my favorites.

I have always enjoyed historical themes and WWI was one of them. I also love the character Snoopy's antics from the Peanuts comics, where he would imagine his doghouse was a Sopwith Camel doing battle with the Red Baron in the skies over war-torn France. These planes were influenced by that a little bit.

On a technical level, it's considered impressive if you can add multiple colors of the "seed" part in the same creation although it doesn't actually affect your official score. It's a bit of casual "flexing".

We would actually go on to lose the Iron Builder round to our competitors, however it was an amazing experience that really put me and my brother on the map in the LEGO® community. We were even interviewed and featured in the official LEGO® Club Magazine about this round of the Iron Builder contest.

Home Improvements

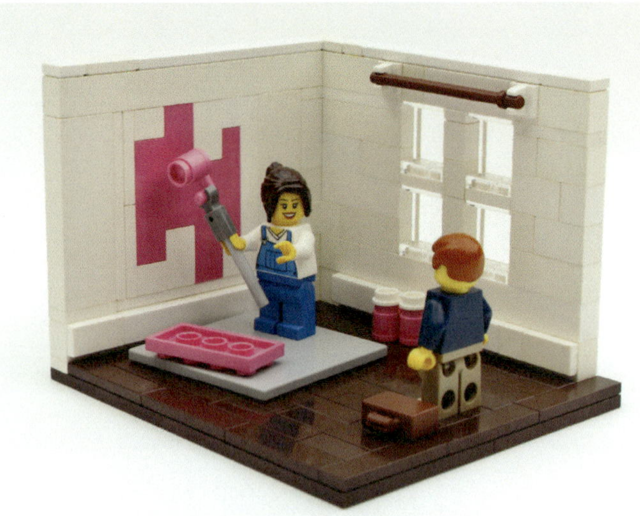

Oh, the pink cup! This challenge was pretty much the exact same concept as the Iron Builder above, only on a significantly less competitive level.

The pink cup itself was a bit of an annoyance to use because of the bright pink color! The point is to highlight the piece, however the shade of hot pink had the danger of standing out too much!

Thankfully, most of these builds turned out to be really fun and comedic. Most notable for me was the microscale amusement park. This was inspired by classic PC games such as Rollor Coaster Tycoon. The pink ferris wheel seats were perfect for the vibrant colors of the park!

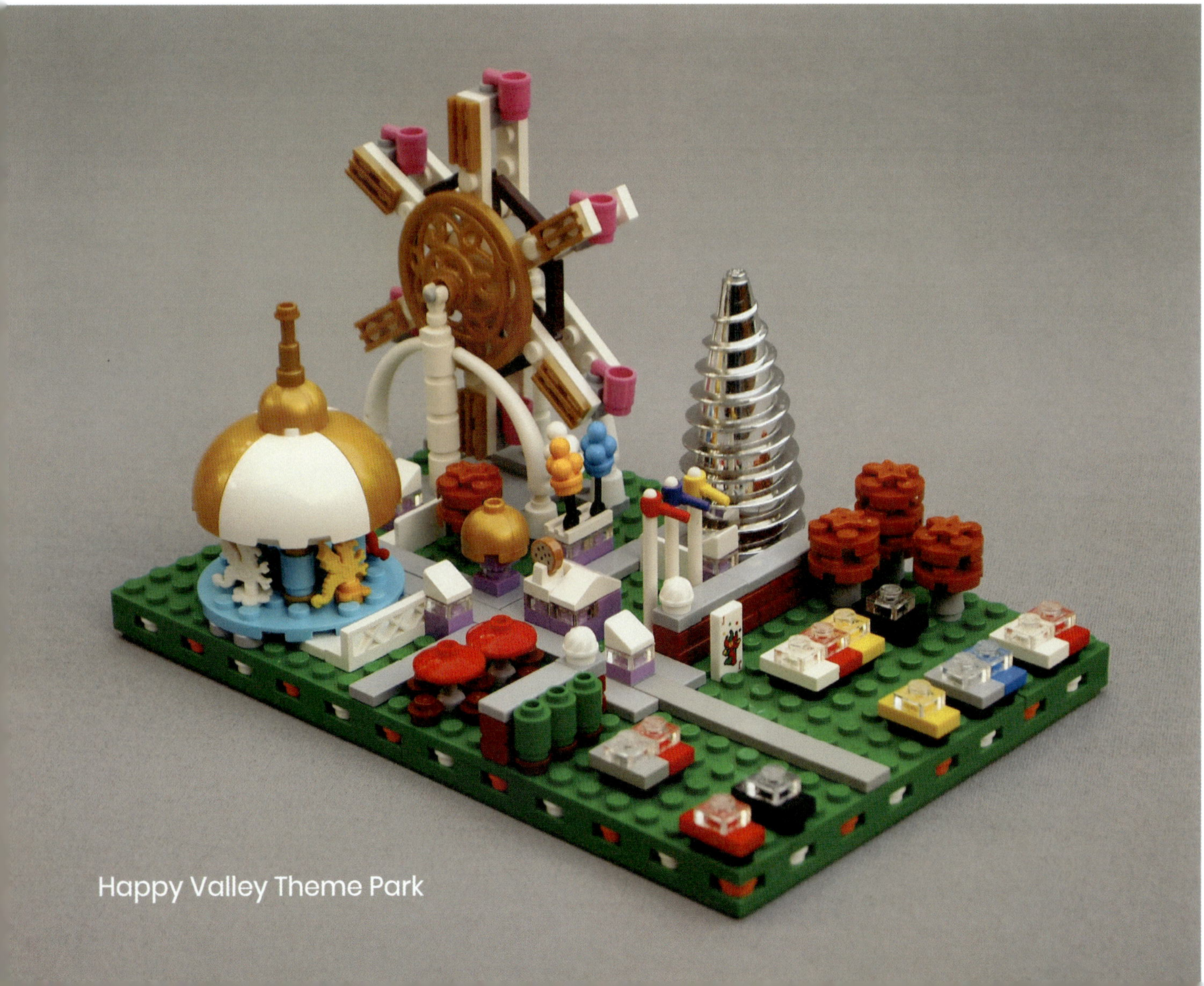

Happy Valley Theme Park

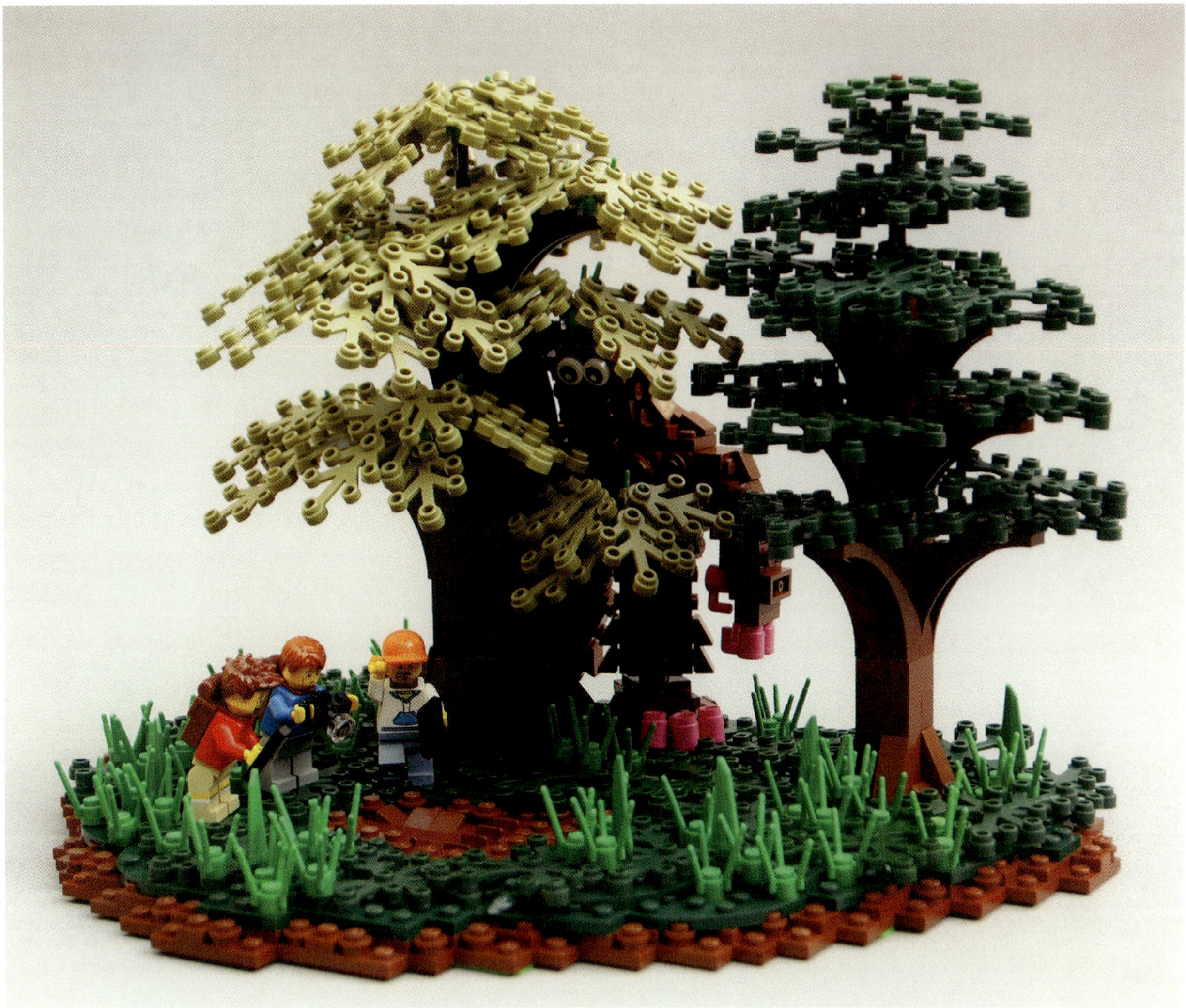

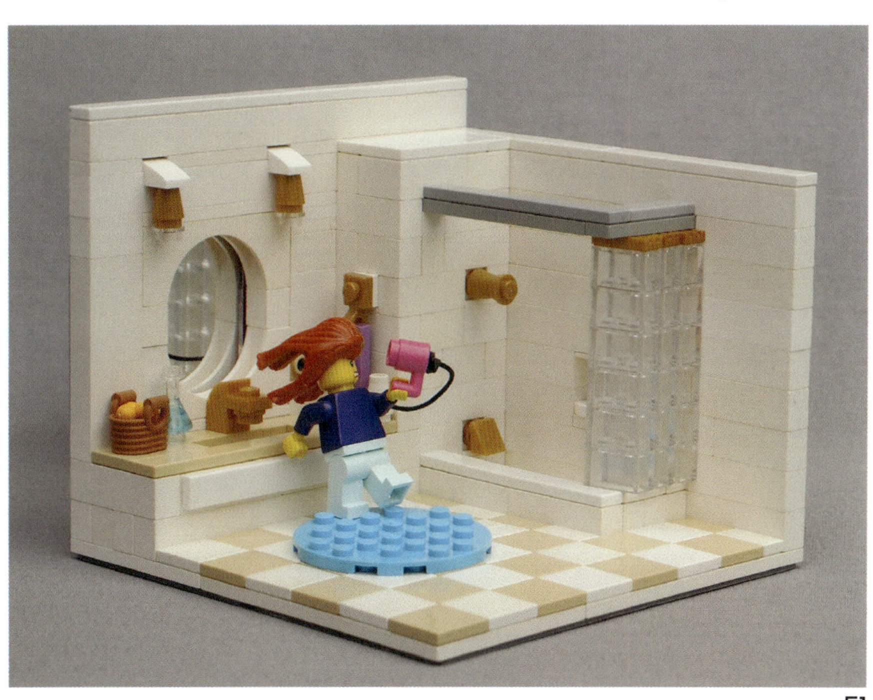

Sasquatch Snapshot (above)

Bad Hair Day (below)

One difference between the ABS builder and the Iron Builder was that I was part of a larger team, the Dark Orange house. (All four groups were named after LEGO® colors). I would go on to win this round for team Dark Orange.

Also, "ABS" comes from the type of plastic used for LEGO® parts themselves.

There were a lot of fun details in these builds! I particularly liked the giant muddy footprint left behind by the elusive Bigfoot in the top scene. The pink cups were meant to be his fingers and toes.

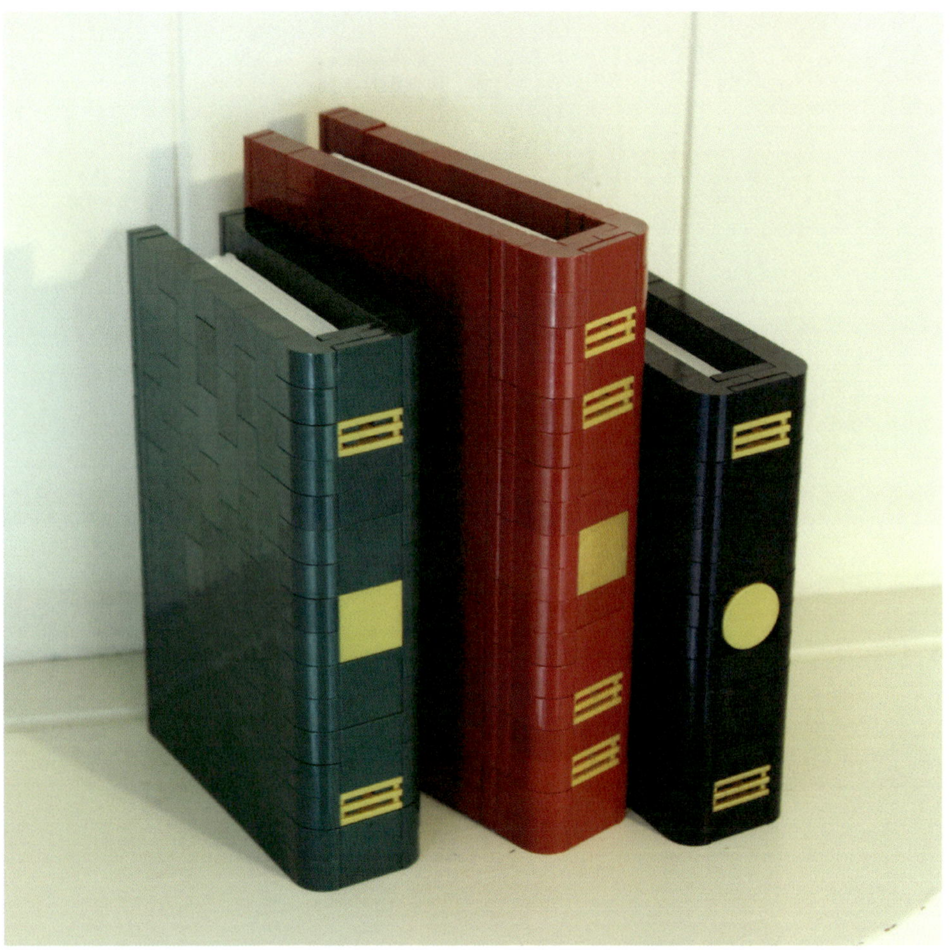

Pages of Knowledge
I wrote the book on NPU! ;)

NPU means "Nice Part Usage" in LEGO® terms.

It may be difficult to see at first but the seed part used here was the dark red curved slope. It can be seen standing out on the coffee cup handle on the opposite page.

The life-size books (left) came out very well and utilized a ton of interesting techniques. The curved slope worked amazingly for the edge of the book's spine.

Some of the hard-to-see building techniques used here were the white grill tiles used as the edge of the pages, along with the fact that no studs are visible anywhere on the entire book. The bricks are even inverted on the smooth edges of the cover flaps.

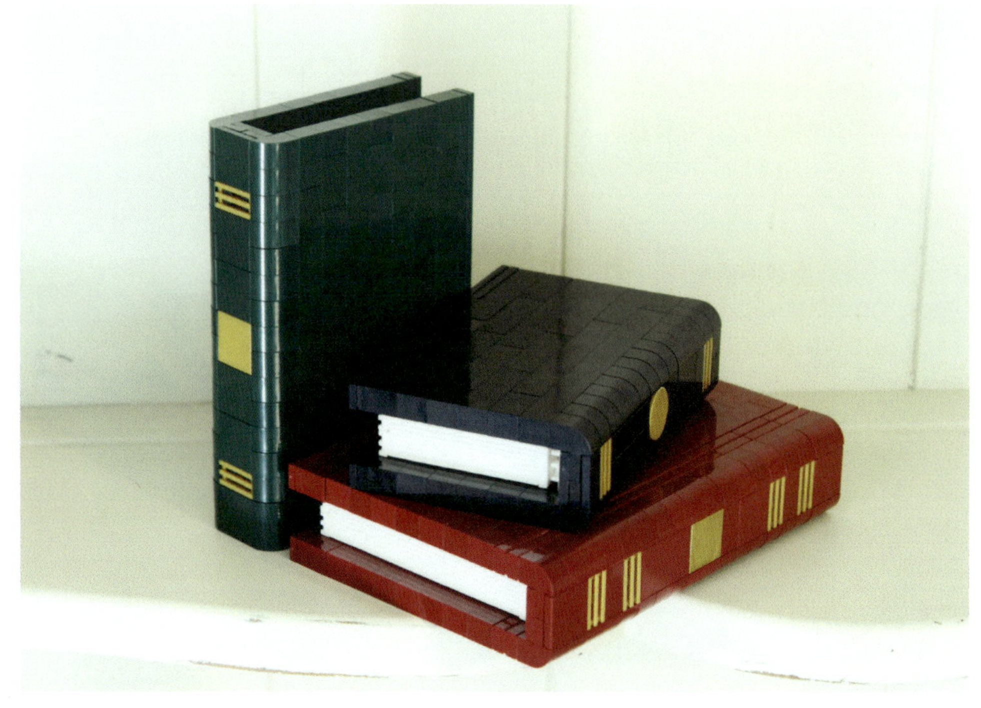

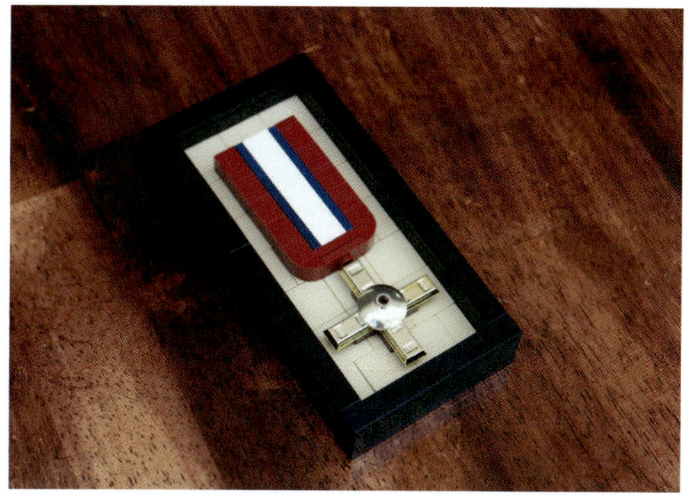

Like most of these competitions, you want a few smaller builds to fill in the gaps of the larger creations that take longer to build. The **Medal of Valor** (above) and coffee cup, **Morning Coffee** (right) are great examples. Shooting for a lifelike appearance with simple but effective presentation leaves a lasting impression.

Below, the curved slope is used in the wings and hull of a fantasy warplane, **Absworth dr12**. This build fits into a subgenre of the LEGO® community, where real-world creations are reinterpreted into a fantasy setting, which makes an insanely awesome mashup.

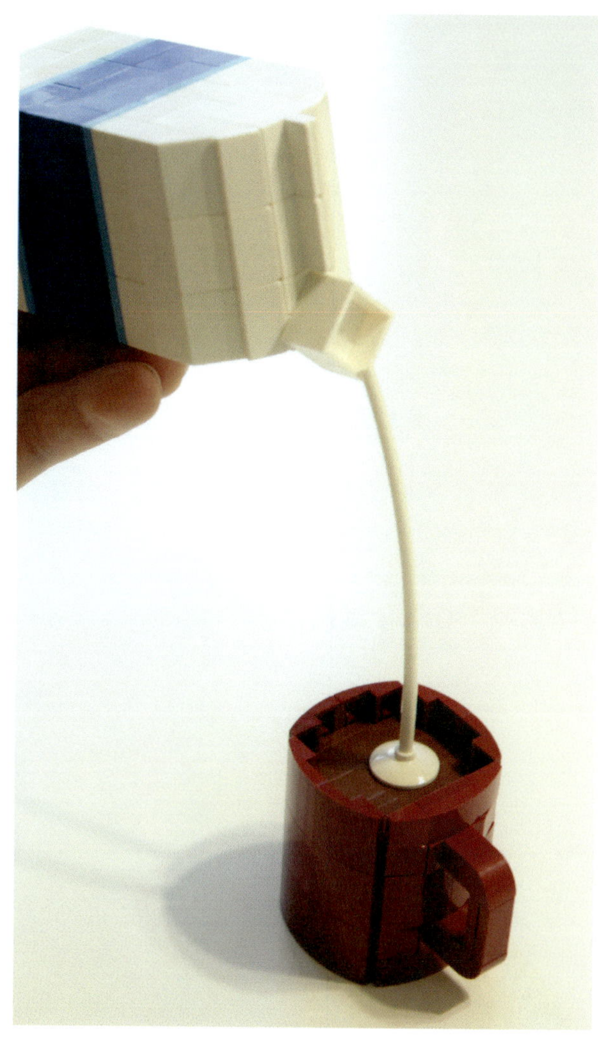

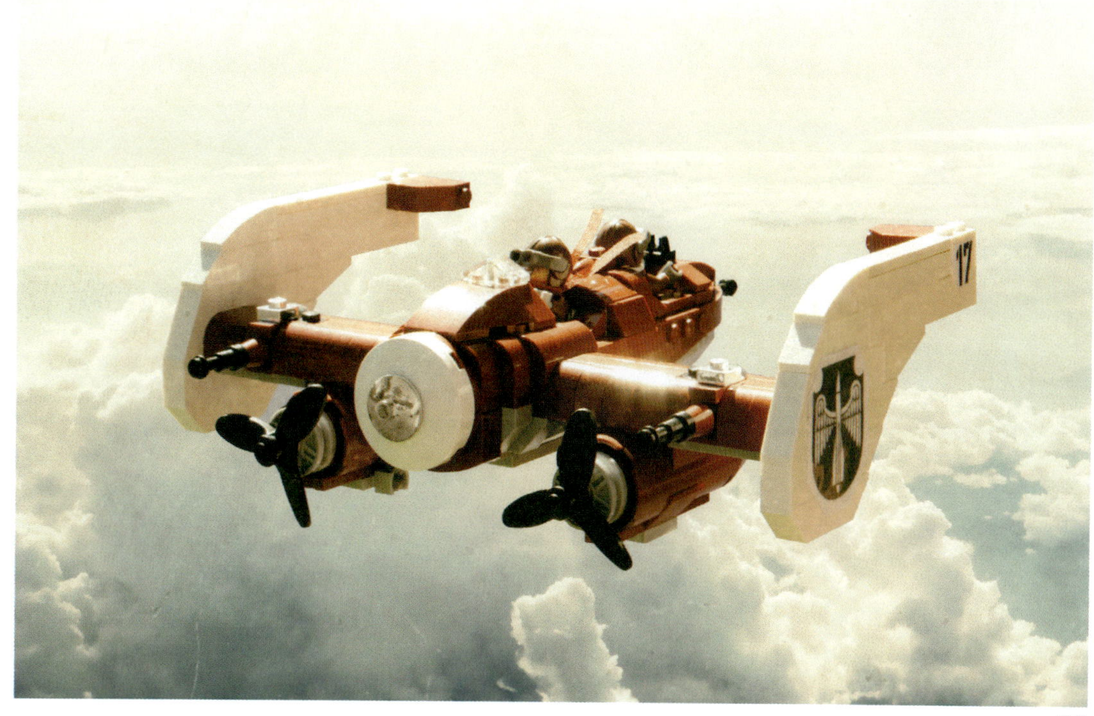

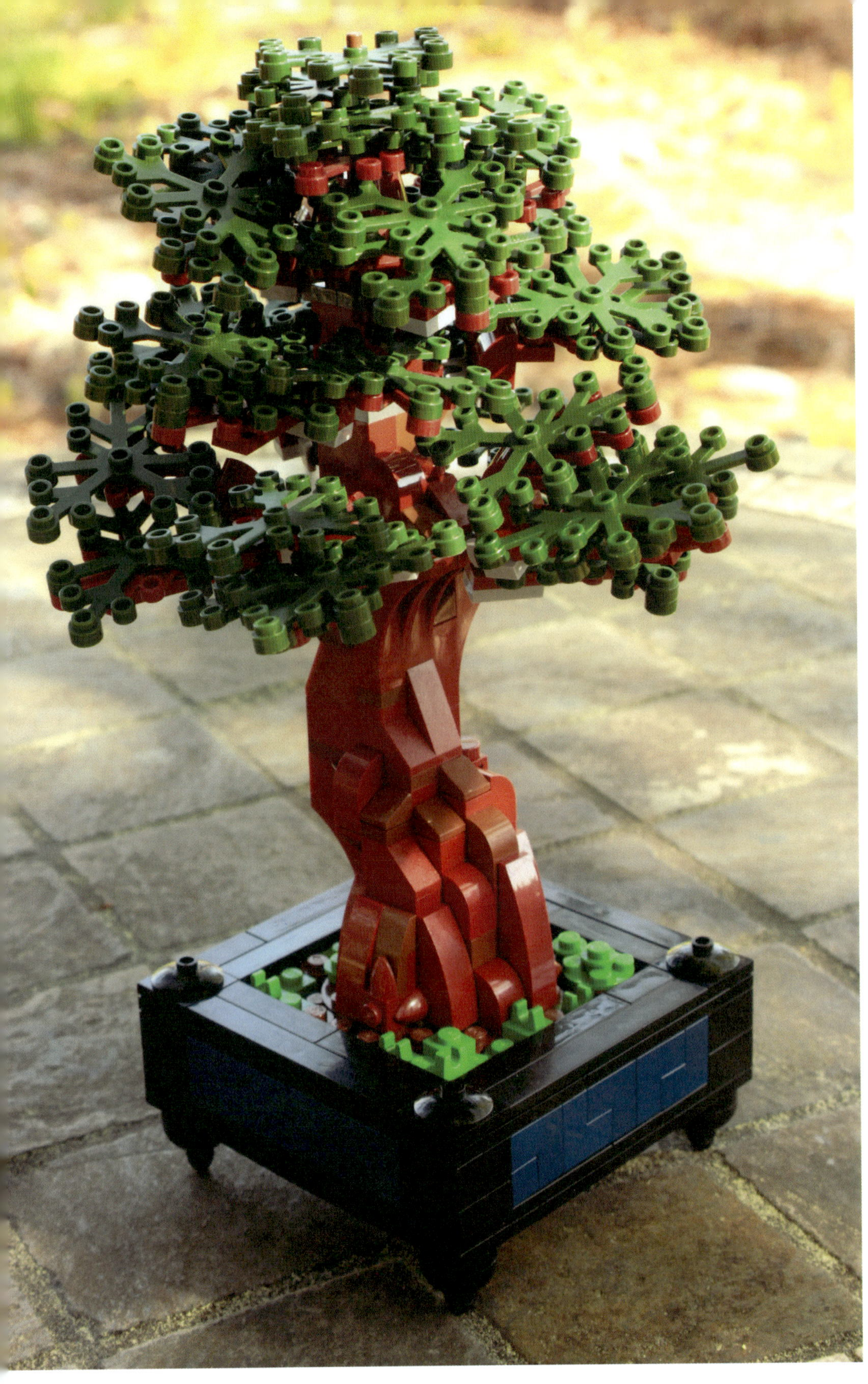

One of my favorite elements in LEGO® creations is the foliage. Trees and landscapes have always been an important part of anything I make.

This LEGO® **Bonsai** was an interesting tree, in that I got to build it in dark red - a unique color for trees.

Dark red is popular with LEGO® trees, but normally just for the leaves. Here I was able to use it for the branches to go underneath the green and make the tree look more full and realistic.

These dark red "branches" looked great with the trunk and a few brown pieces, to add texture, leaving lots of room to add the curved red slopes.

To contrast the red tree, I had fun with the black and dark blue decorative base. Most bonsai trees grow in elaborate pots, so this adds to the realism.

Game Over - I'm not 100% sure where the idea came from for Pac-Man, but I couldn't have made this little red ghost pursuing our pellet-munching hero without that dark red slope. It's a very simple build but it gets the point across very quickly.

Desert Flower - One of my favorite entries for the ABS builder contest was the cactus (below). In my opinion, it is the perfect entry for a Seed Part Challenge as the majority of the build highlights the red slope with contrasting color, great composition, and presentation.

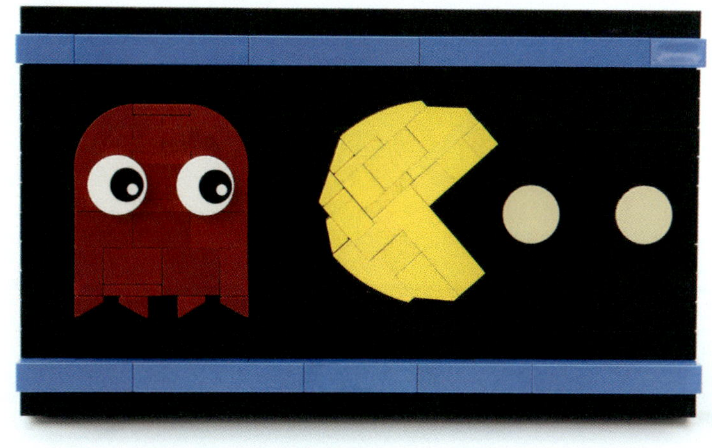

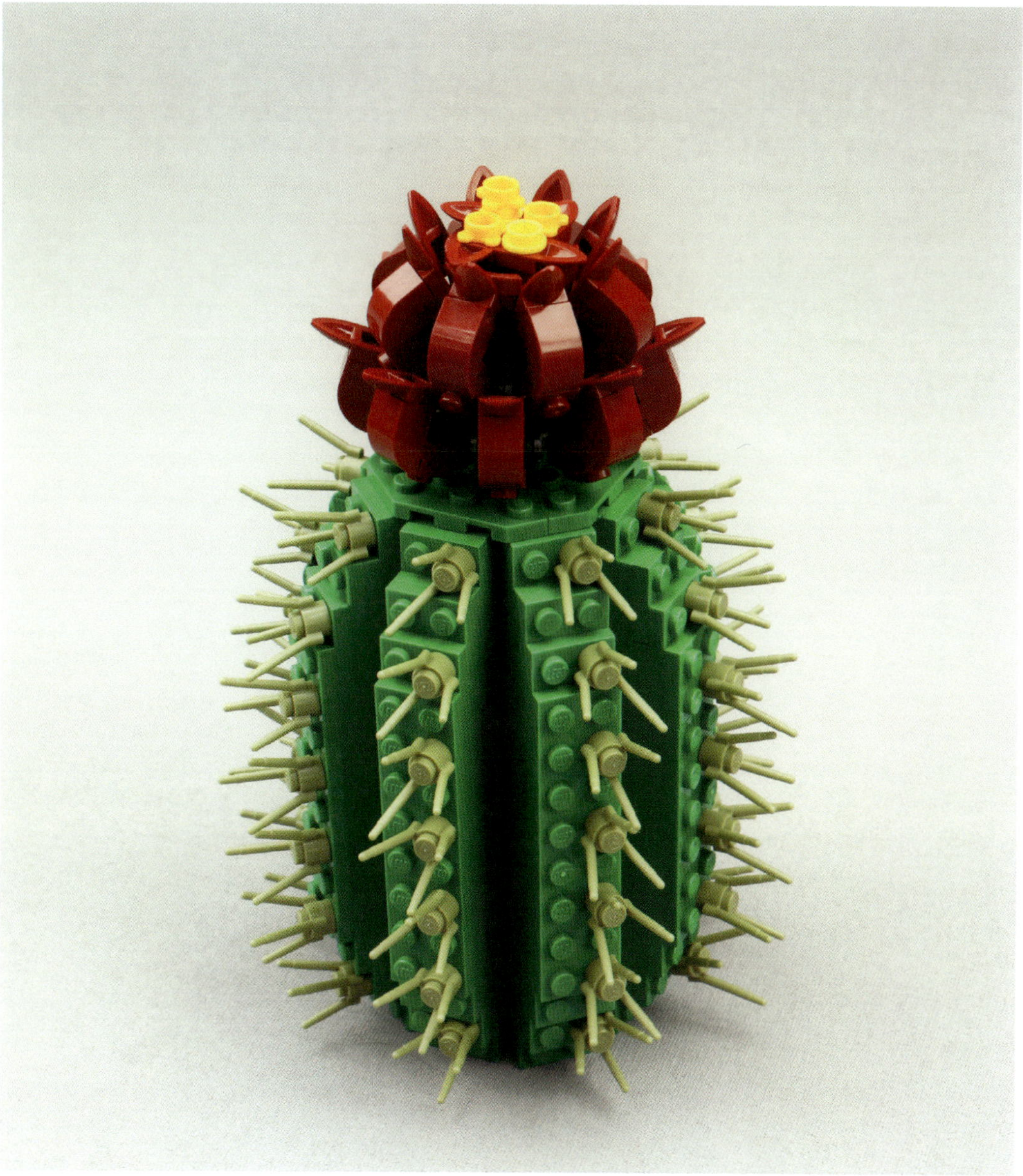

During a pre-buildoff at a convention with our iron builder competitors, me and my brother built a cactus in 30 minutes flat while our competitors built a rose.

This was a mini promo for the Iron Builder. Since that fateful day, I have been building cacti as often as possible. They are strangely one of the most satisfying things to build!

SCIENCE FICTION

One of my more unusual themes is the world of science fiction, a theme I admire and enjoy. However, in many ways it is very different than my typical style and has remained a smaller chapter in my career. I mostly use it to explore techniques, designs, and characters that I normally couldn't use in my signature themes.

Traditional science fiction in LEGO® uses high levels of detailing called "grebles" or "grebling", often to convey a techy and industrial vibe. As far as color is concerned, most anything goes. Sci-Fi is recognized as being wacky, off-the-wall, and otherworldly.

Unlike Castle, the rules of Sci-Fi are incredibly loose. Your imagination can run wild. This can be a bit overwhelming, and consequently, I have pursued Sci-Fi a bit less than other building styles.

But I've always loved classic Sci-Fi media, whether it's British time travelers, or starships going "where no man has gone before". It can be a super inspiring theme as well, always looking towards the future.

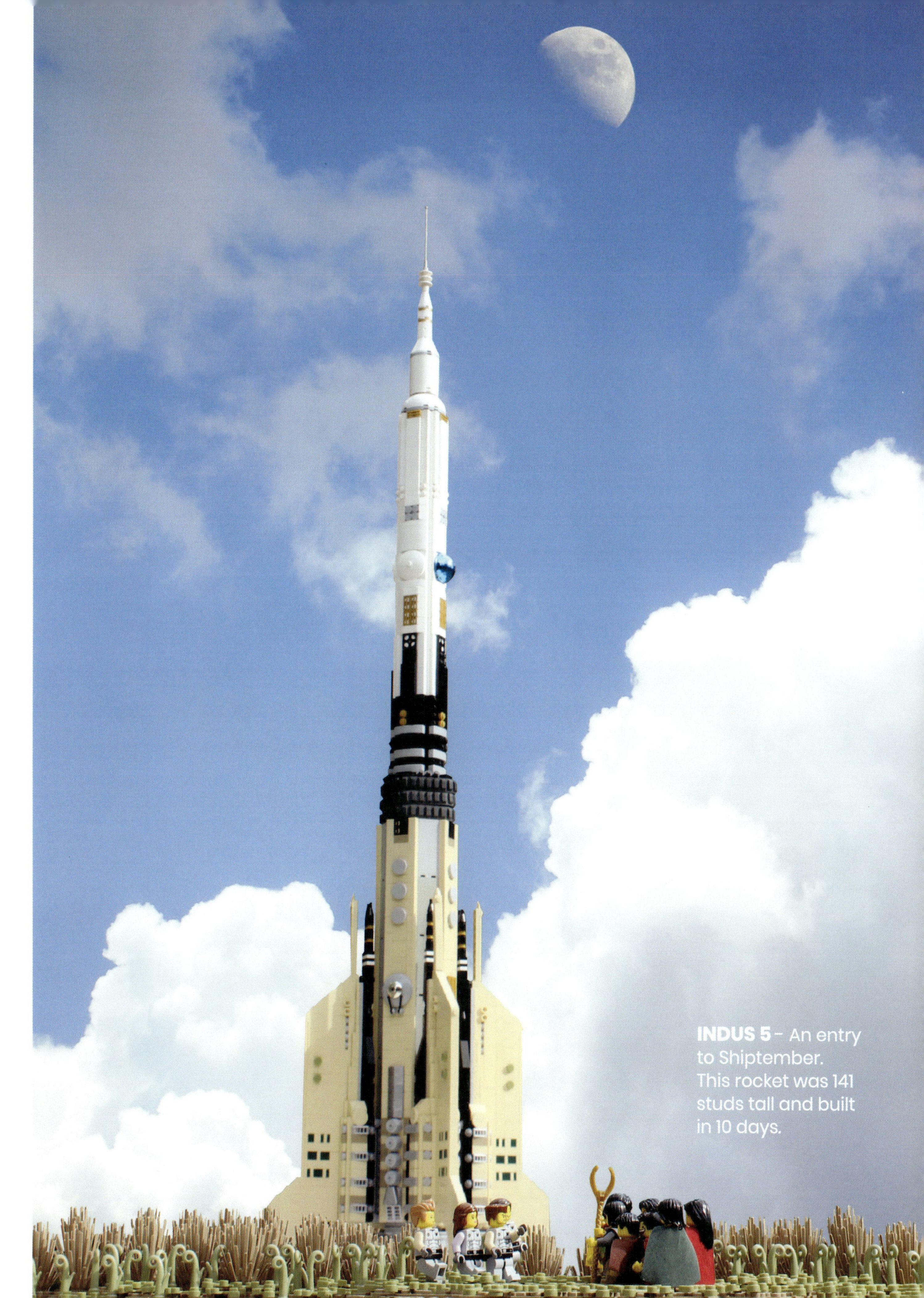

INDUS 5 – An entry to Shiptember. This rocket was 141 studs tall and built in 10 days.

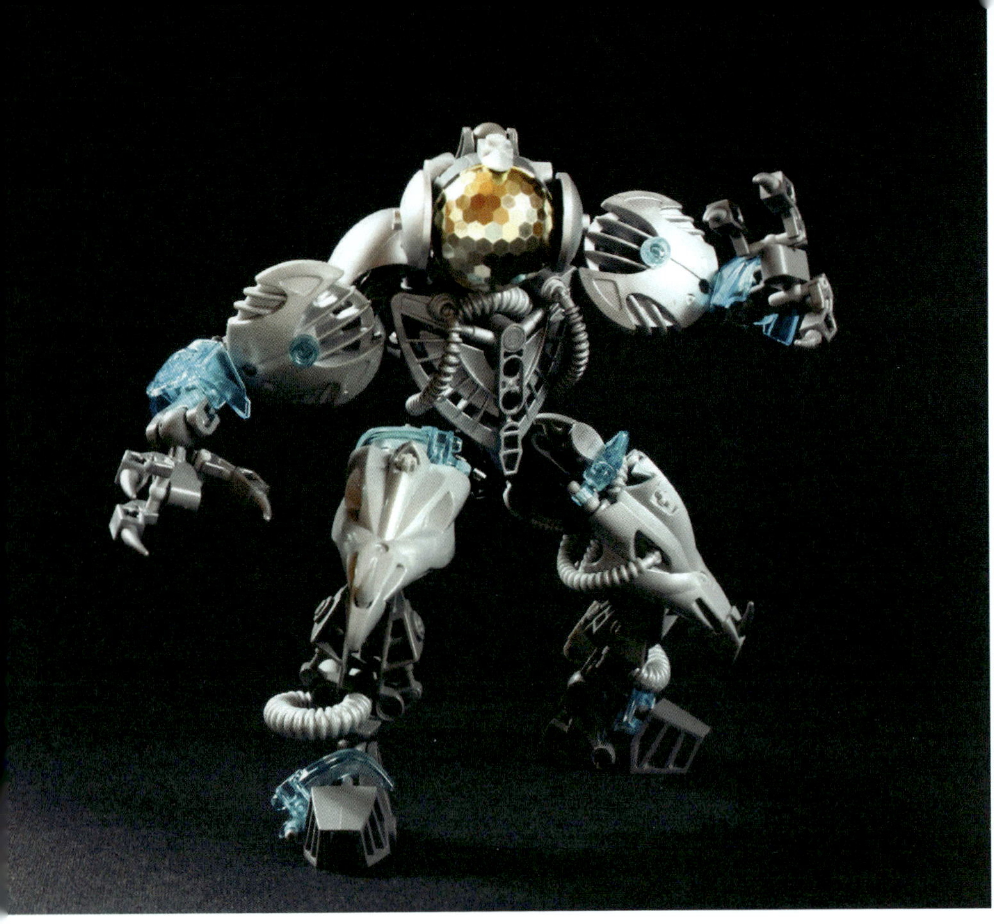

One theme I love but barely have the opportunity to explore is Bionicle, one of the more exciting Technic themes.

Tributron, left, is possibly my favorite example of this bygone yet beloved theme. He was specifically built as a tribute to a friend of mine, who also happened to be the same friend who beat us in the Iron Builder contest.

Interestingly, the silver hoses were the seed part in the competition he was taking part in.

Villatron, right, was the sequel to Tributron. Both of these characters used a combination of Bionicle System (LEGO® parts) and Hero Factory, the infamous reboot to Bionicle. Some fun things about these characters are the compound chrome eyes - the type of piece I would use in future builds similar to these guys.

I was starting to enjoy more dramatic photography at this point, by incorporating dark backgrounds and more direct lighting. Photography is a surprisingly important aspect of LEGO® presentation.

For the posing of these characters, I have to give credit to my brother Mark! It really brought them to life.

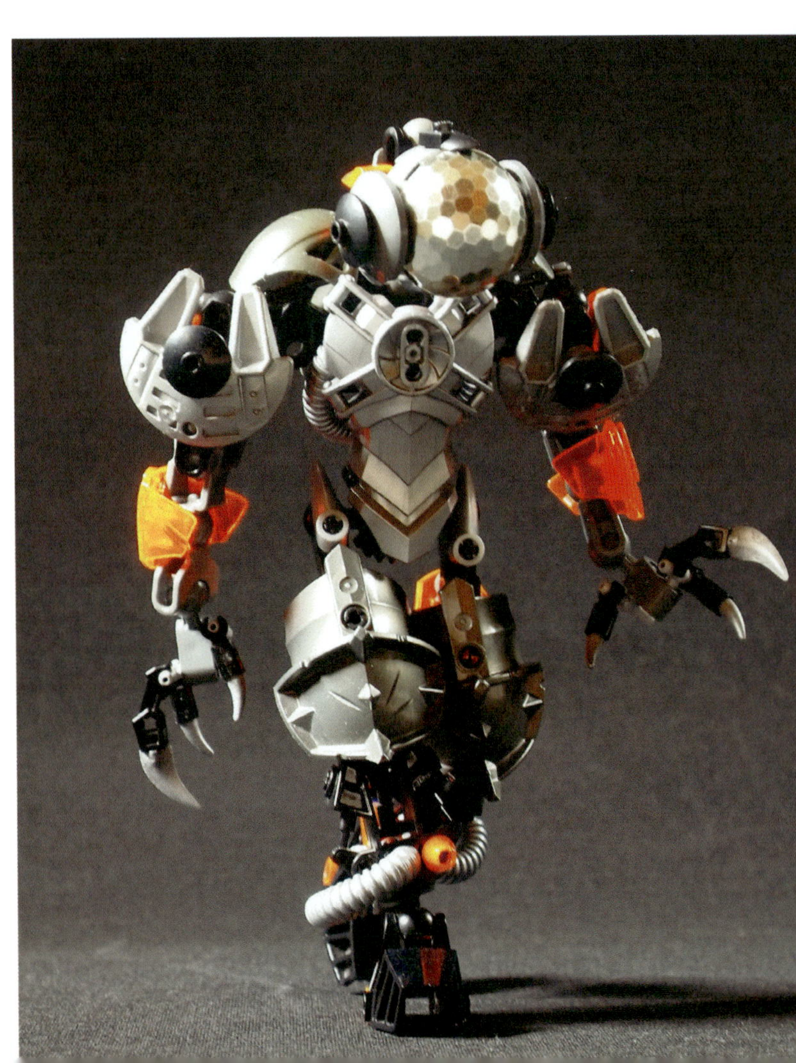

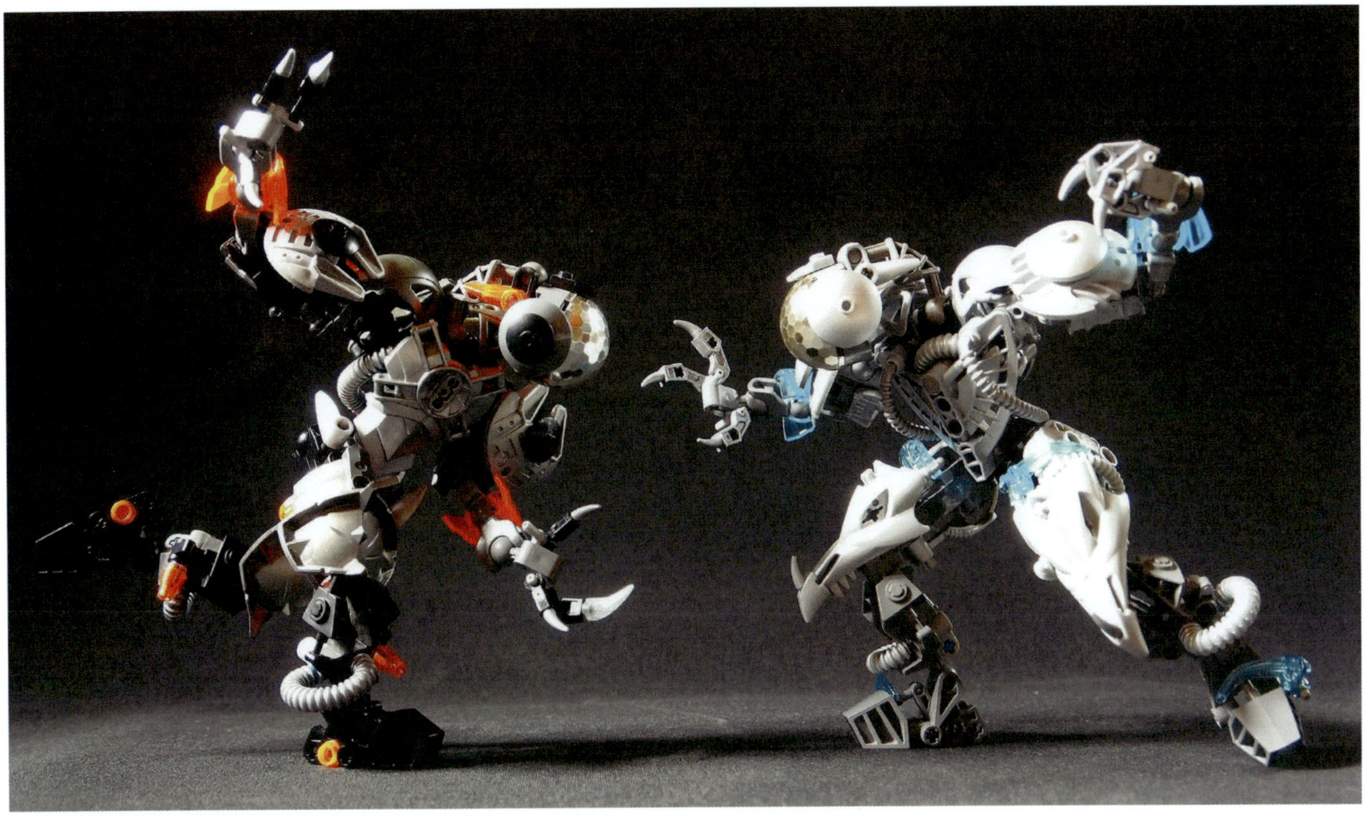

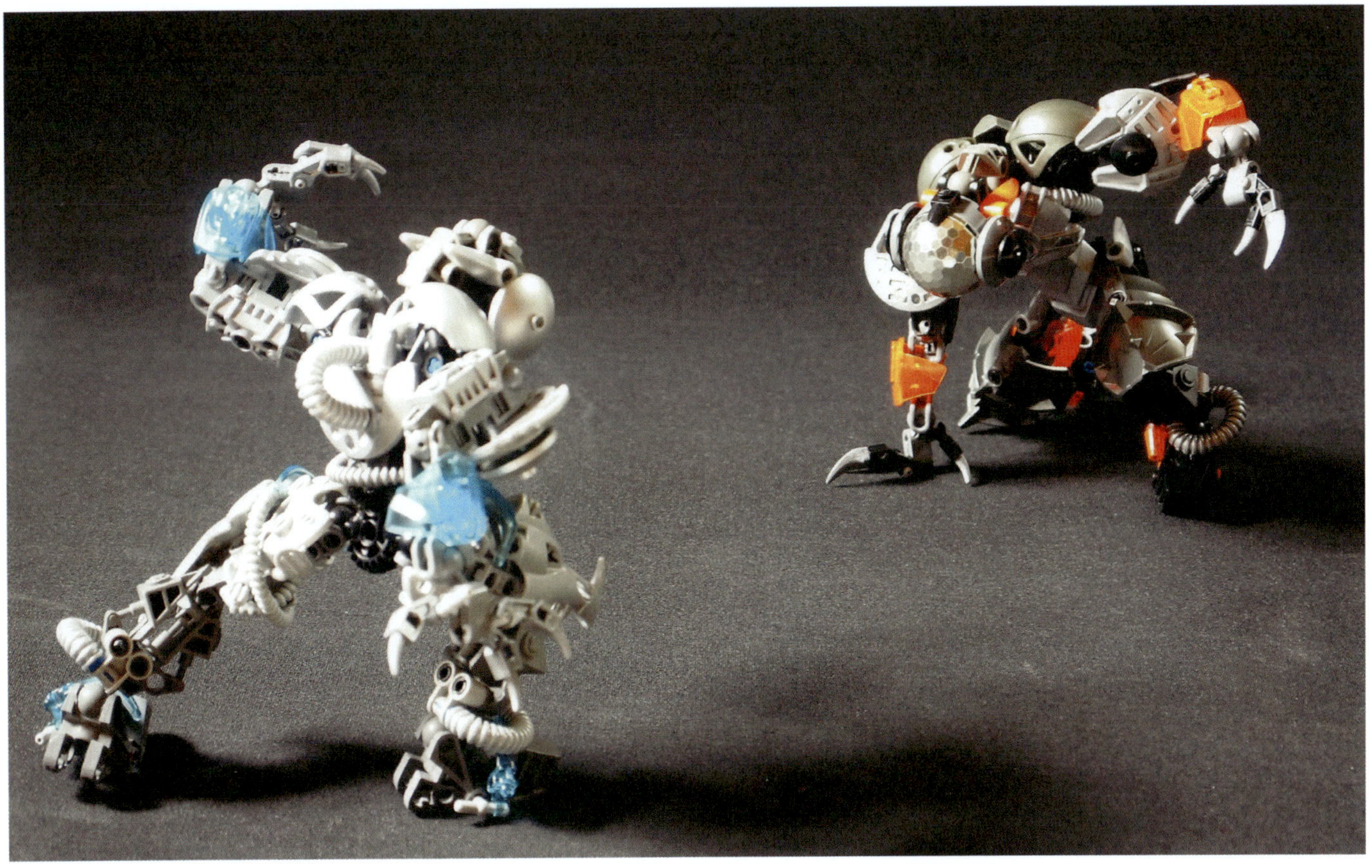

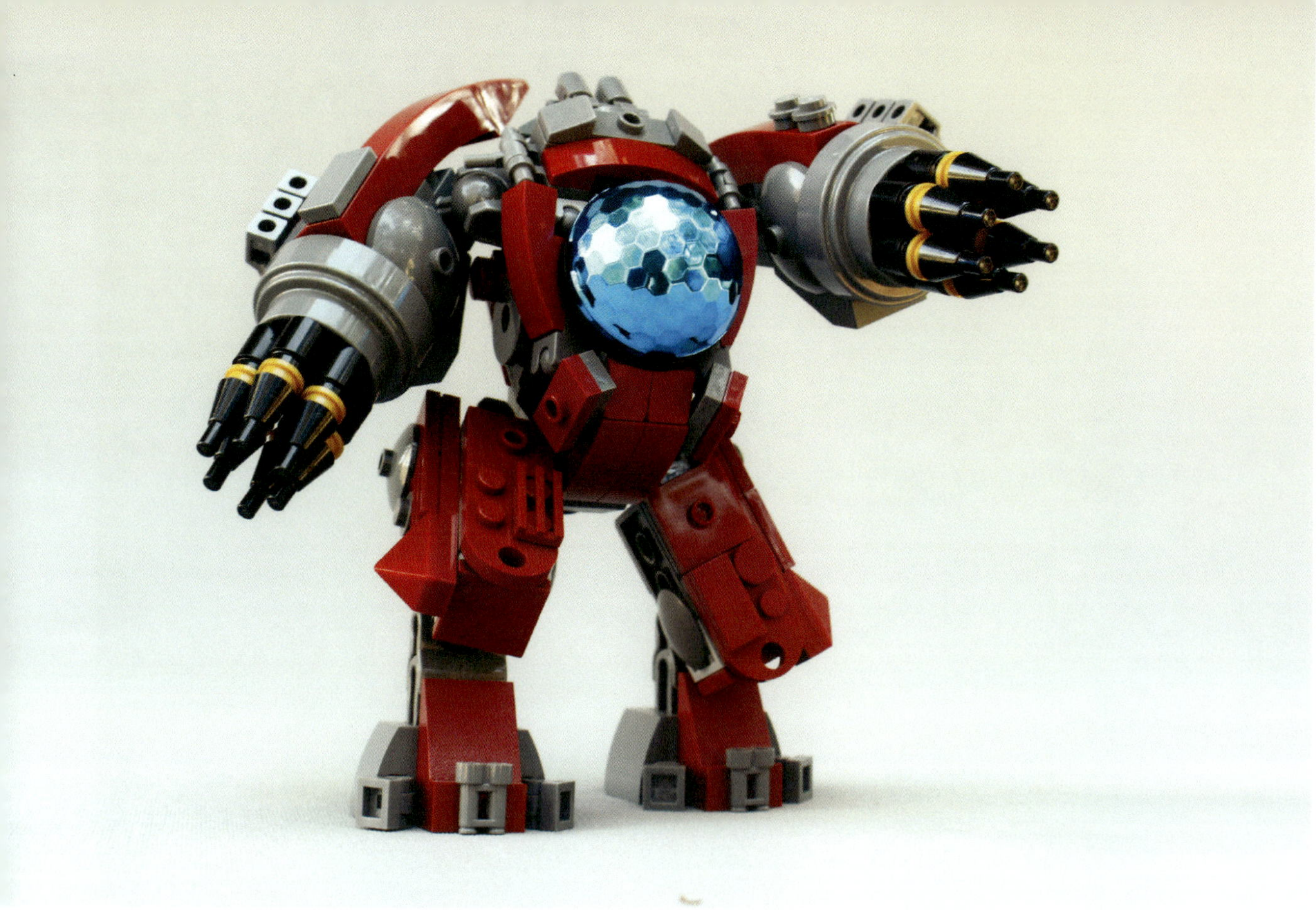

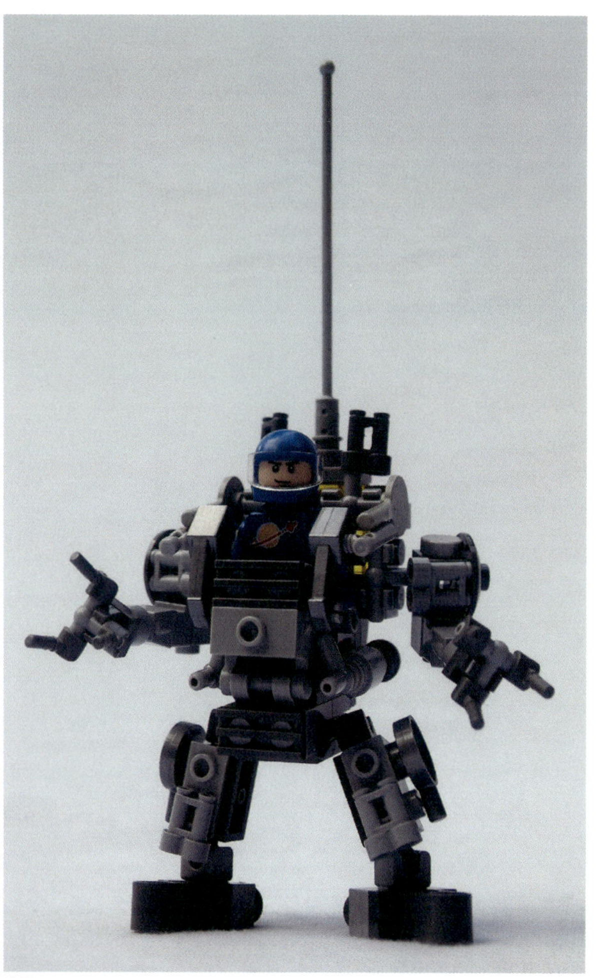

When people think space, they usually imagine spaceships and hovercraft. But there is plenty of room in Sci-Fi left for the ground. Mechs are a staple in Sci-Fi genre, and are some of my favorite creations from this theme. Above, we have the **AFS Karhu** who has missile blasters and the dome compound eye again in blue.

An important part of all these creations is the "grebling", a fancy way of saying 'extra detail'. But it specifically relates to mechanical detail like joints, bolts, and pistons. It tells the story of how the machine moves, interacting with its environment, and mimics the appearance of hydraulics and wires.

You can see the "grebling" on his shoulders and the corners of his limbs.

On the left, we have a Classic Space Mech I never got to upload to Flickr. His grebling was really fun and super detailed. It's designed around a spaceman from the neo-classic space theme.

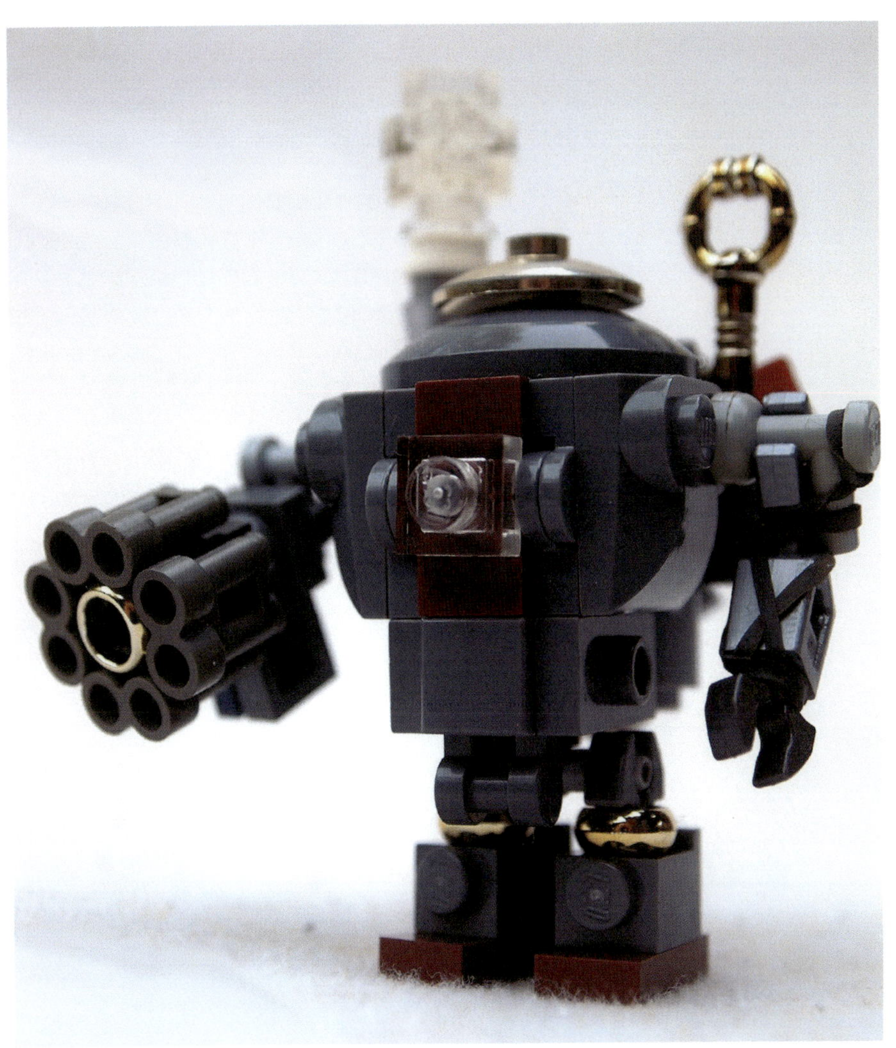

In this top right corner we have the **Vapor Ma.k**. He's a steampunk Mech and his gold and brown elements give him an old-fashioned science fiction feel.

This mech incorporates the "a lot in a little" style very well by cramming lots of detail in a little space, like his gatling gun made from binoculars, his antenna array made from a golden minifig key, and his rubber-band-strapped arm.

This little guy is a type of Mech known as a "Ma.k" and they are designed to look as if they have a minifig inside.

Below we have his squad, which was meant to look as if it combined the best elements of steampunk and apocalypse.

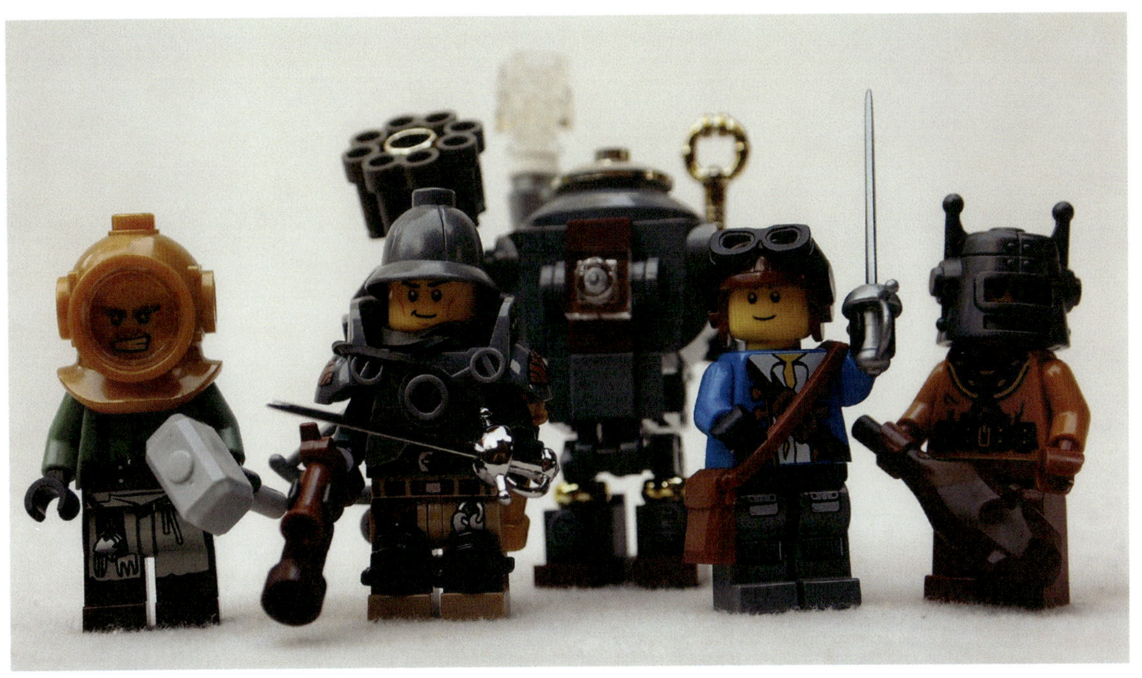

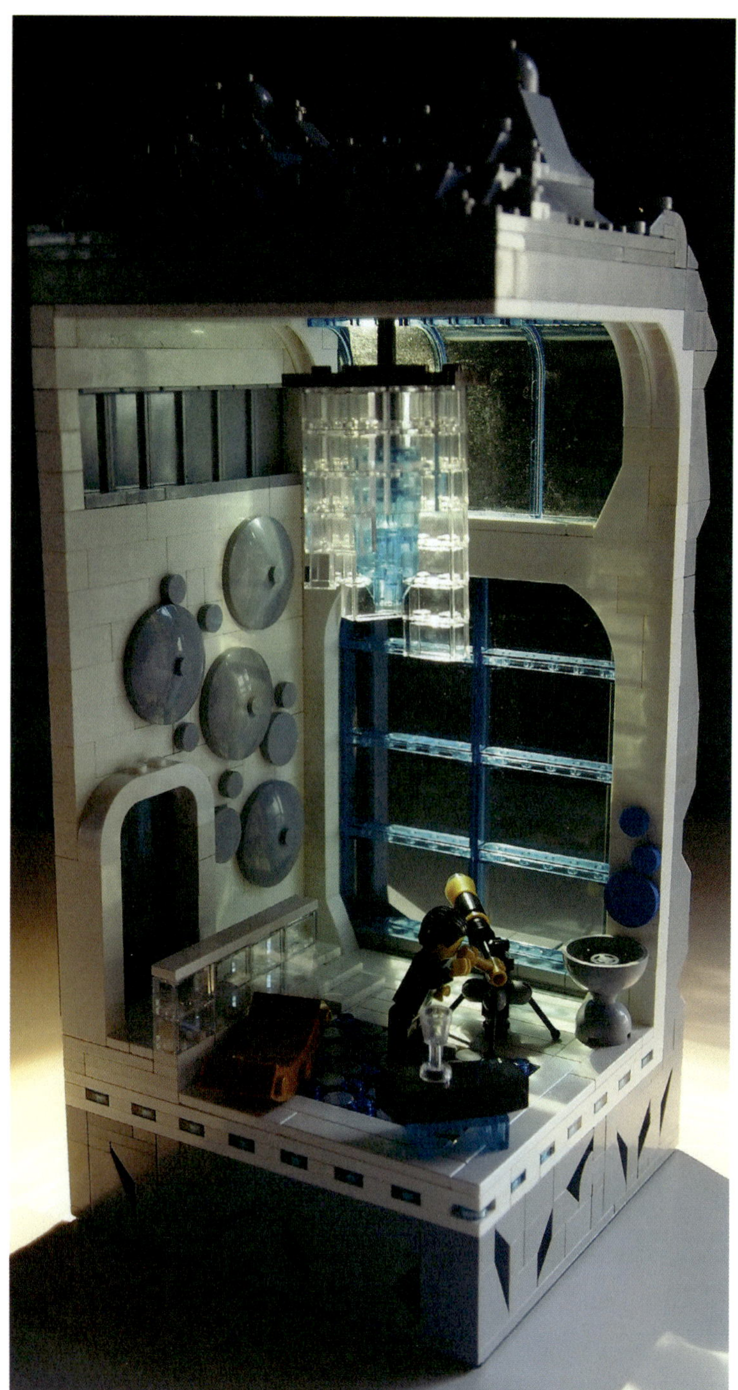

Although most of my general designs are inspired by history, there are some rare exceptions.

On the left, **Commodores Quarters** is an example of a more modern interior. With more emphasis on glass and stone and cooler colors, this scene was a refreshing take on interior details like the furniture and decor.

I had fun with the couch and the coffee table, as well as the circular chandelier, which evoke a nice contemporary vibe with just a few bricks.

Interestingly, the layout itself is very similar to the ones I do for castle themes, with the corner view of the two walls, the light hitting from a specific angle, and even the decorated base has a familiar pattern, (white and blue) which is seen often in this book.

Adding to the modern theme, there's a circular motif throughout this creation like the art on the walls and in the pattern of the rug. The blue over the vase is built to represent an abstract fountain.

This build evokes a slight feeling of loneliness, with it's sparse and clean look, but it's also minimal and relaxing. (Also, a cool detail - there's Moon dust piled on top of this creation.)

On the right, we see the **GSB Redshift,** one of my better entries to the annual Shiptember contest hosted on Flickr. Shiptember is a high-profile contest with a challenge to build a spaceship that is at least 100 studs long in only one month. The Redshift measured in at 105 studs! As fun as this challenge was, I have mixed emotions regarding the Redshift. Although I was well into my career at this point, I would still consider it "earlier" work for me.

The back half of it I am most proud of, the grebling is fun and intricate, with well-integrated side windows and even some sticker work. the front is where things get a bit sloppy in my opinion. I made the mistake of putting off the majority of the work until the last few days of September, and only finished and uploaded the build within one hour of the contest deadline!

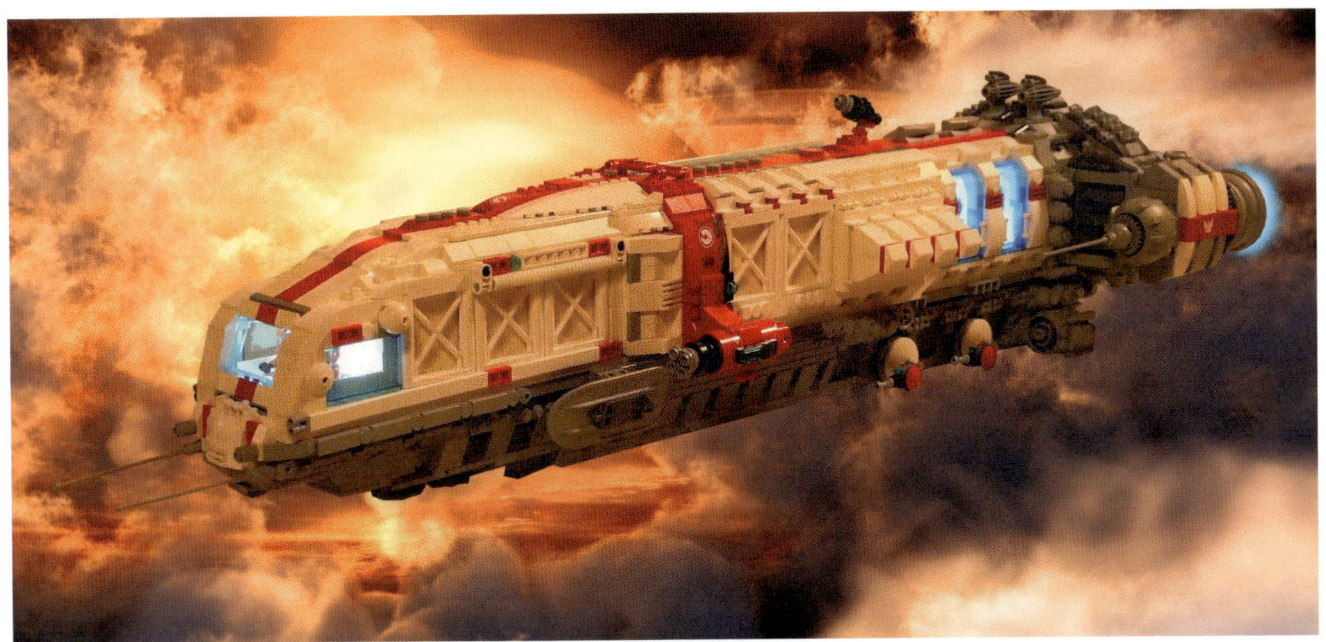

With better time management, I bet I could have made this ship a lot nicer. In the original design, the front third was going to be more of an arrowhead shape with the top of this triangle being the main cockpit. It sort of has a greyhound bus look instead! Thankfully, there were some fun features that keep the ship interesting. The center houses two flashlights that light up the vessel.

Since the Redshift, I haven't made a serious attempt at a spaceship again. But who knows, maybe one day I'll rebuild this thing.

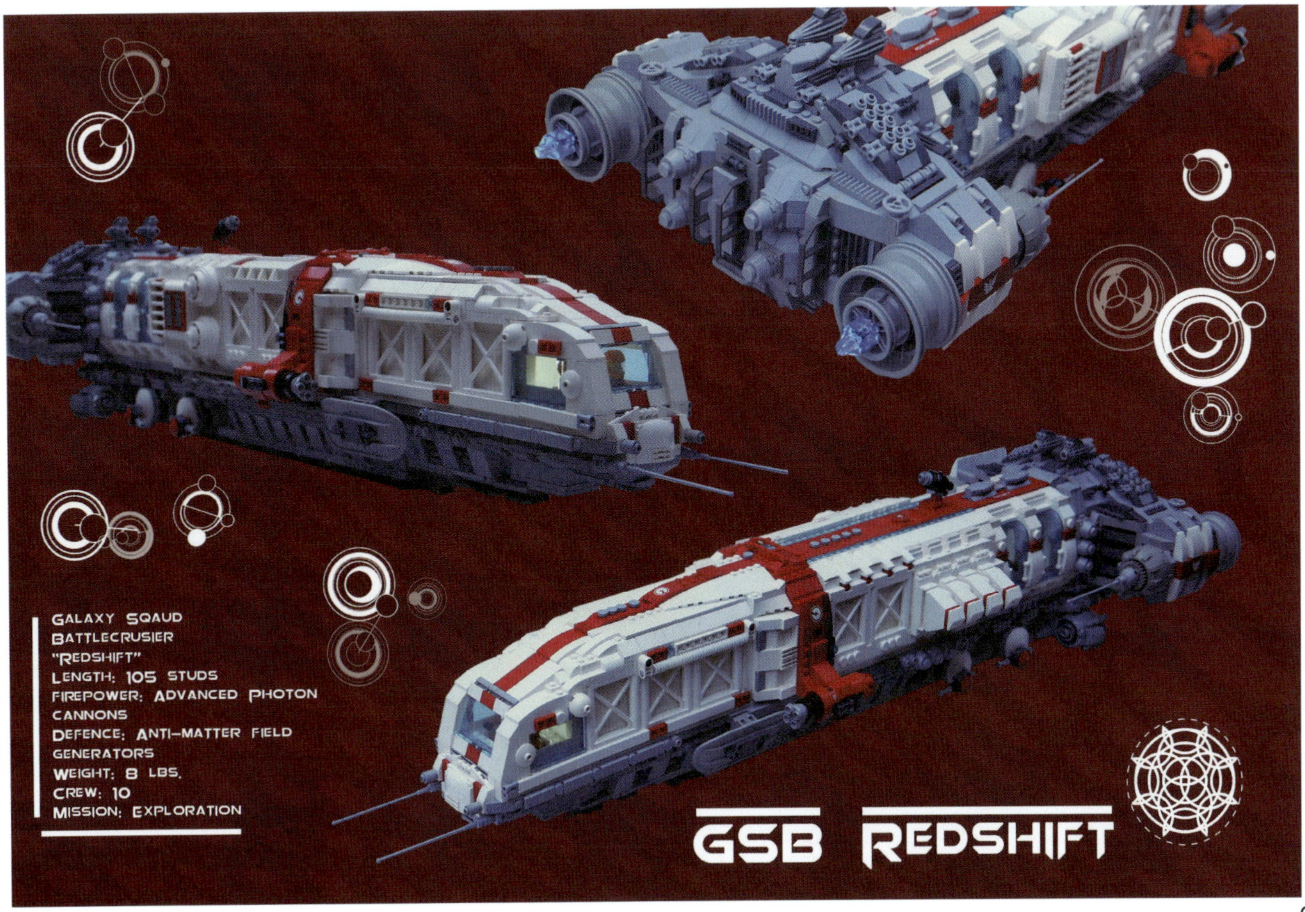

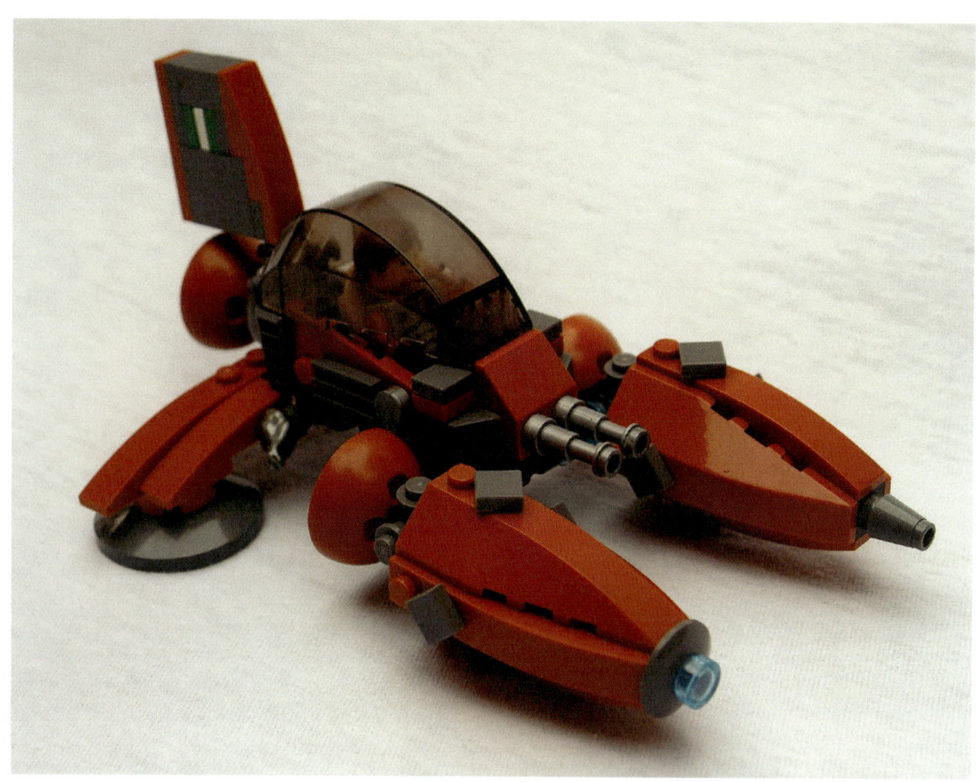

Every now and then, a new LEGO® trend pops up in the community – a fun design, character or theme. A fresh perspective on something old, or a simple challenge.

One of these was the "Vic Viper", a ship with a specific shape – two prongs at the front, two wings at the back, and a tailfin on the top.

One thing I wanted to do for the **Copper Viper** (above, below) was the color. The dark orange was a unique choice as most spaceships relied on brighter colors. There's also a tiny cockpit that barely contains the driver.

The **CLR-24** or "**Cappellan Legion Racer**" (opposite page, top left) is another example of those popup trends. It was loosely based on a design known as the "cycycle". Those were known for racing, however these are intended for combat and look more robust.

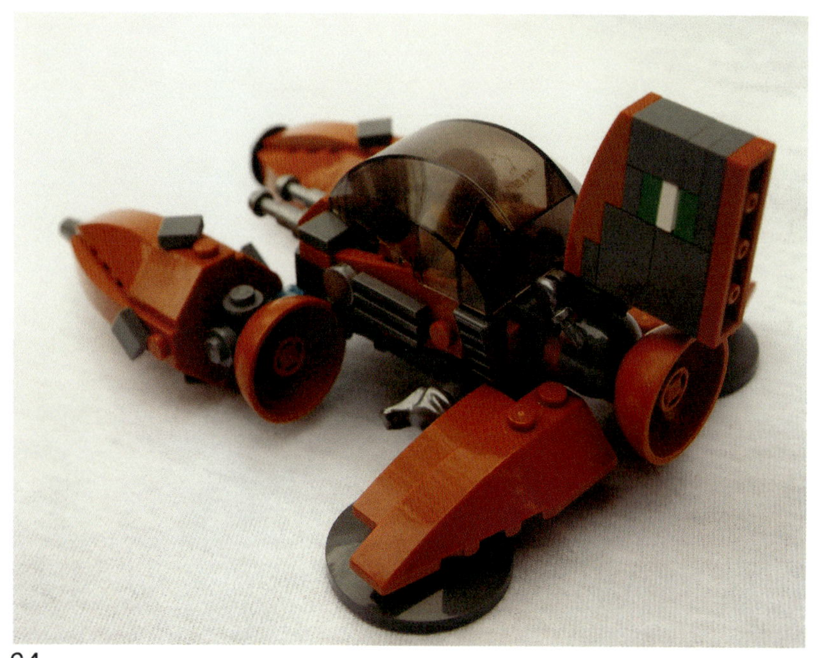

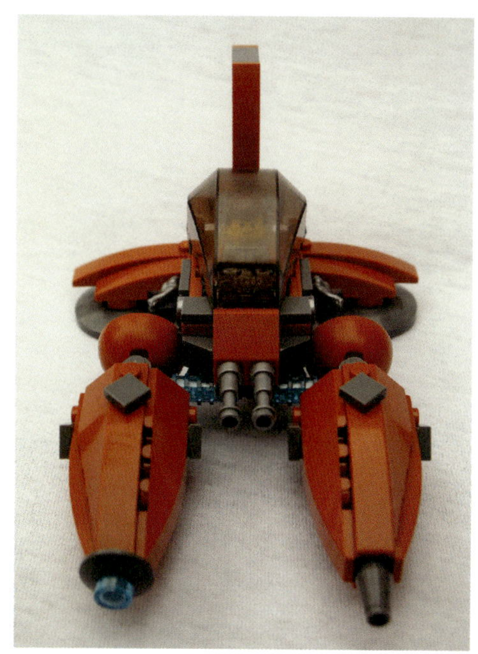

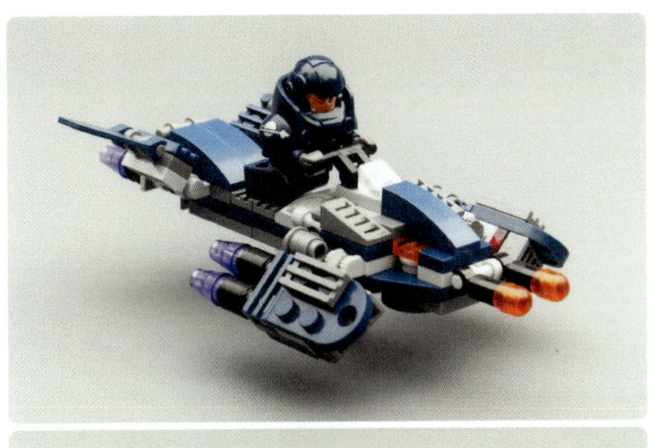

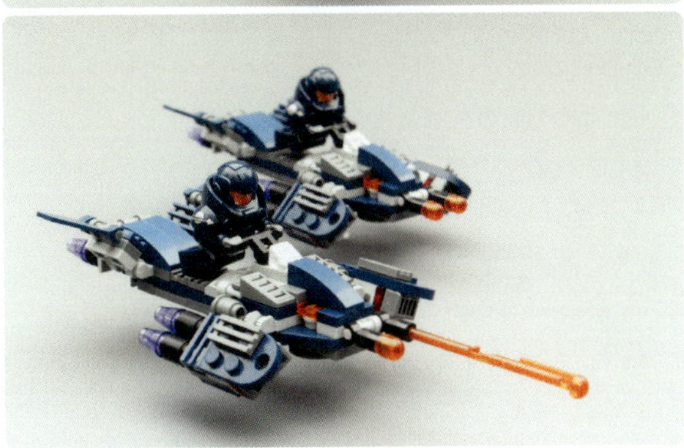

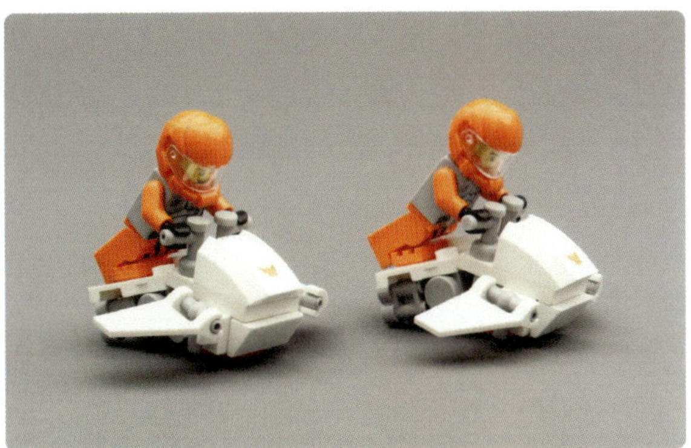

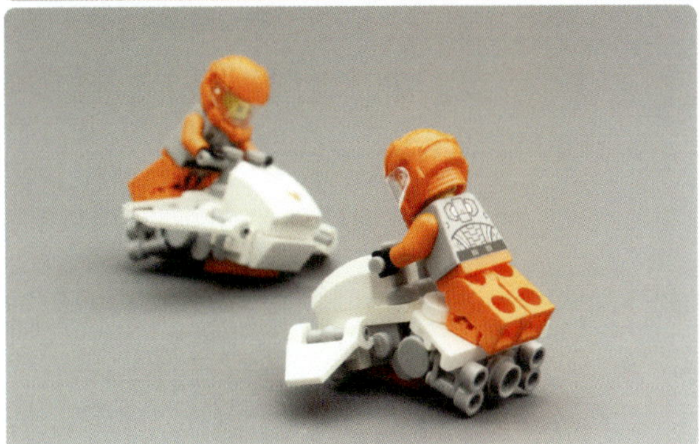

The **B10 Gnat** (top right) is easily my most delightful spacecraft to date. They were made to look like tiny jet-skis for space and employ the "lot in a little" philosophy - very small but detailed.

The **White Raven G-12** (right) is one of those builds that was built for no reason at all, just tinkering with designs, and I came up with my favorite space ship I've made yet. It's a clean look with just the right amount of grebling and a color scheme that's easy on the eyes. I wouldn't change anything about it.

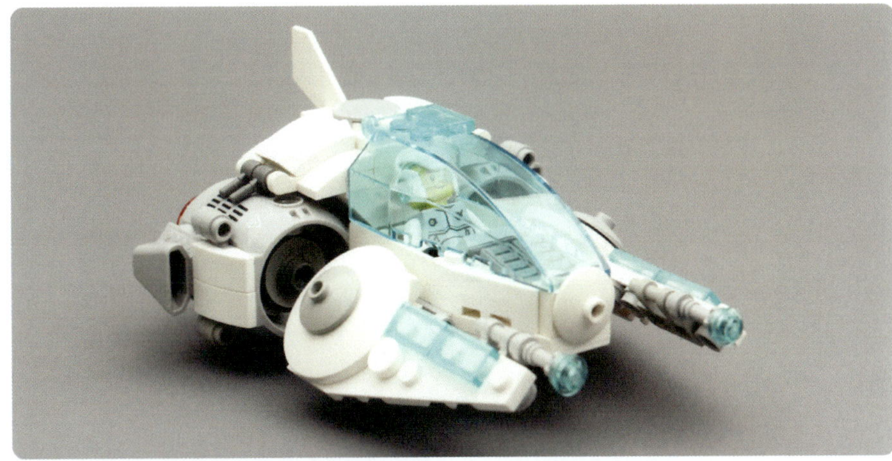

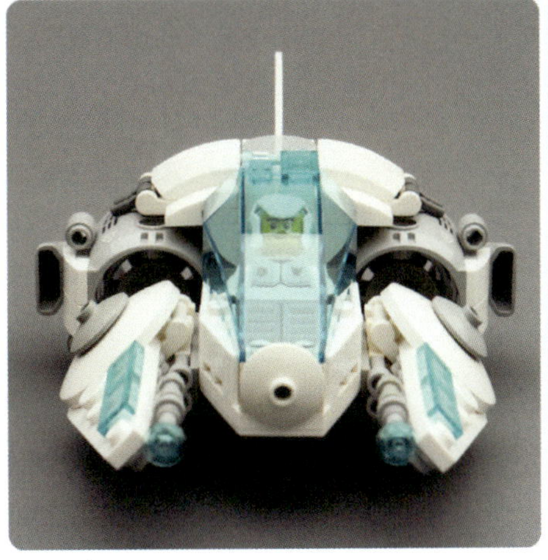

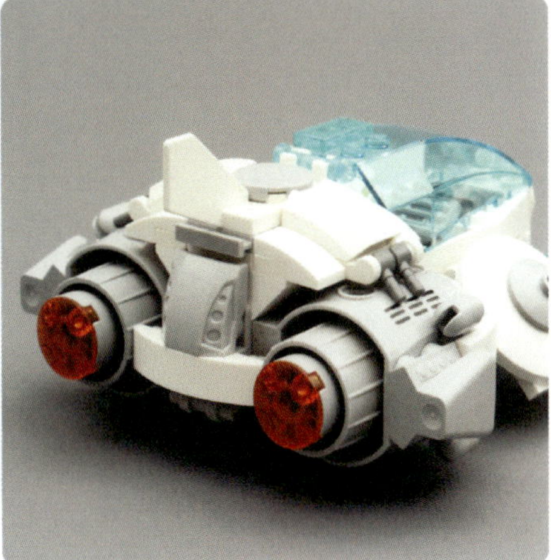

FLORA & FAUNA

Growing up, I always had a huge appreciation for the great outdoors. I loved exploring. I loved studying and learning about animals and all the different ecosystems. Anything I could get my hands on in relation to those topics - stuffed animals, books, documentaries, zoos, aquariums, I couldn't get enough of it. You could almost say that nature was in my nature.

It didn't take long to see this passion expressed through my LEGO® creations. Landscapes were first and the creatures came next.

In this section, we will be taking a closer look at both of these themes separately and combined, along with rockwork and grasswork, water and trees. And of course, lots of animals.

But not just realistic animals, I also love building dragons, and other fantasy, imaginary, and extinct beasts.

This cheerful orange fellow to the right is one of my best, a seahorse built as my entry for a college art competition in the 'sculpture' category. Although I only received an honorable mention, I did get kudos for my unorthodox medium.

This seahorse has some fun details! I especially like the colors. The orange, purple, and green are secondary hues on the color wheel. I also love the seashells on the ocean floor base.

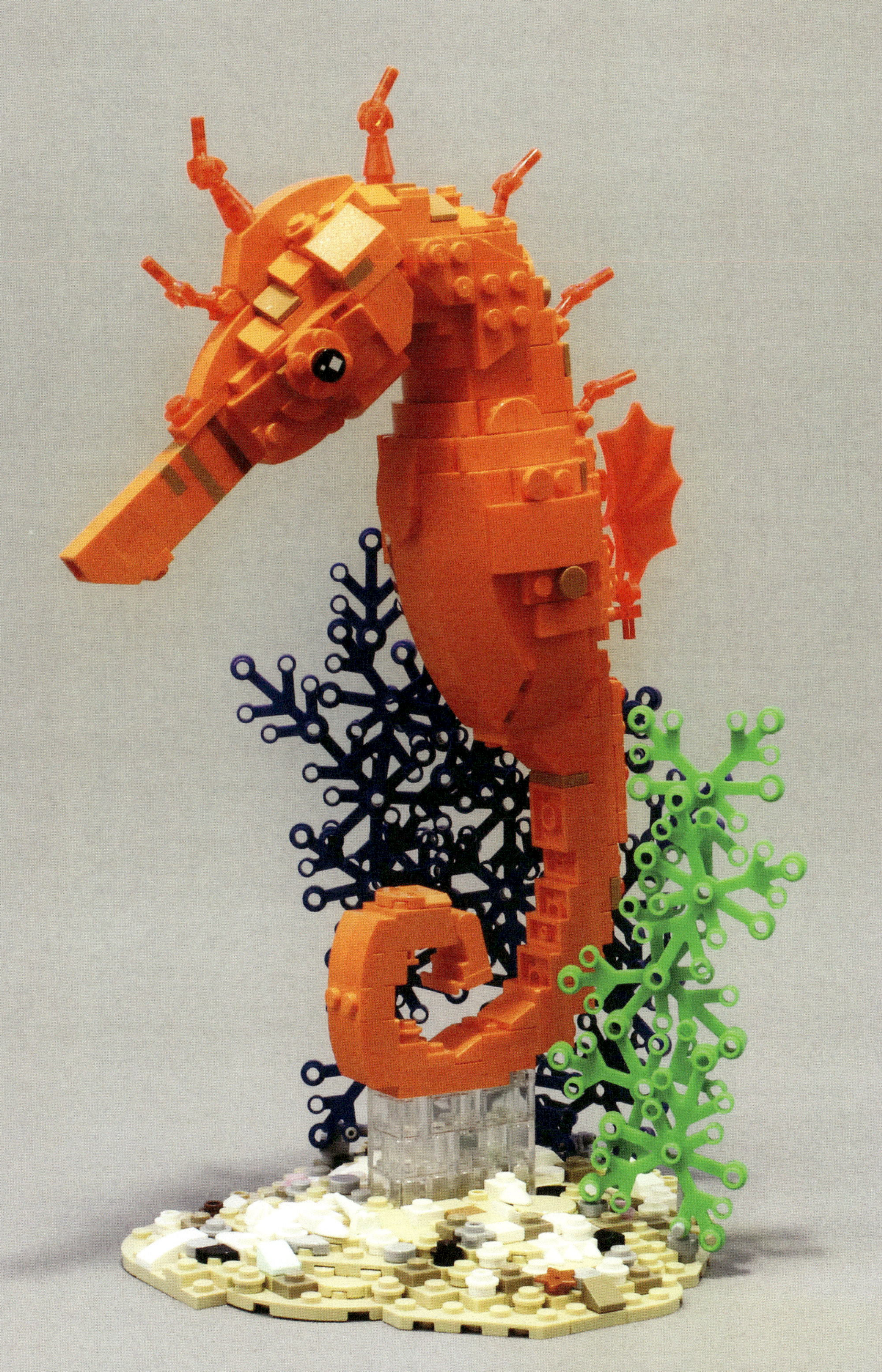

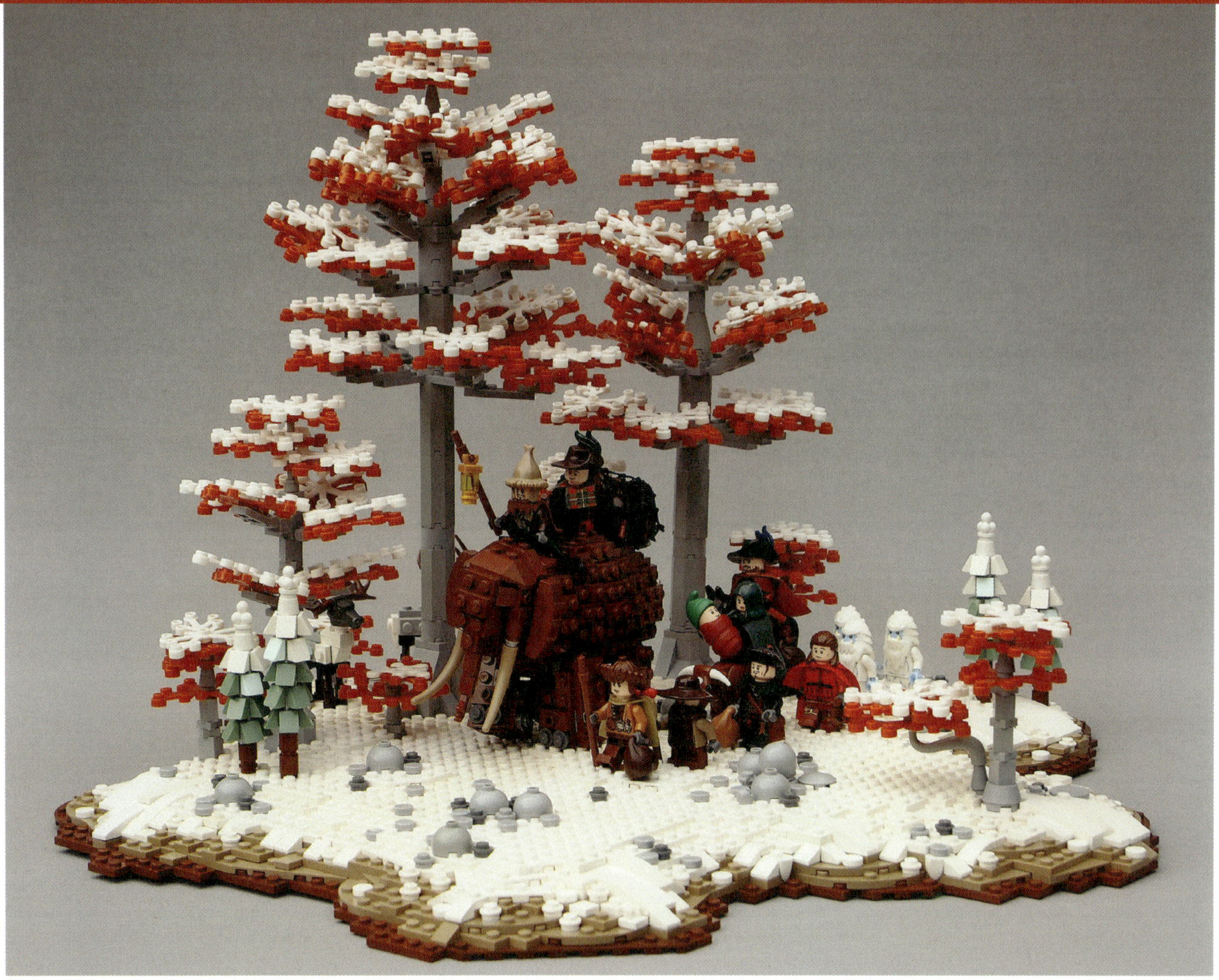

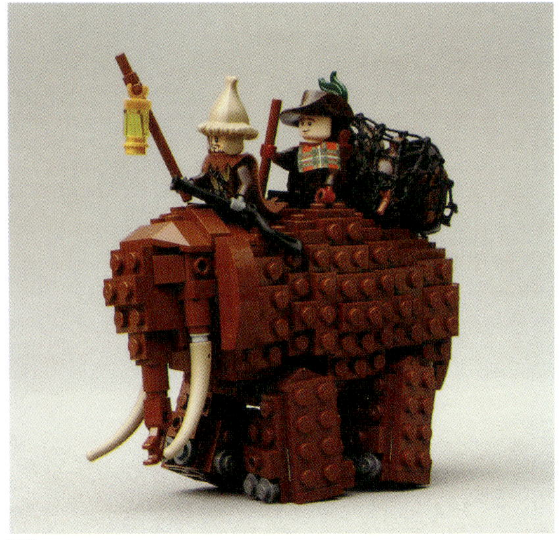

The **Convoy in the Coniferous** ended up being one of my more iconic creations. There are so many fantastic highlights. Let's begin with the colors. The earthy tones provide a brilliant "wildernessy" feel, with the orange popping against the crisp white and soft evergreens. The wooly pachyderm and other characters stand out against the gray tree trunks and stones.

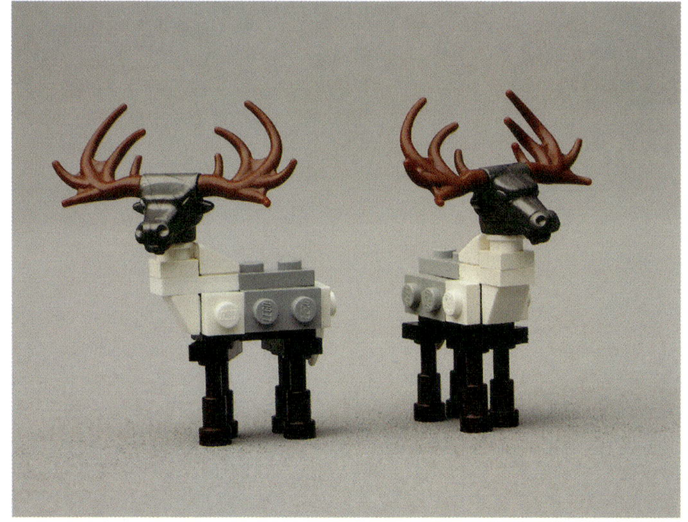

The characters in this creation are just as important. Front and center is Bayen, an "Elemoth". A running gag for my characters was to have hybrid animals and he is a cross between an Elephant and a Mammoth. Following and riding Bayen are a young family, and alongside are two merchants, a minstrel, a dwarf, and a small troop of yetis migrating south for the winter.

The other animals (left) are a very old deer design I created years ago using third-party elements for the heads. They were meant to be elk, but turned out looking more like caribou. Perhaps they should be known as "Elkibou"! The build itself was built for the Isles of Aura. Where's the floating island? The larger creations in the theme were meant to not have an island in order for the landscape to feel larger and more widespread. In the story, there were plenty of islands that were too big to see across and this made it easier to not have to worry about a rock underbelly.

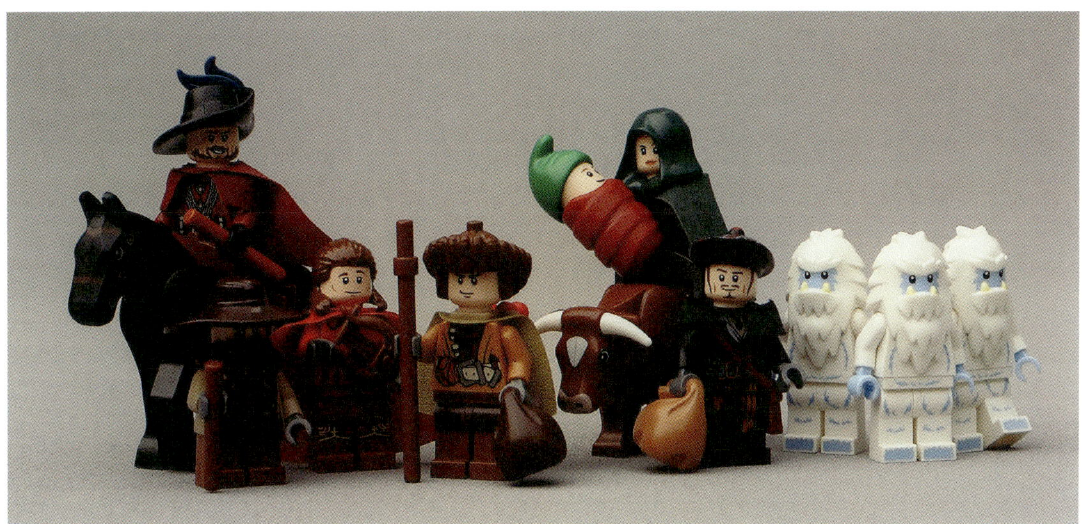

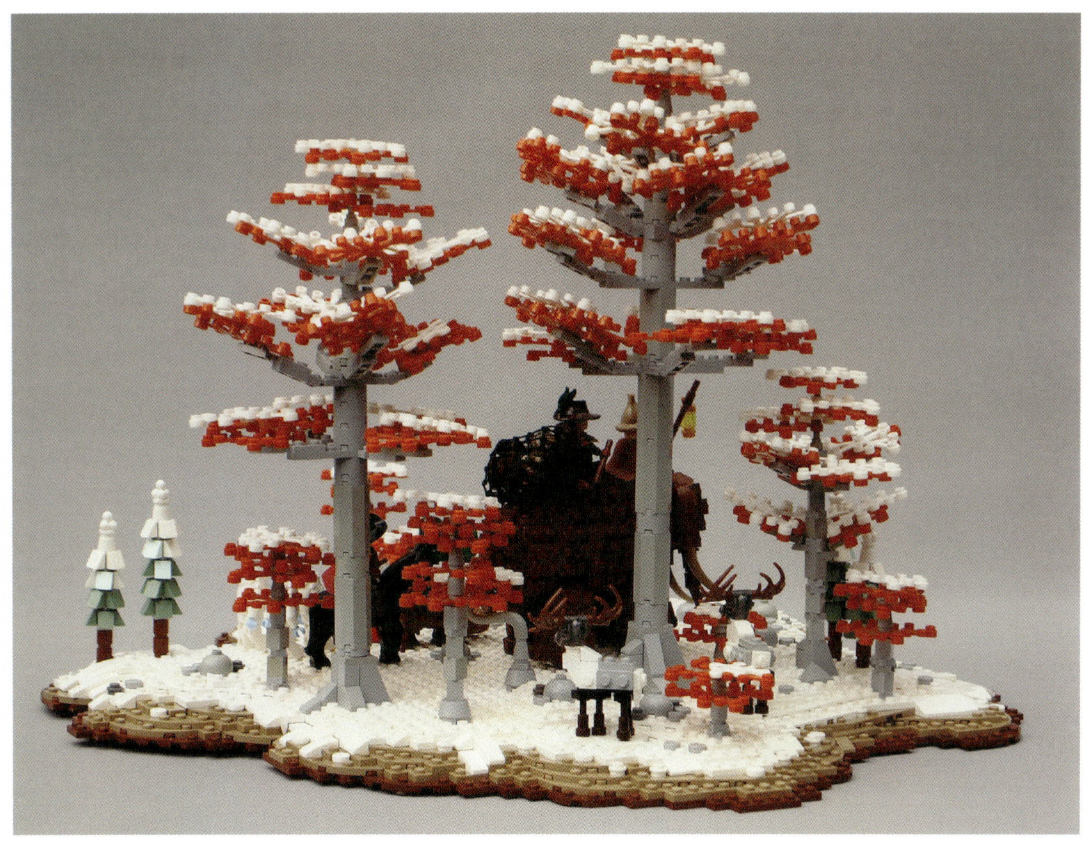

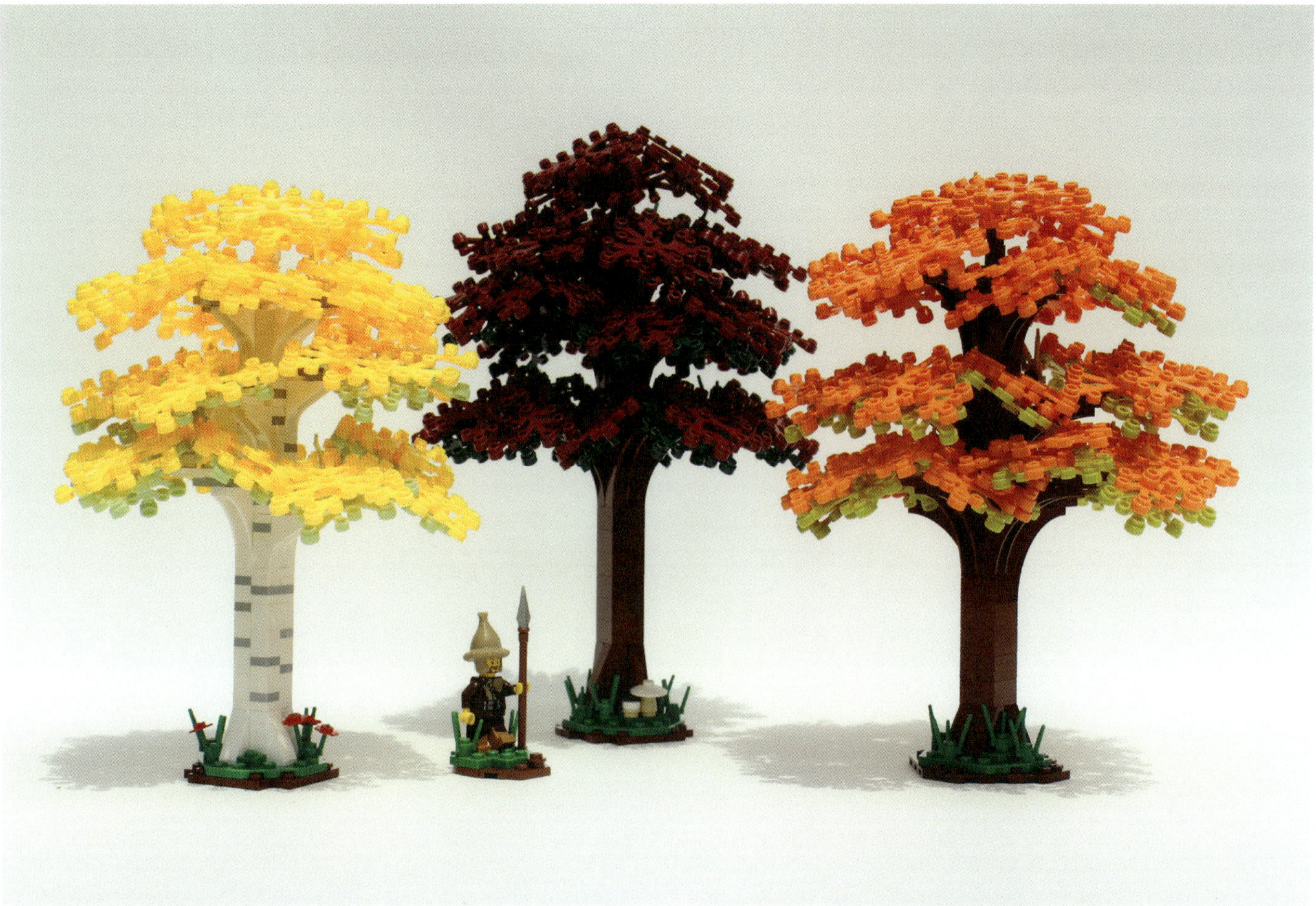

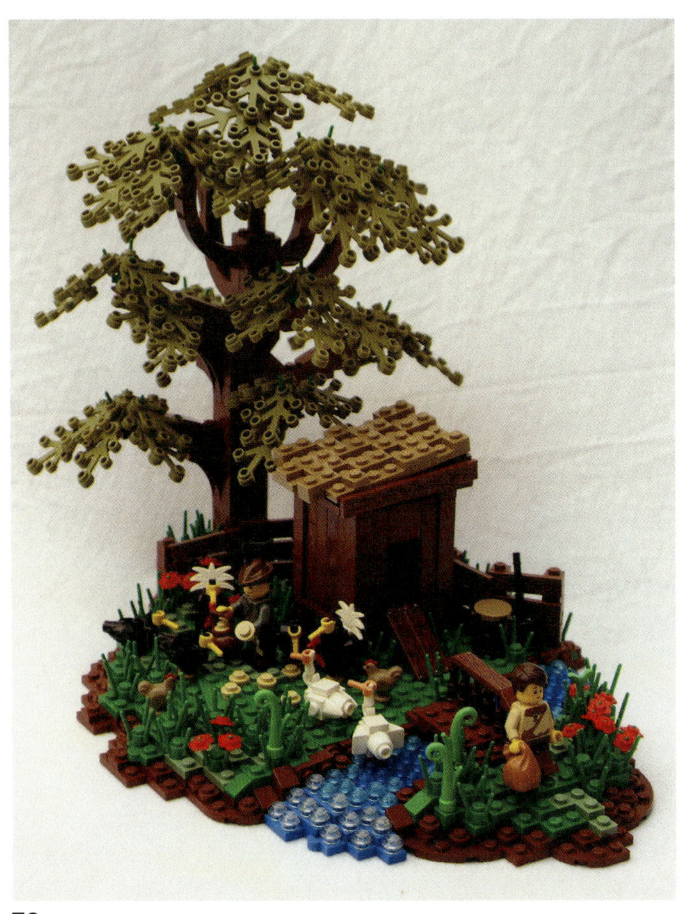
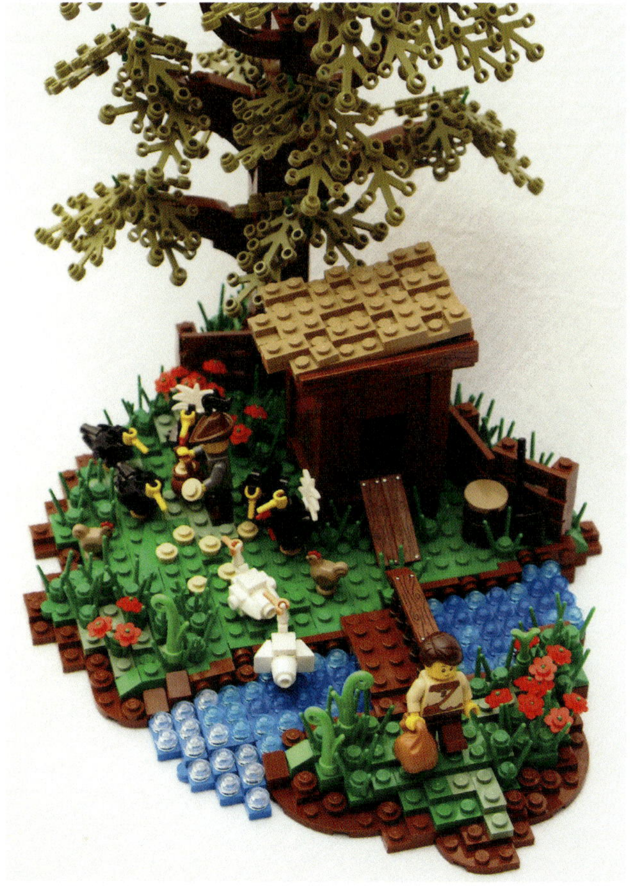

One of the most enriching parts of landscapes is to try new techniques for relatively simple things. Trees offer a treasure trove of opportunities for new designs and styles. That brings us to these grass-stalk trees. These are designed to incorporate irregular and natural leaf patterns and are made with common parts so they are easier to use on a large scale.

The grass stalk trees provide a simple "quick and dirty" solution to getting lots of irregular shaped branches and leaves with simple parts. The design is very straightforward – place a 3-prong grass stalk at the edge of a branch and loop the leaf pieces onto it! It produces an unusual tilted branch, giving it an organic look. If you have the same shape and weight on each stalk, it remains well balanced. I'll go through some examples here.

(Top left) We have a birch and some oaks. These striking trees really stand out because of their bright colors. However, aside from the red tree in the middle, they are third-party leaves. For a long time, builders like me had to resort to using aftermarket parts if we wanted colors like yellow or orange. However, LEGO® took notice and has now released their own similar colors of leaf pieces.

Below left, we have the **Poultry Farmers**! Along with its excellent tree, we have geese, turkey, and chickens. This was built for a Classic Castle contest.

(Right) And here we have **Robin of Locksley's Camp**. Even merry men need a day off once in a while!

This creation goes to show just how big a scale you can use for this leaf design.

Eventually I would go on to find stronger techniques with a similar effect for these leaves, (the grass stalks themselves aren't a very sturdy connection point) but for anyone just starting, it is a simple, efficient way to make your tree look natural.

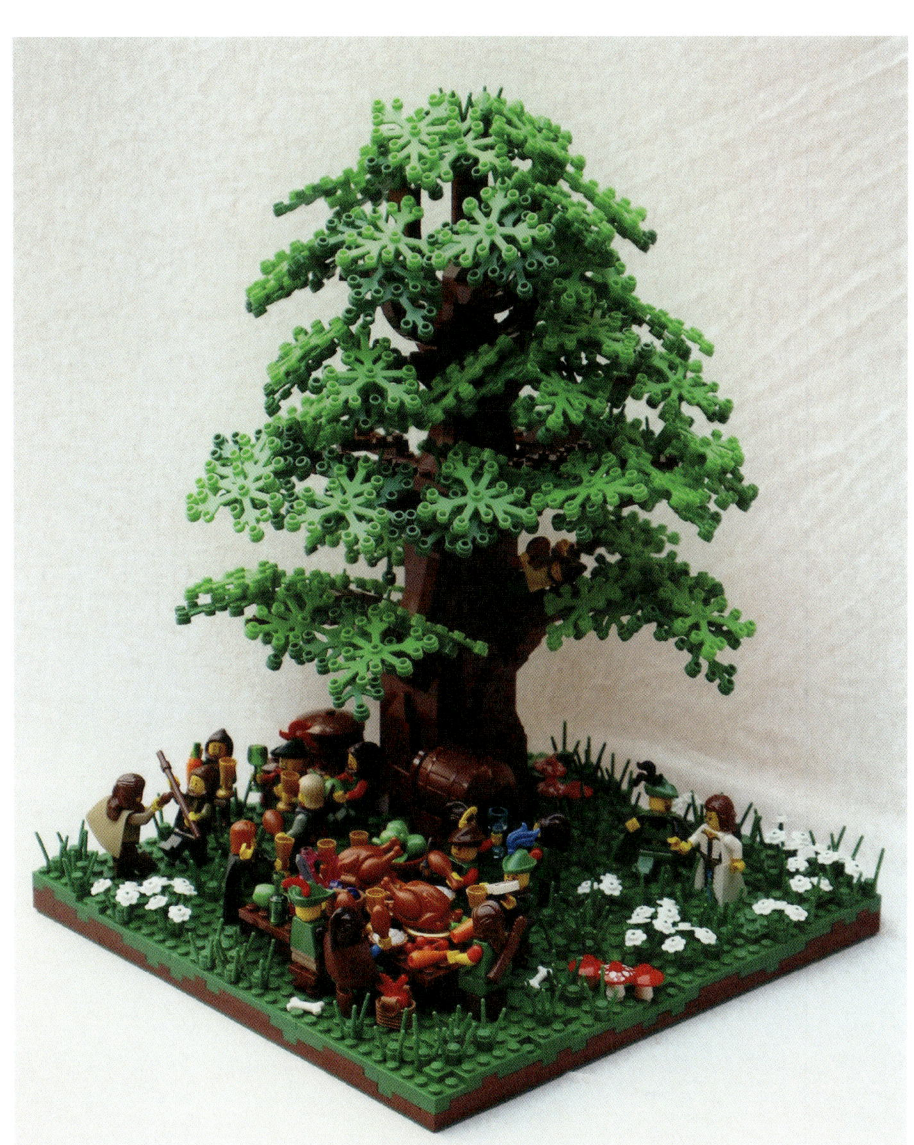

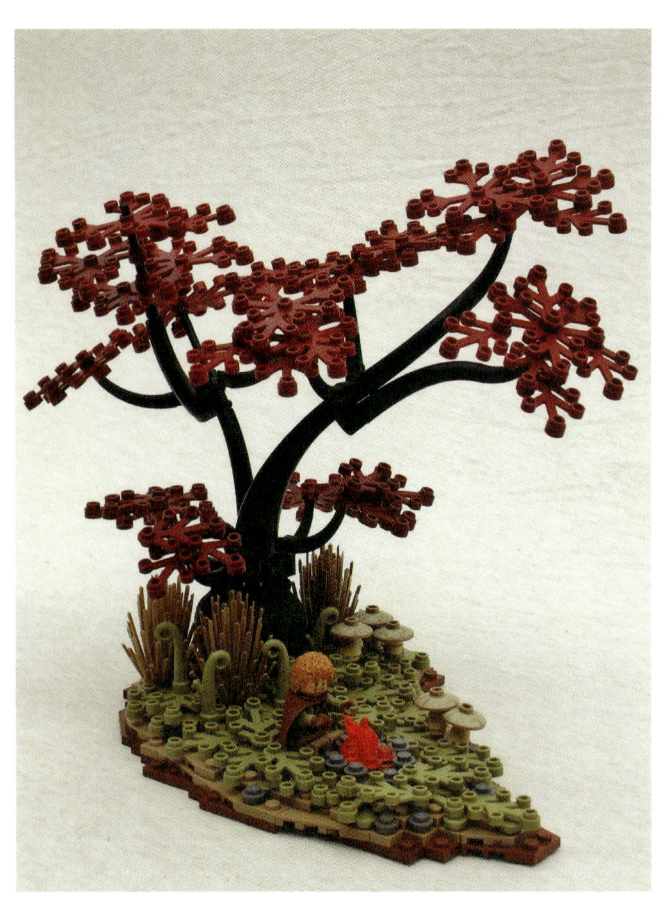 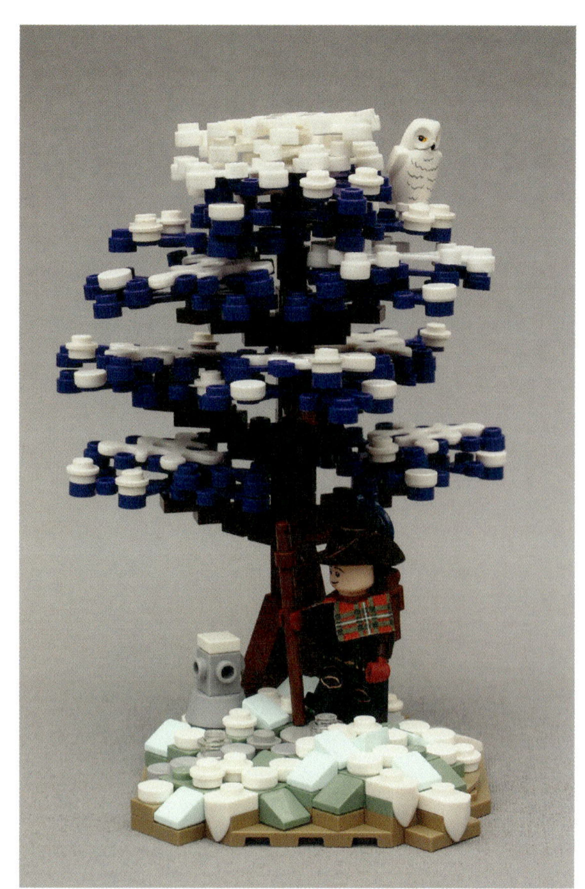

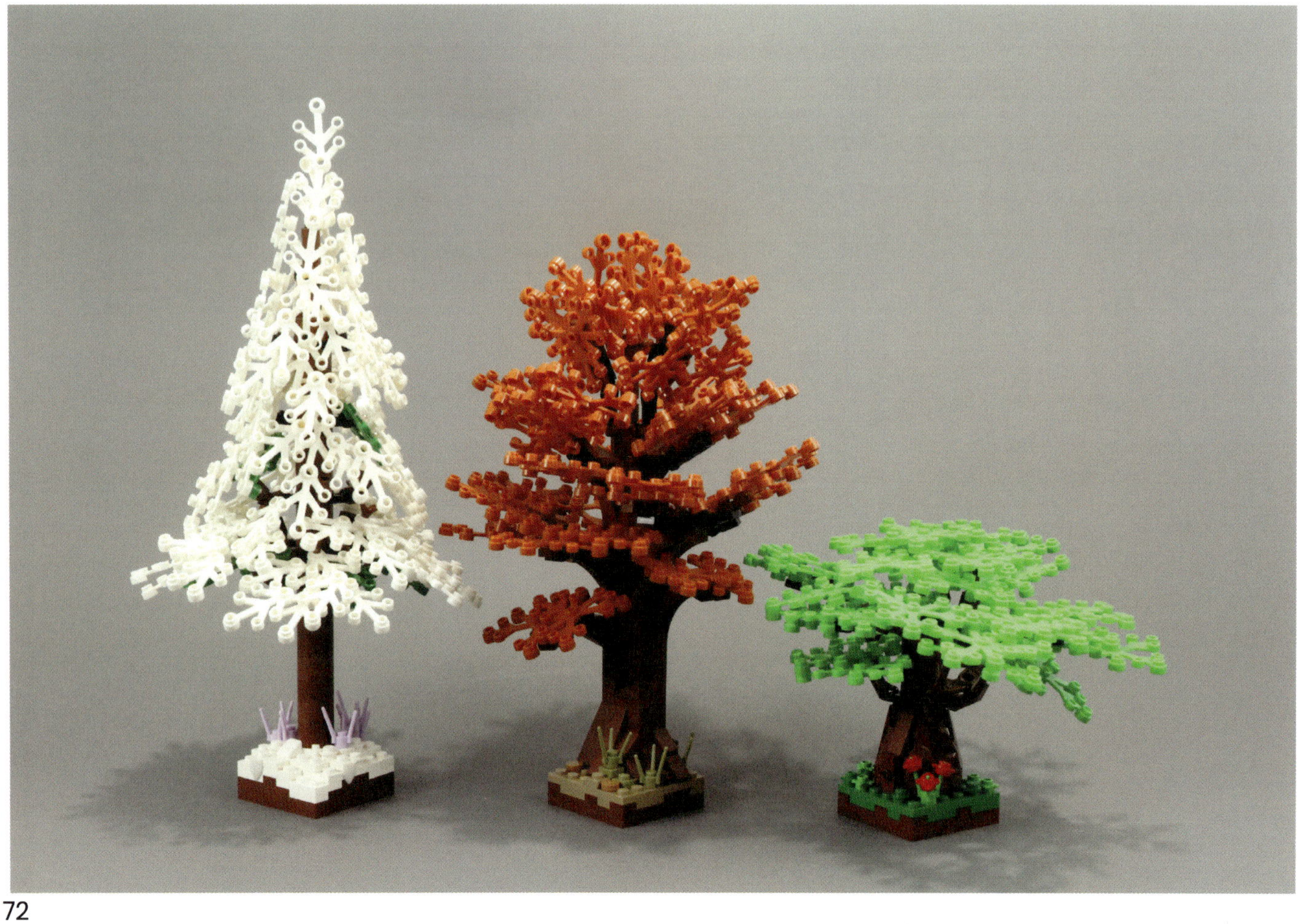

There are many different ways to create trees out of LEGO®. A few examples shown here are the tree made with animal tail and horn pieces (far left) as well as the dark purple tree (left) made only with plates and bricks. The rest of the trees were created with a combination of technic ball joints and occasionally minifig robot arms! The main thing to keep in mind when building trees is to create an organic and free-flowing look as much as possible.

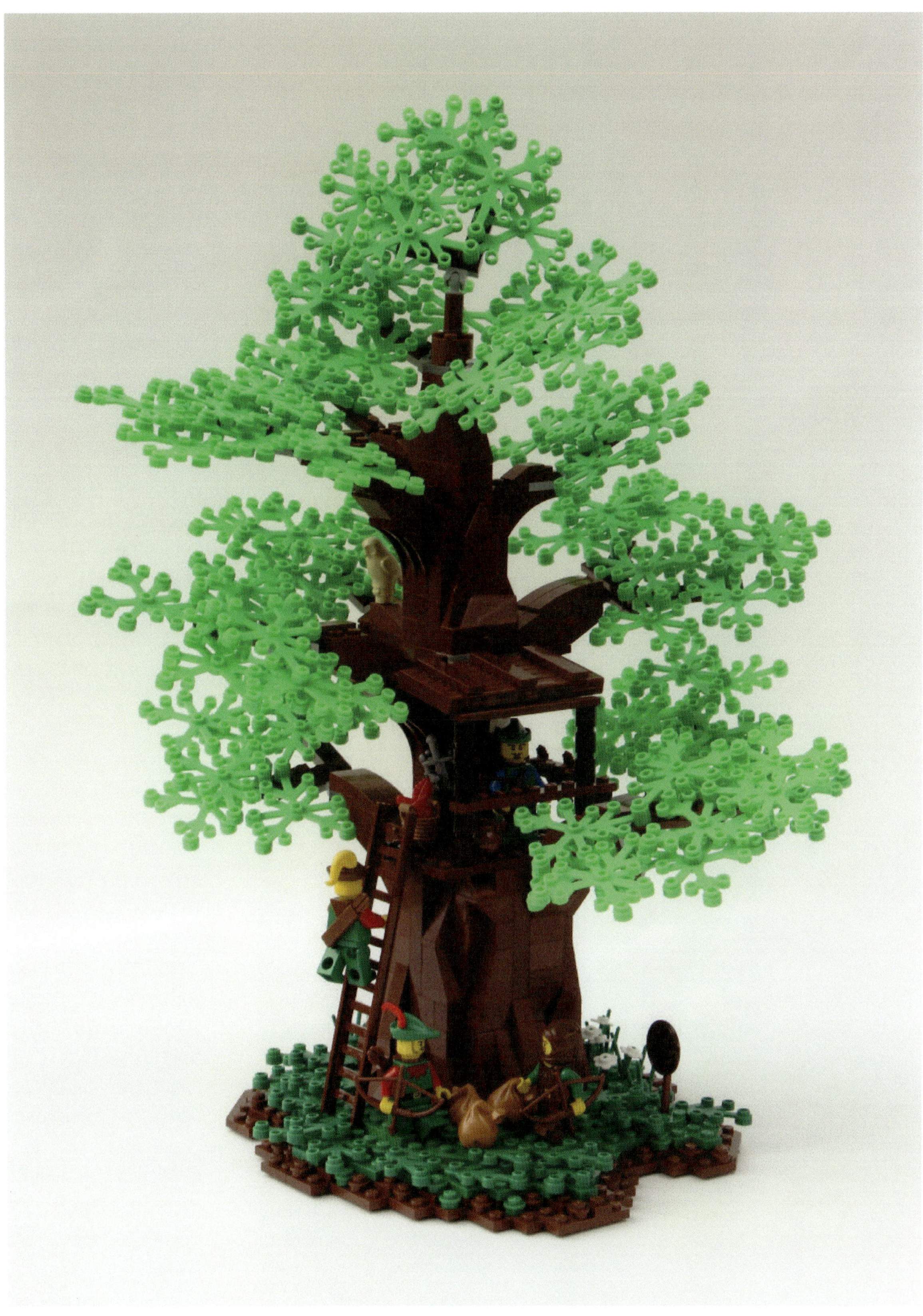

The Progression

Landscapes were a huge part of my early career. However, over the years things have changed a lot and here we'll take a look at the stages of that change in detail.

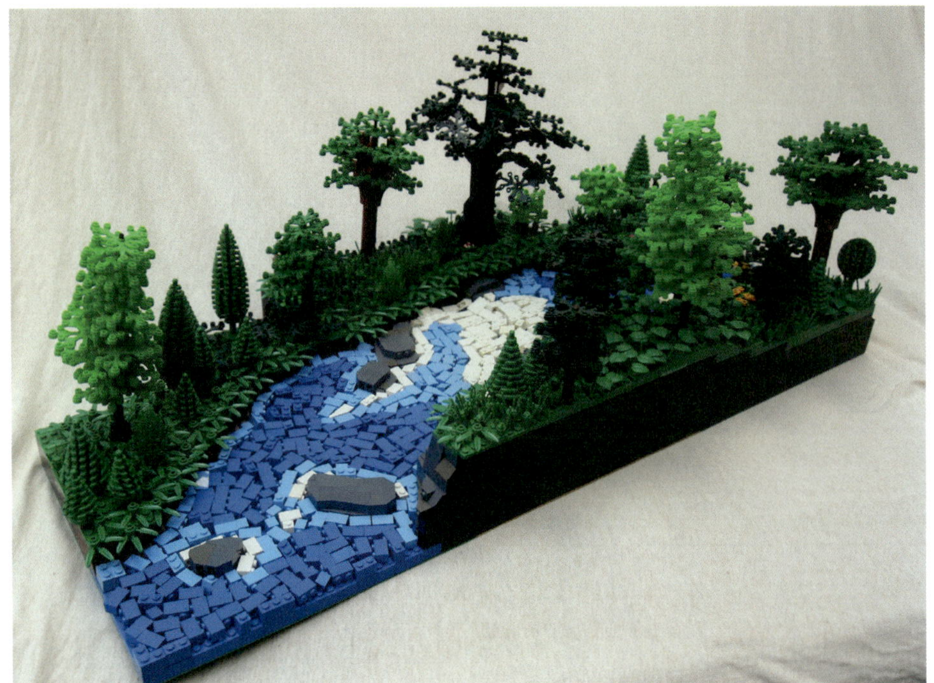

On the left, we have one of my earlier major landscapes called the **River of Life**.

This river scene has a lot of "interesting" techniques that don't quite stand the test of time and are a bit dated now, but at the time, they were considered revolutionary.

The water, most notably, is made from loose bricks, almost looking like a mosaic. This was created in part because we didn't have any other pieces that would work and I had to use what we already had on hand. It's not as polished as it could be but it was a very unique style.

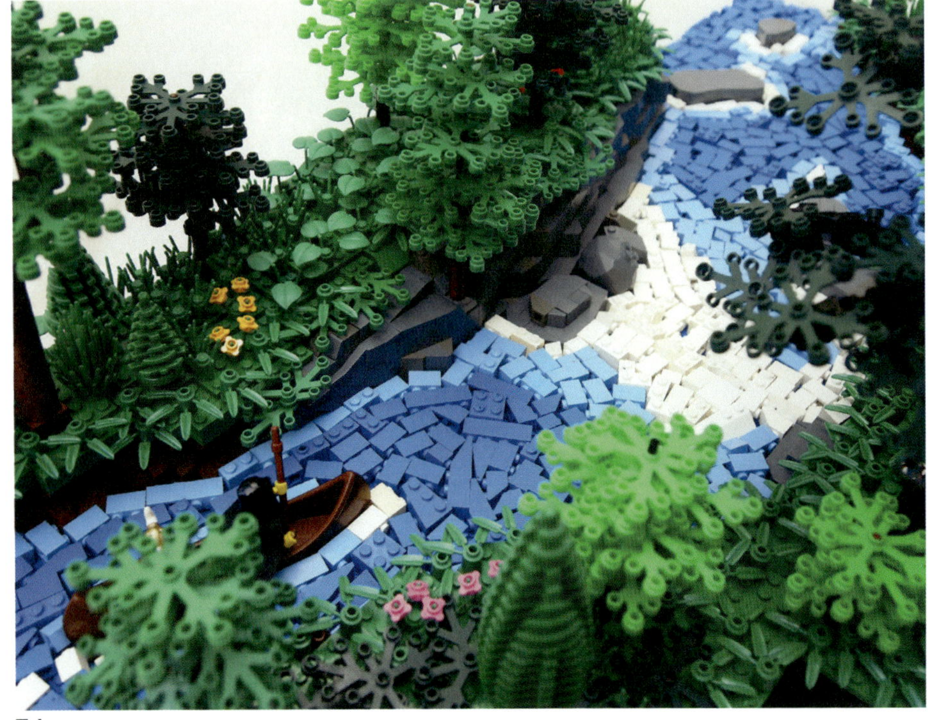

The foliage is perhaps overdone, with too much on the ground and not enough in the trees (of which some are are prefab, something I would never do these days) but one thing that holds up nicely is the rockwork. It's mostly SNOT (studs not on top) and have an elegant freeflow that works well wtih the riverbank.

Overall, the aesthetic was headed in the right direction with a vibrant look.

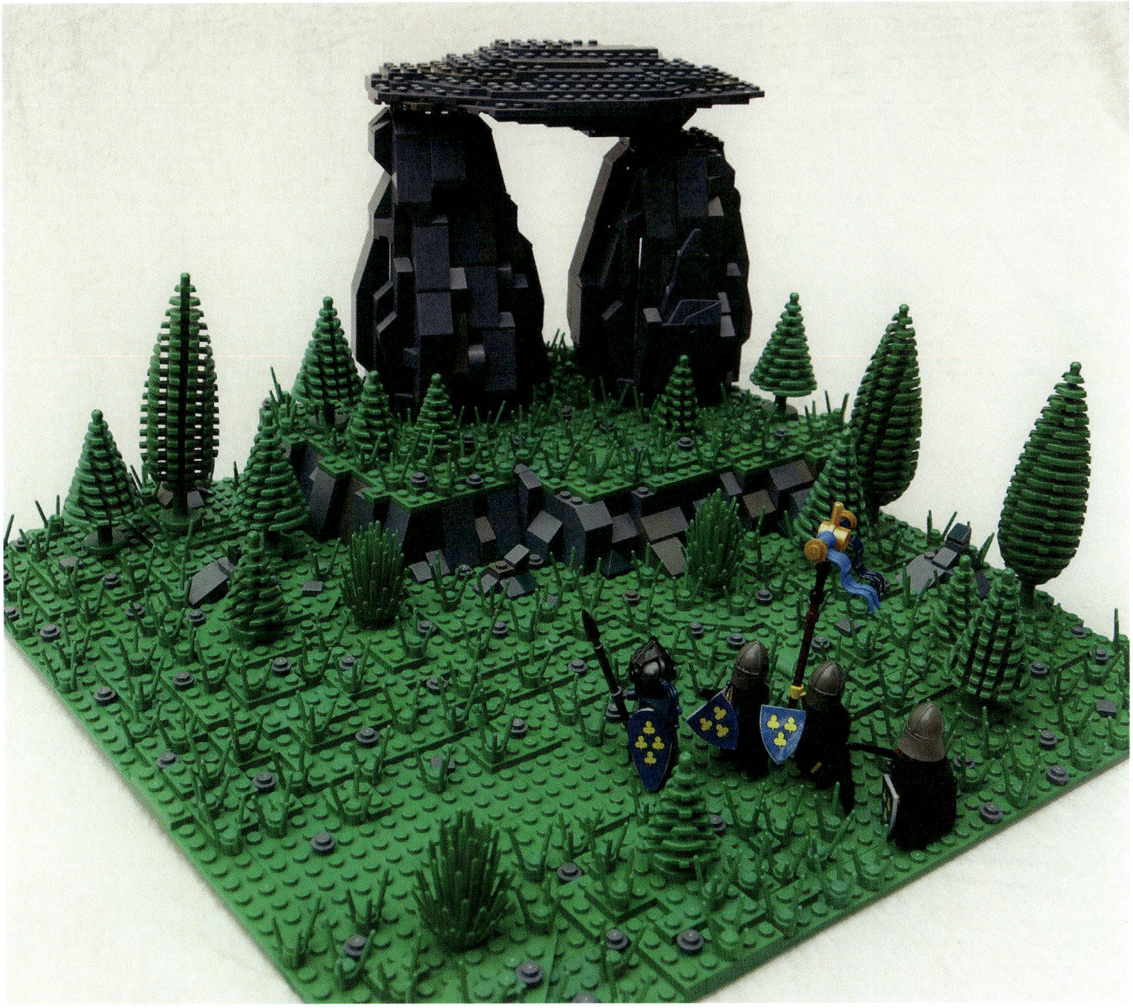

I was having more fun
with rocks with **The Arch
of Ran Gor** (above, right)
aiming for a rather stacked
Stonehenge look.

I would start to use less
foliage in future creations
like this one, but there are
a few things I had to learn.

First, there's not enough
color! Just green and gray.
And we still see prefab
trees at this point.

I was, however,
experimenting with better
presentation. Now the
creation can be viewed all
from one angle.

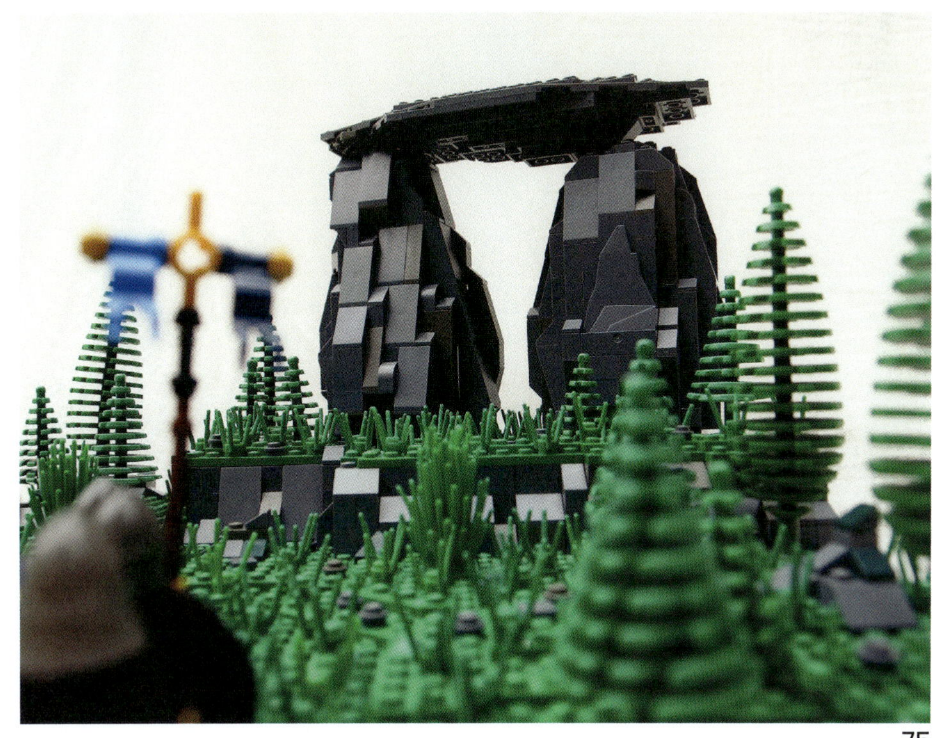

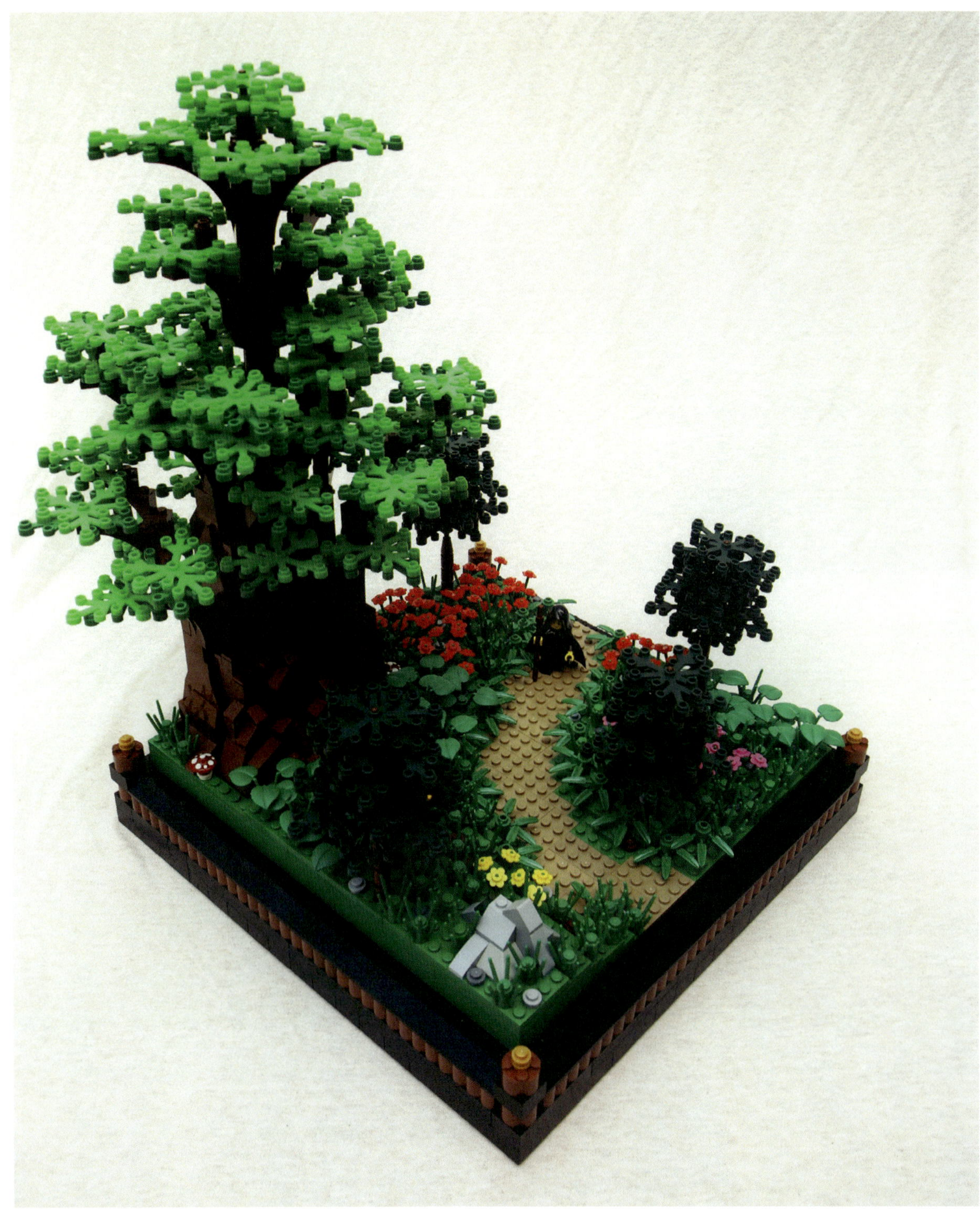

In the creation above, **A Walk in the Forest**, I begin to fix the lack of color, especially with the dark tan path (unlike earlier with the Arch of Ran Gor), lots more flowers and rocks and even some mushrooms. We also have more diverse and defined trees - smaller dark green ones making the larger green tree stand out. There are still a few small persisting issues. The signature tree has a trunk too large for its branches, and appears a bit "overweight". I was also sticking with a square base for this landscape. Later I decided to move away from square baseplates in general except for small and sometimes medium creations. The presentation continued to improve though, as this is a 360-degree MOC but still has an excellent main shot.

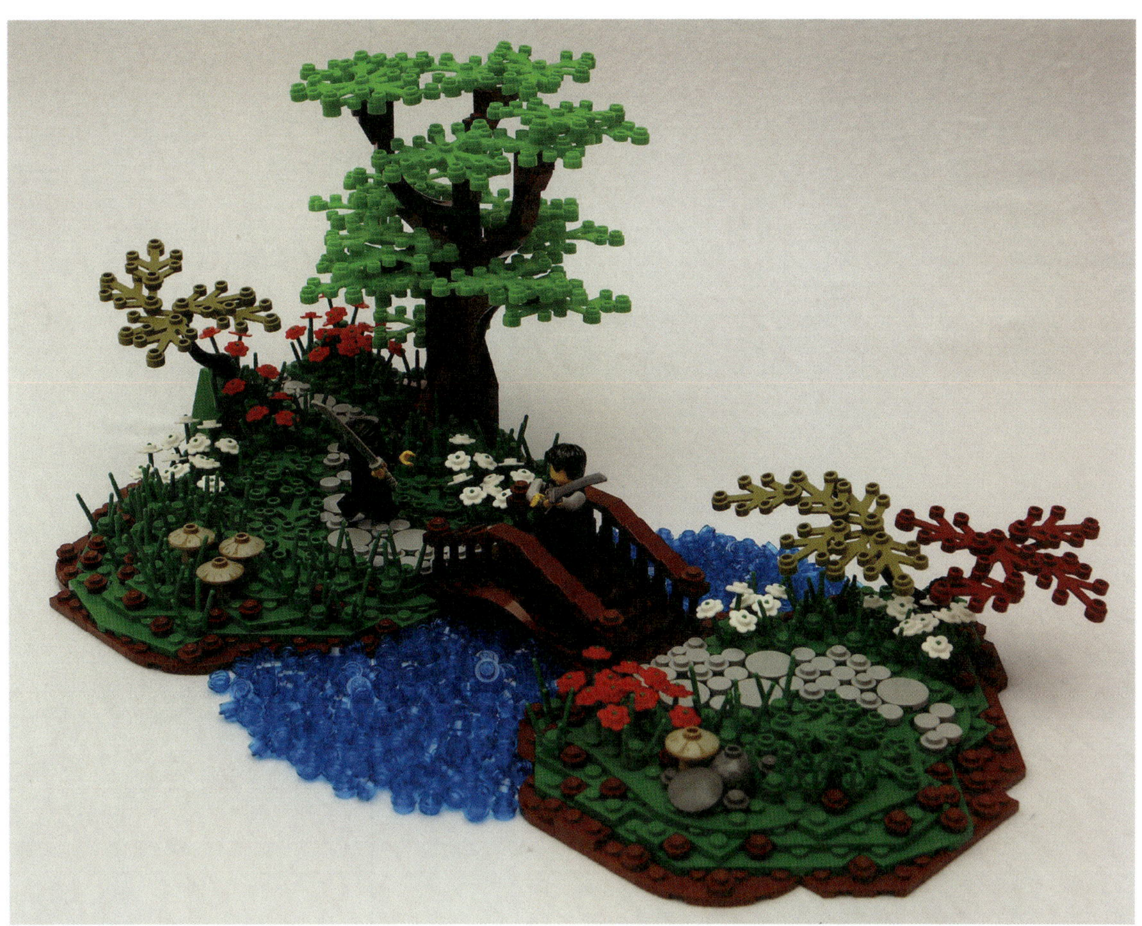

Japanese Garden Ambush (above) Here's where my landscape started to achieve more balance, with color, scale, and details in general.

First and foremost, that sprinkled stud water was a big improvement over the loose brick water – it's a subtle texture with the same concept, but not nearly as jarring to the senses.

The color begins to shine as well. By holding myself back a little as to the sheer volume of plants, the things that remained popped out better, like the cobblestone path, the bridge, the small waterfall, the fir trees, mushrooms, and the characters.

Balance (meaning, adding lots of engaging details without overwhelming the viewer) would become an important criteria for my builds in future.

The Encounter of a Lifetime (below)

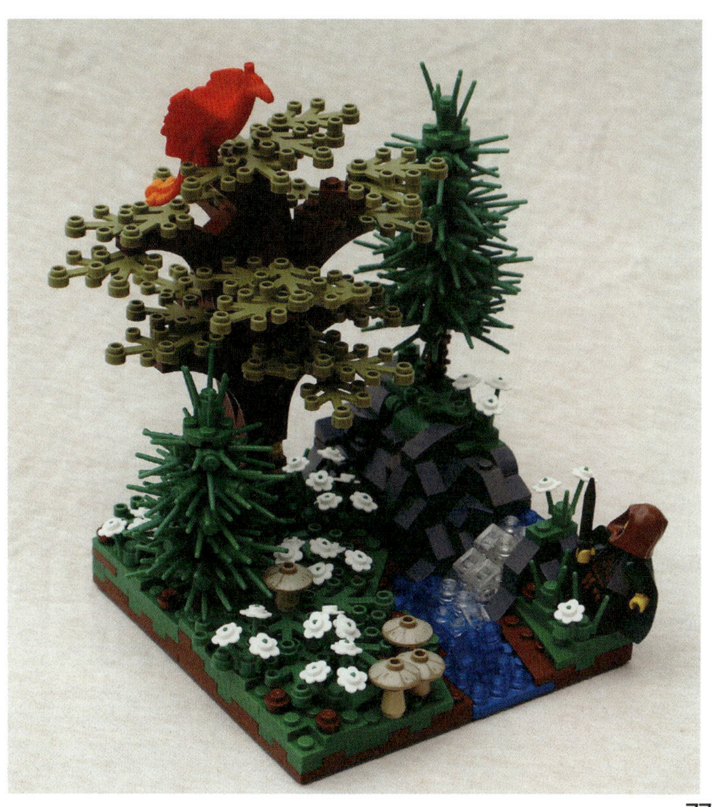

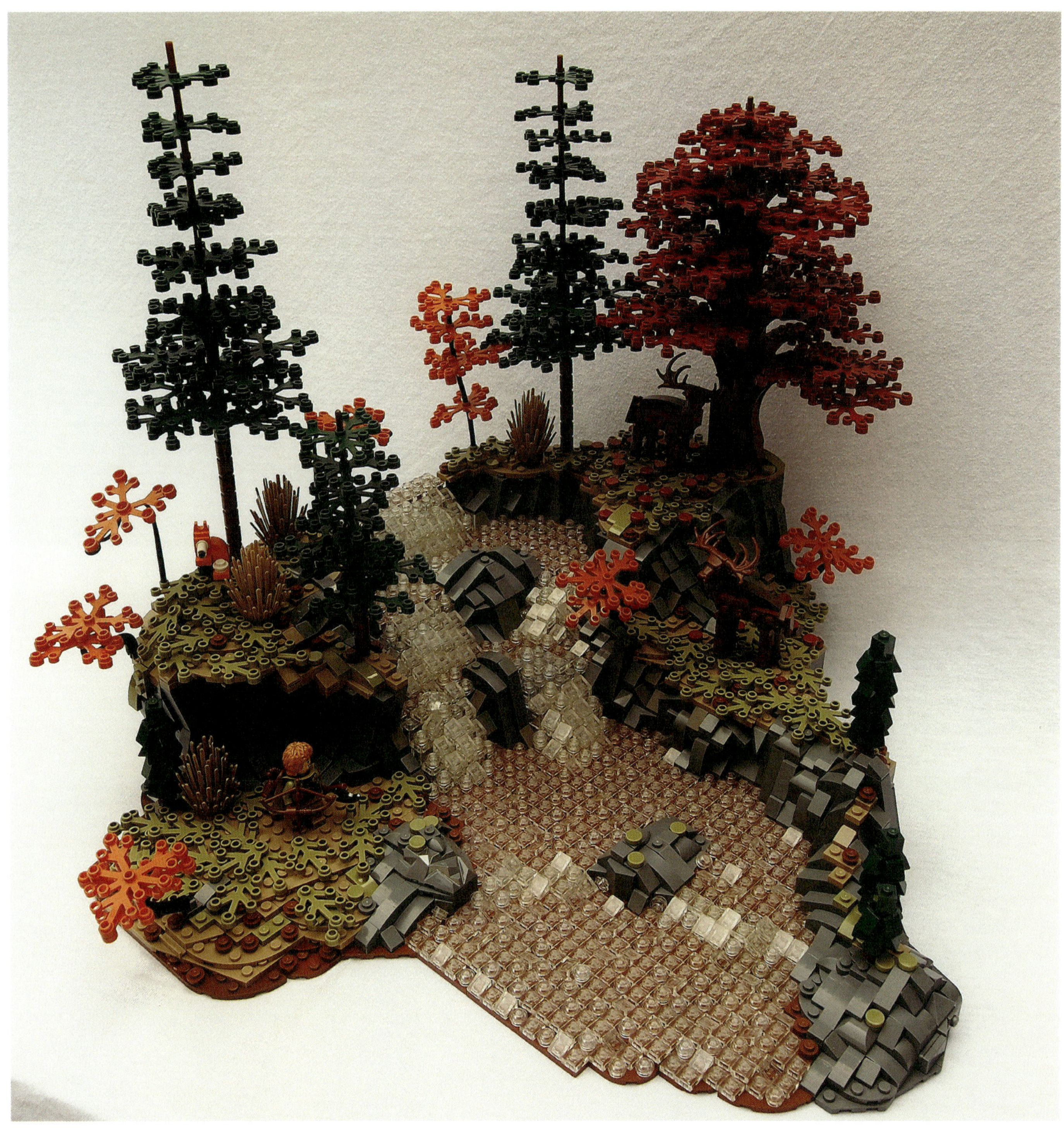

Friðsælt Falls - I started to realize as I built more and more landscapes that if you're just doing a landscape, your presentation had to be amazing. Not to mention, my brother and I started getting our hands on fall-colored leaves. This opened up a huge avenue that I called my "Fall Phase". Technique-wise, the smallest evergreens are made with cheese slopes, and the rocks are becoming more dynamic here. The woodland creatures - two moose standing on the hilltop and the small orange fox - also added a nice touch of character.

Crystal Falls - At this point, I couldn't decide if I wanted to go for clean landscapes or ones that were packed with interesting details. Both were fun but had their own setbacks.

The cleaner landscapes suffered from less color and vibrancy. The more detailed ones were too busy.

At this point, I think you know where I'm going with this - it all came down to balance, and a combination of the two ultimately won the day.

Side note - the glowing waterfall was lit with tiny LED lights. This was one of the first times I lit a waterfall, and I enjoyed the effect.

My brother and I would often return to lighted water for some of our larger signature creations that we would usually bring to conventions.

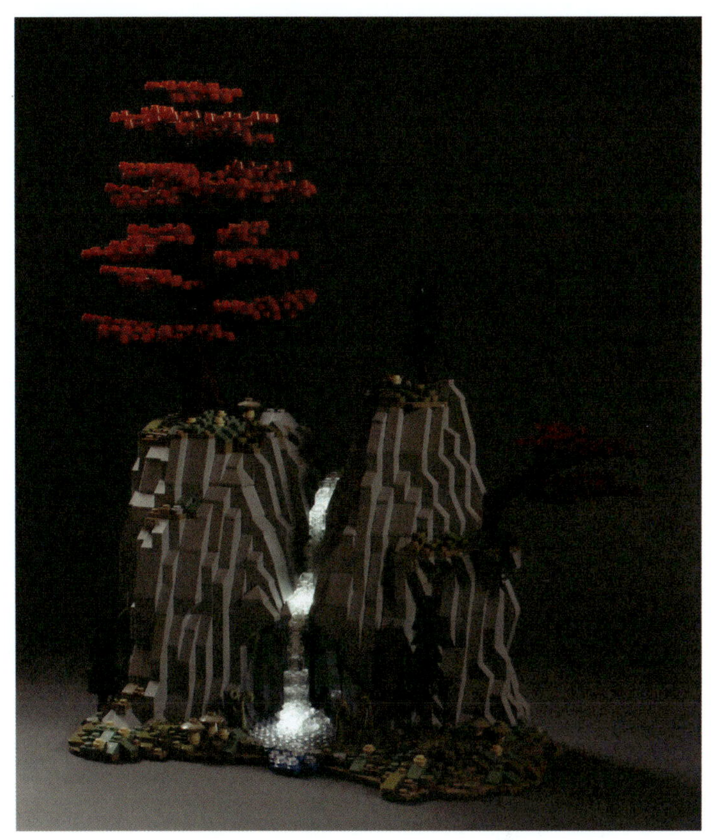

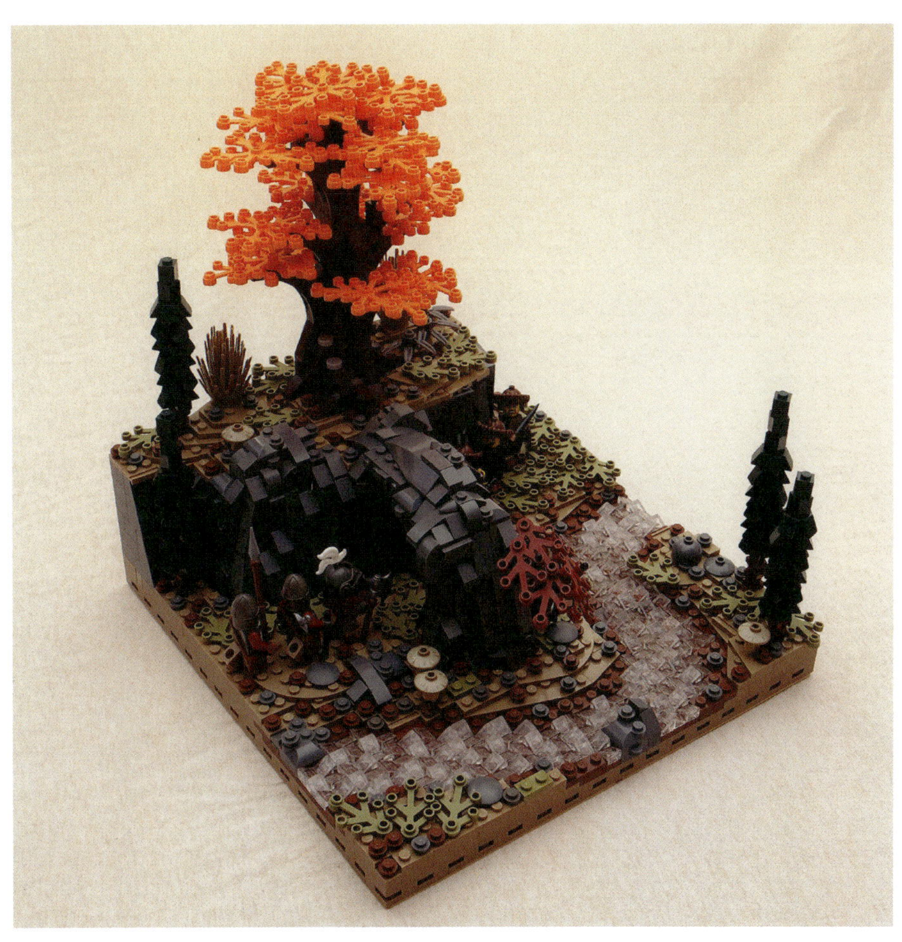

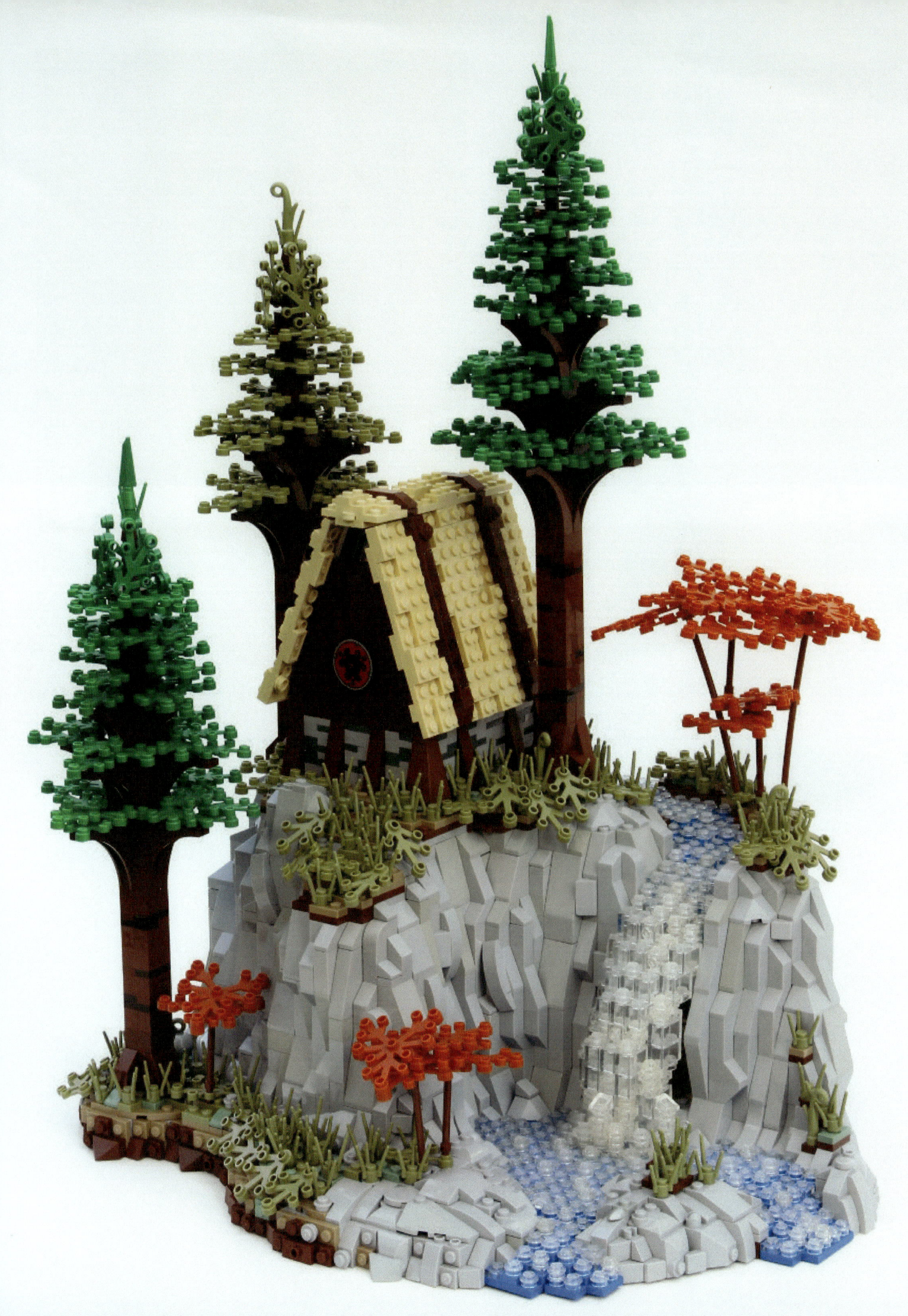

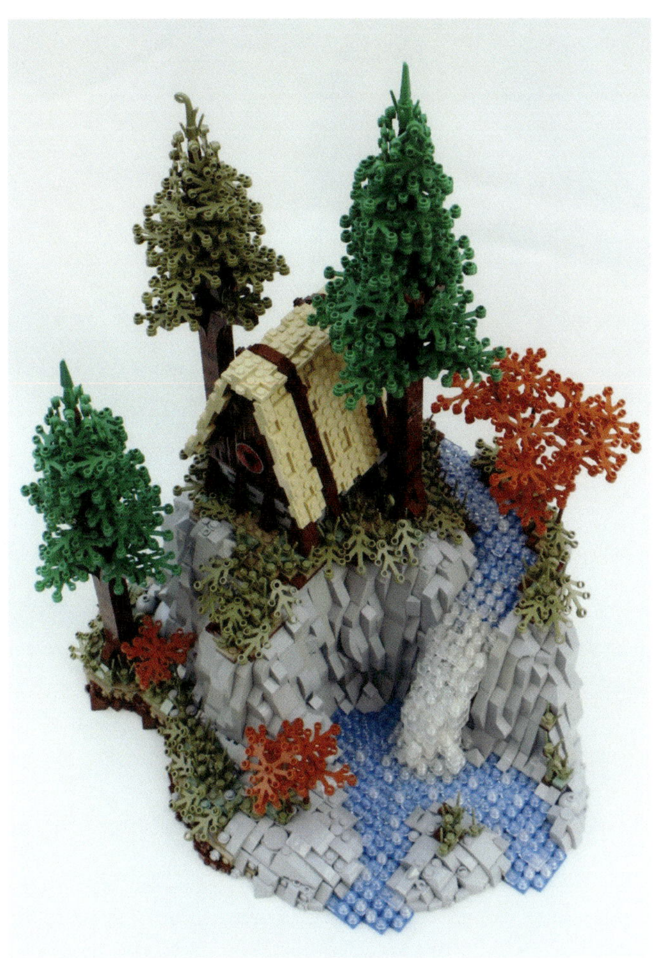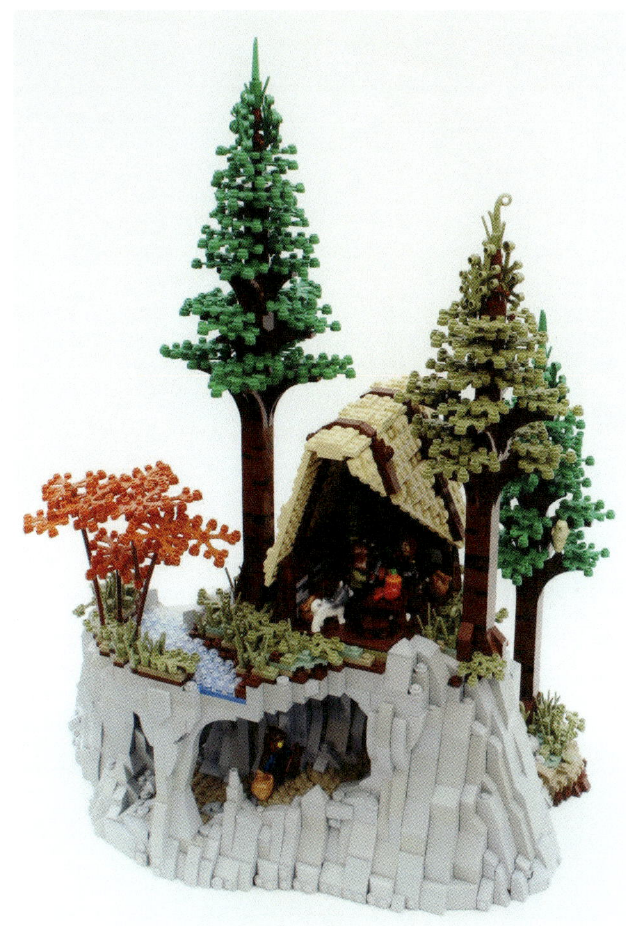

The final entry in this line of progression is where everything comes together! In the **Huntsman's Lodge**, I'm really leaning into the irregular baseplate, the flowing landscape looks so organic, with a little more spilling over from the water, which is snapped down but still has a turbulent texture - not to mention the awesome waterfall that hides a secret underground tunnel. The blue underlay color beneath the clear bricks pops perfectly against the orange trees, which also contrast against the green firs. These cool colors bounce off the earthy tones of the olive grass and reddish brown dirt. Another fun feature is that the grass has an overhanging look, with leaves looped on the grass stalks.

The rocks, which I am most proud of, were a combination of SNOT (studs not on top) and upright bricks. They achieve that tricky balance, and provide a clean and detailed look all in one, making an excellent canvas for the rest of the details.

When I upload my creations online, they often come with a fun and descriptive story, and this was no exception.

"Even the lonely hunters and trappers of the great northern forests need a warm place to find shelter and rest now and then. This communal abode was built on top of a mountain spring. A secret alternate entrance is hidden beneath a waterfall to prevent thieves and wild beasts from stealing their hard-earned larder. The tunnel also serves as an escape route if the enemies should be too dangerous to fight."

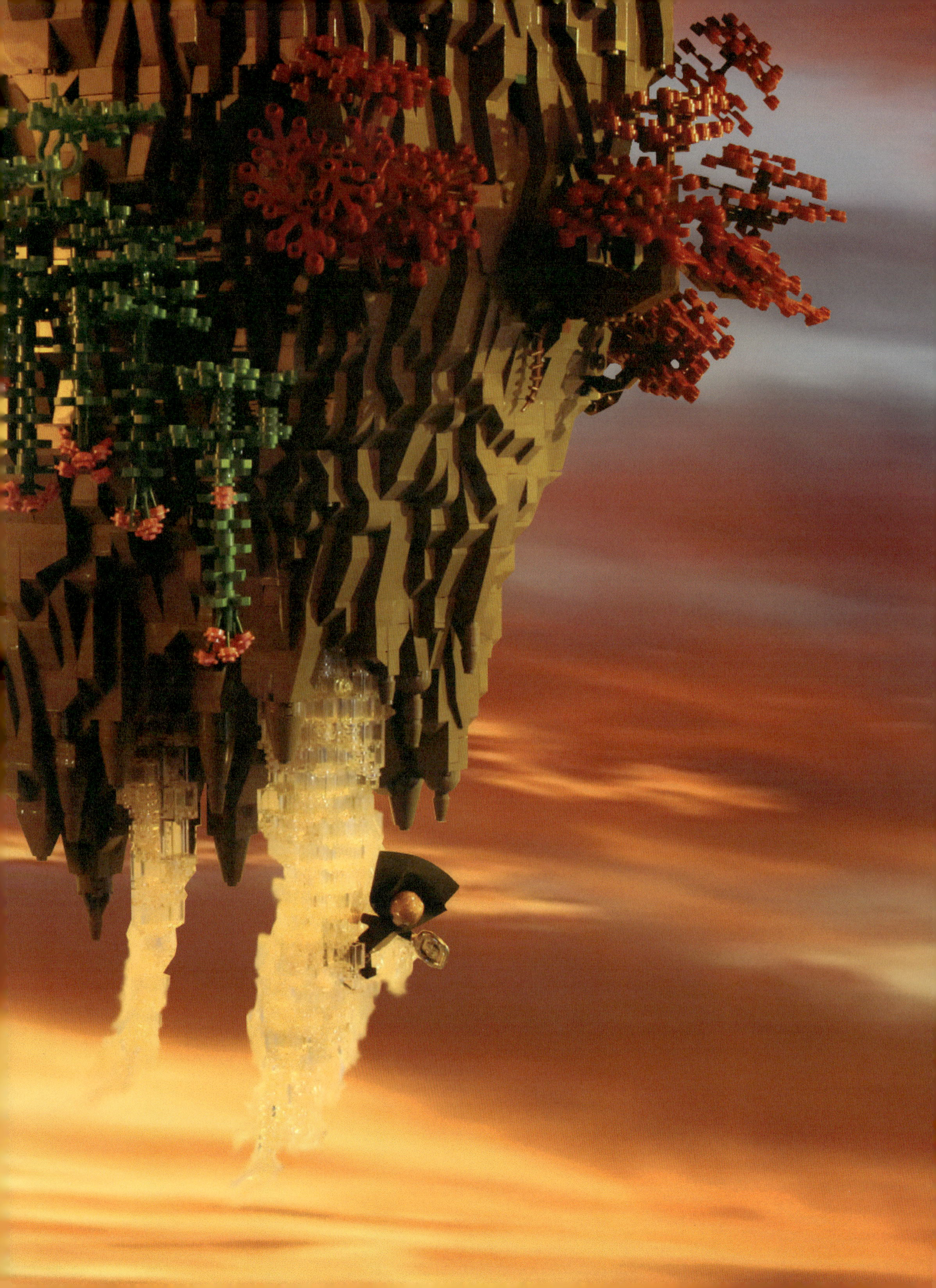

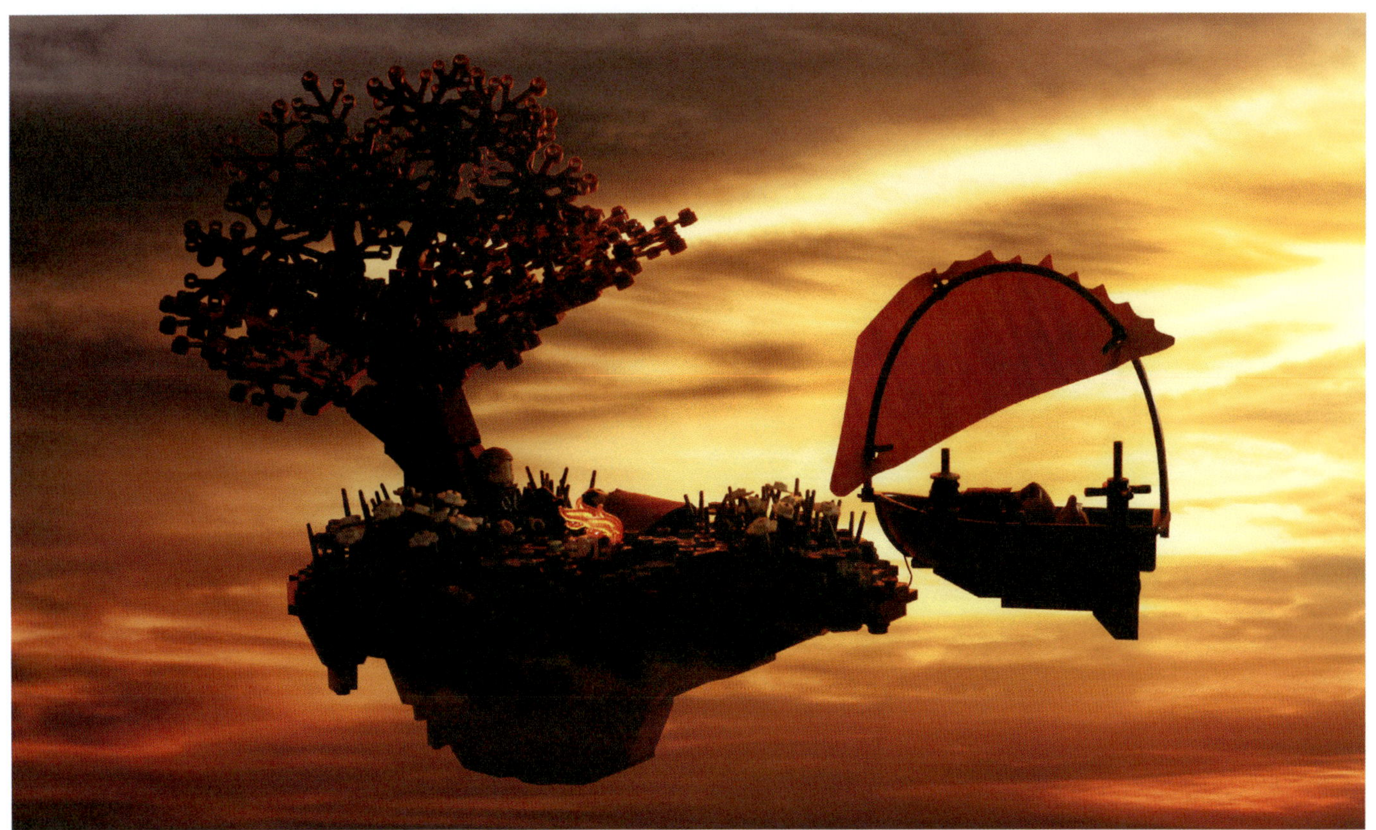

Every now and then, it's fun to get dynamic with the lighting and atmosphere of a creation. With these sunset builds from the Isles of Aura theme, the builds were photographed in warm lighting and then superimposed onto the sunset background in photoshop.

Photoshop is actually a valuable tool for presentation of a LEGO® creation, along with good photography. Slight tweaks can make all the difference, like the mist effect and how the ship appears to be mysteriously floating in the sky (above).

On the left, **Into The Endless Abyss,** the most notable feature of this build is the fact that it was built and photographed entirely upside down. The photograph is flipped 180 degrees in post-edit for the final effect. The reason for this is that it is significantly easier to build rockwork from the bottom up instead of from the top down.

The landscape in the top picture, **Sunset Slumber,** employs a similar technique to the larger build on the left. The idea is to build the rockwork - intended to be upside down - first, then create a landscape to go on the reverse side. This makes the landscape match perfectly and the rockwork is easy to build. The layers of rockwork and landscape are attached together with technic elements.

Both these builds were created for an ongoing series in the Isles of Aura with floating continents and airships.

Creatures

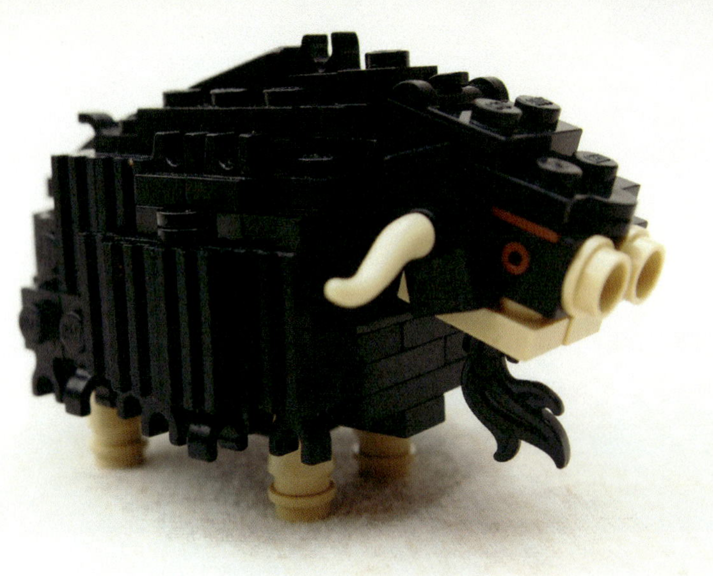

As previously mentioned before, I really enjoy creating animals. Some of my more iconic ones are the miniscale creatures shown here.

The **Musk Oxen** on the left was a big hit when I first uploaded him online. The hairy look and fun details really added up. His eye in particular uses a hinge brick, and a rare black feather plume is the piece used for his 'beard'.

To further emphasise his hairiness, grill tiles and clips were used as extra texture for his coat.

For a while, I was exploring more arctic and cold weather creatures. The collection of them on the middle right is comprised of reindeer, elk, prong-horns, and mountain goats.

All these arctic critters featured here have third party elements like the deer heads, antlers, and claws.

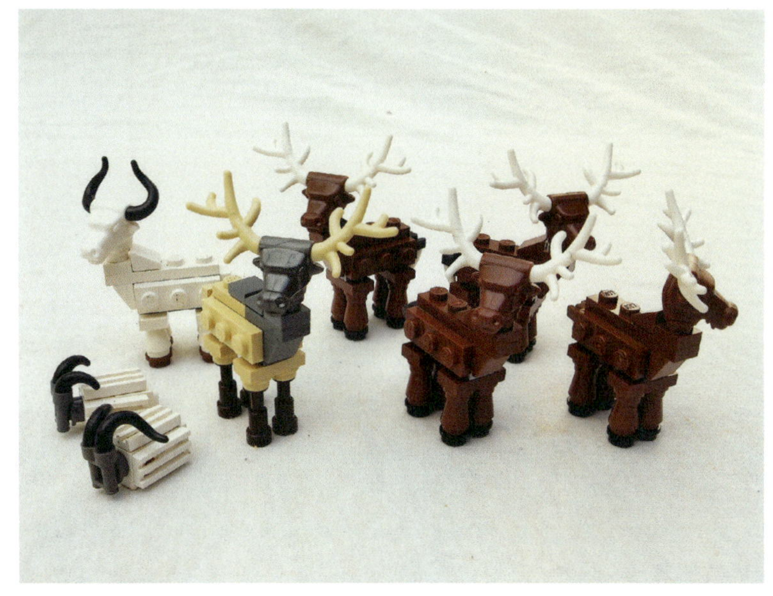

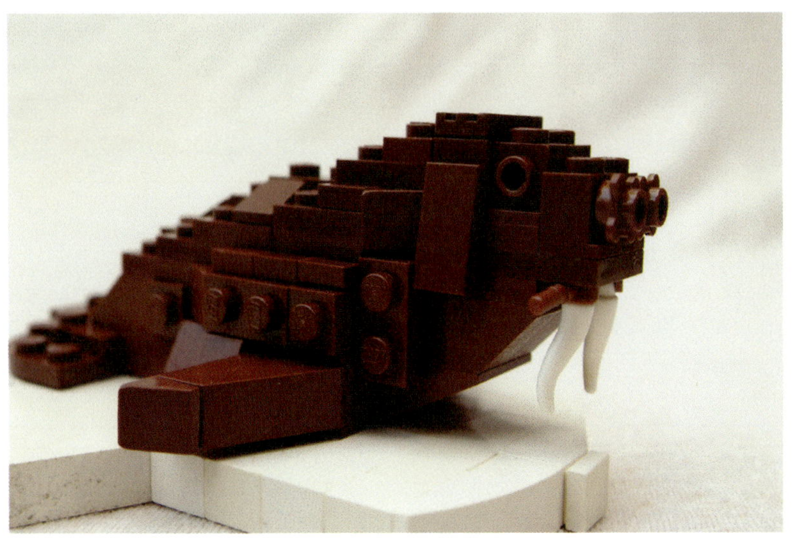

Something to notice about the **Walrus**, perched on an ice floe (left) and the **Giant Ground Sloth** (right) is the utilization of studs along with slopes. Lots of builders avoid studs showing on smaller builds as they can sometimes clutter a creation. But for these creatures, I wanted to pursue a more studded look for as lifelike appearance and texture as possible. They seem wrinkly and hairy, rather than smooth.

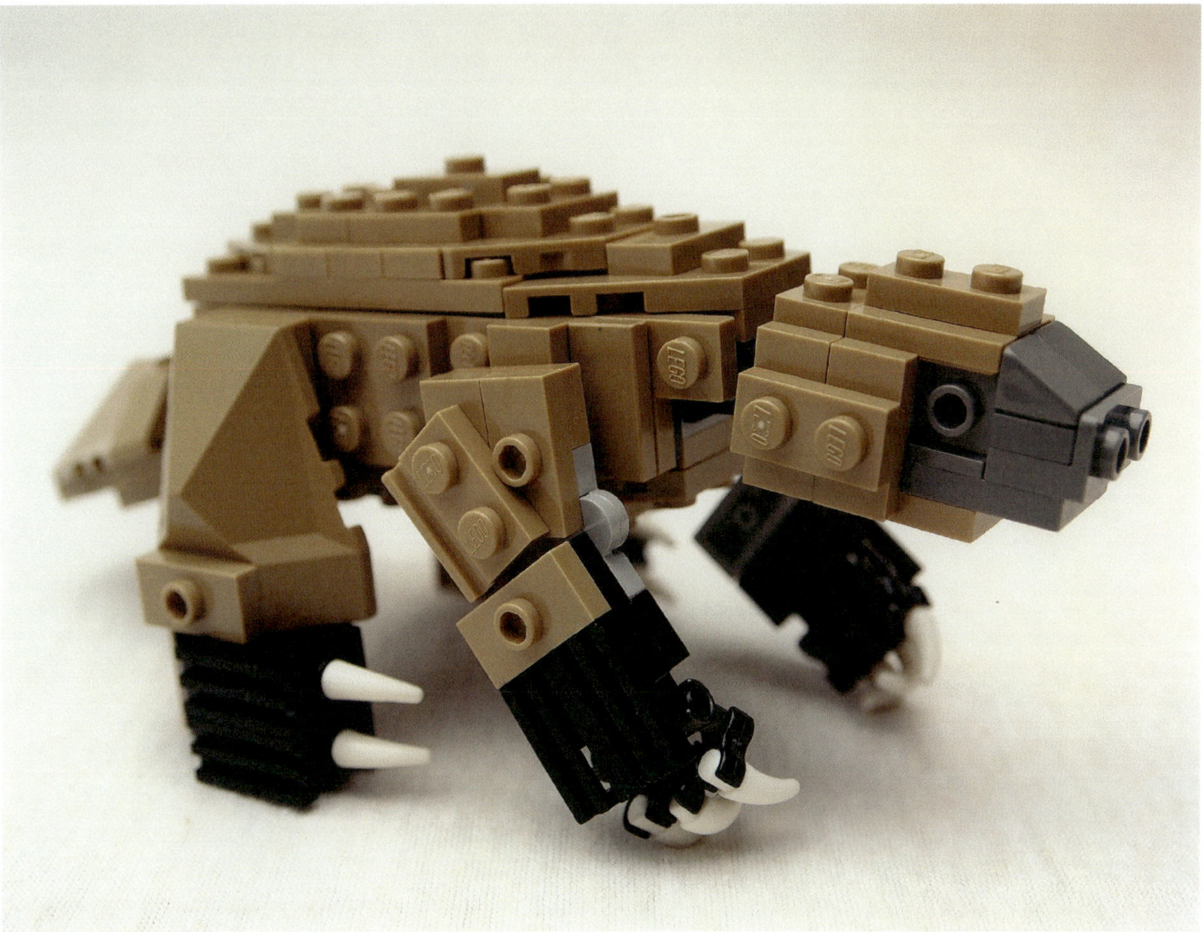

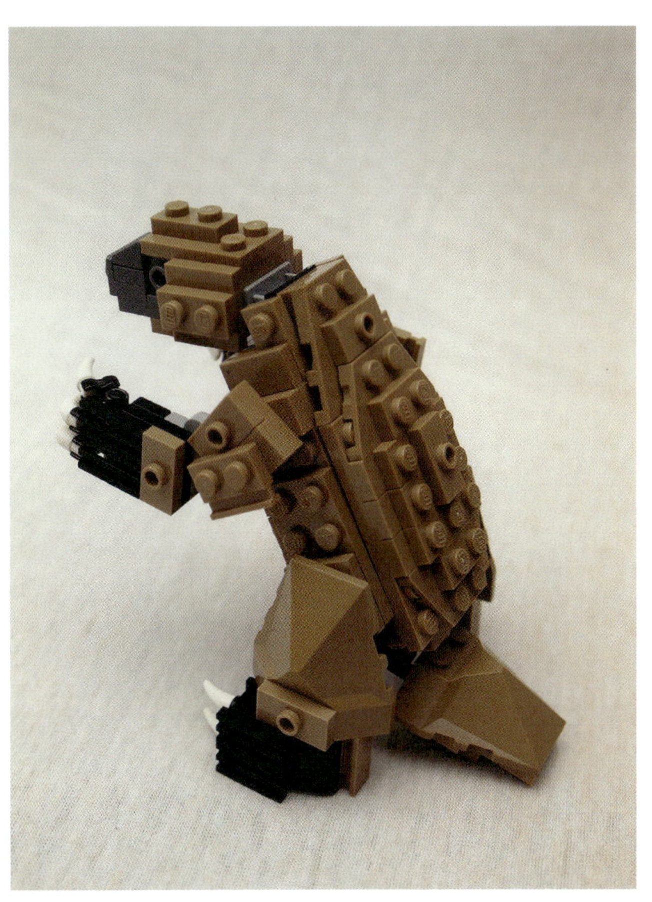

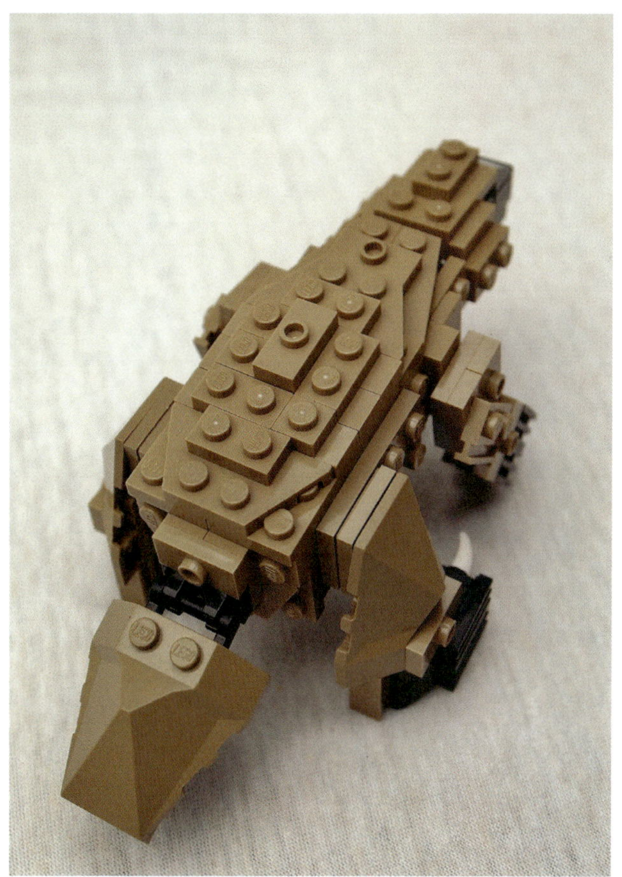

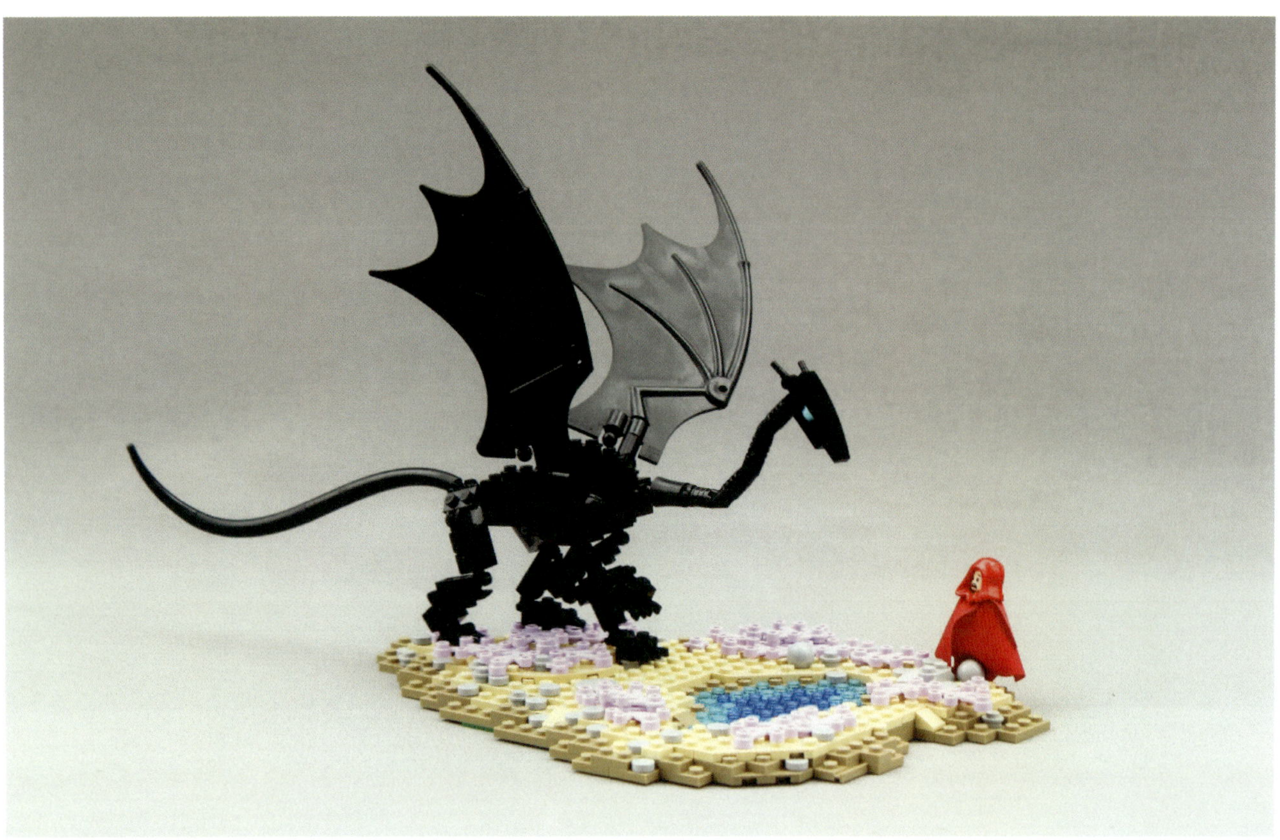

Of all the animals I've built, my definite favorites are my dragons. They're a major cornerstone of the castle genre! In my opinion, any good castle builder should know their way around building a dragon! I think one of the reasons dragons are so much fun is their huge diversity. There is more potential for variation in their design, color, classification, style, and theme than any other animal.

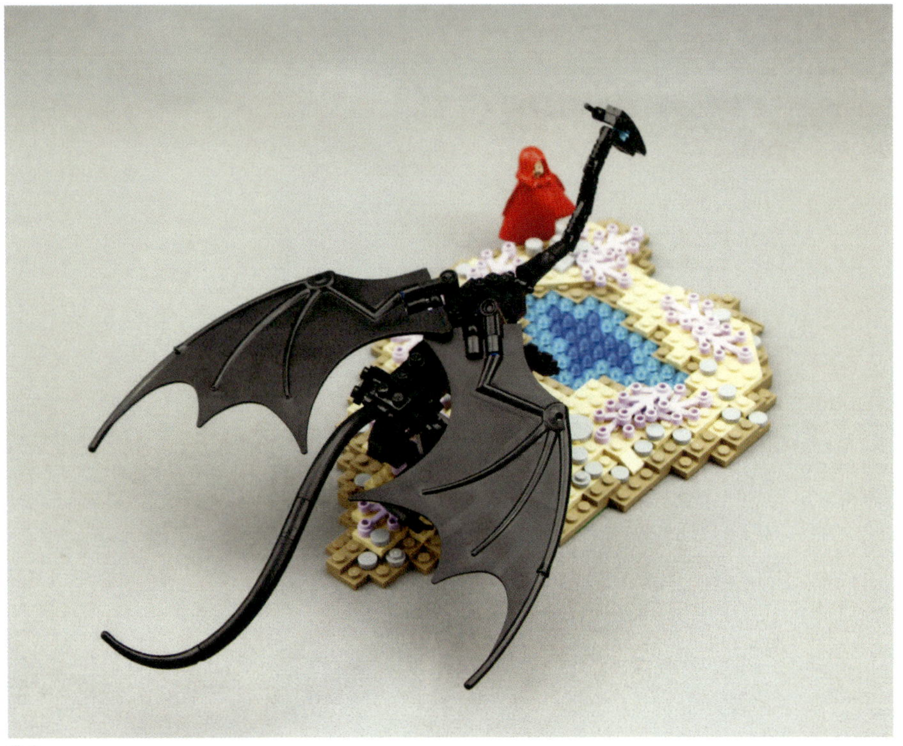

It may surprise some, but dragons have an advanced and lengthy system of classification.

Above and left we have **Ingvarr**, from the deserts of Enns. This midnight dragon is a slender, peaceful beast with a classical design of four legs and two wings.

I was inspired to build some of these dragons for various contests online. Although Ingvarr never brought home a trophy, several others that I'll mention later, did!

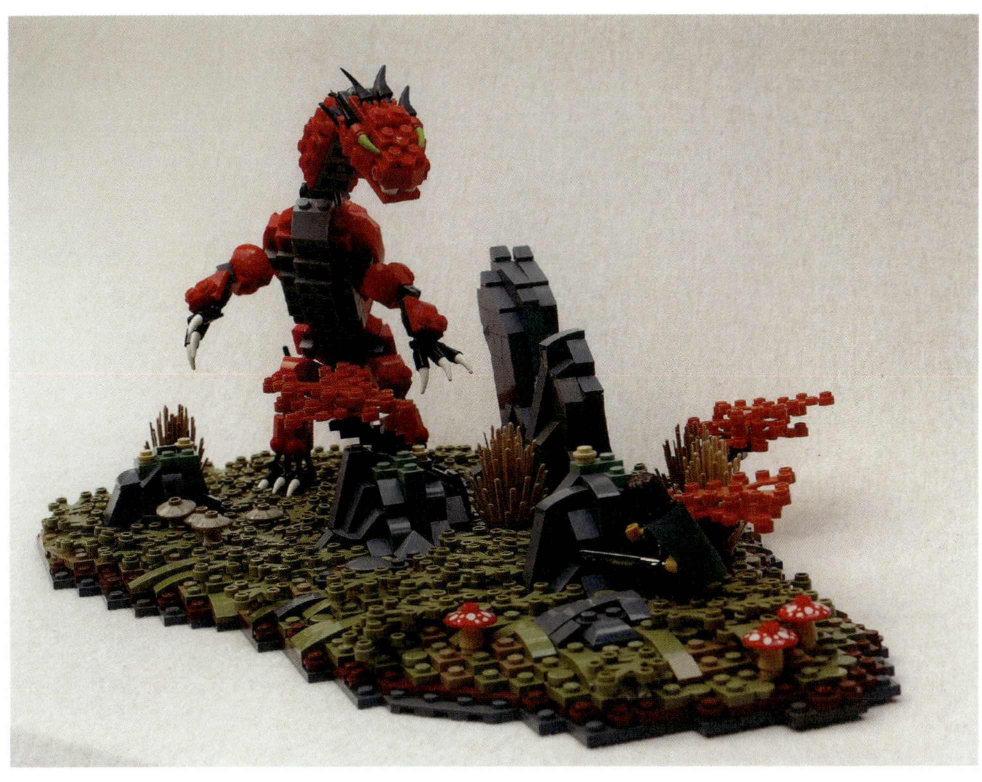

This scarlet creature on the left is known as a **Drake,** a dragon with no wings, and is one of my earlier designs.

Although there are a few things I would change now, (the limbs are maybe a bit too small) there are some things I still really like about the design.

First of all, the pose-ability in the head design. Like with any creature, the head is the most important part of the whole animal. And this guy's head design was actually borrowed from the one down below.

On the bottom right, we have the **Tyrfinger** (which was built for the Iron Builder contest and had to include a green spike piece) – this one is classified as a Wyvern, a dragon with two wings and only two extra limbs.

I incorporated brick-built wings into this design which was rare for me since they were very heavy and hard to work with.

One thing I loved about this creation is the unique birdlike appearance. This was very different from all my other dragon designs, not to mention the bright and bizarre colors almost resembling a peacock.

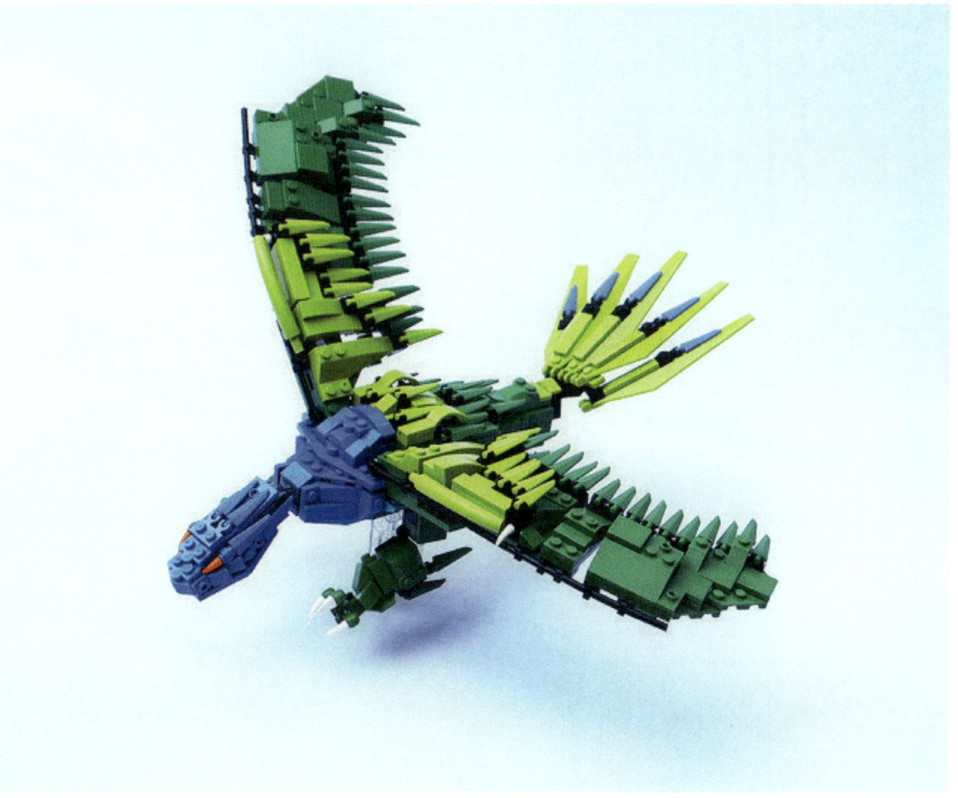

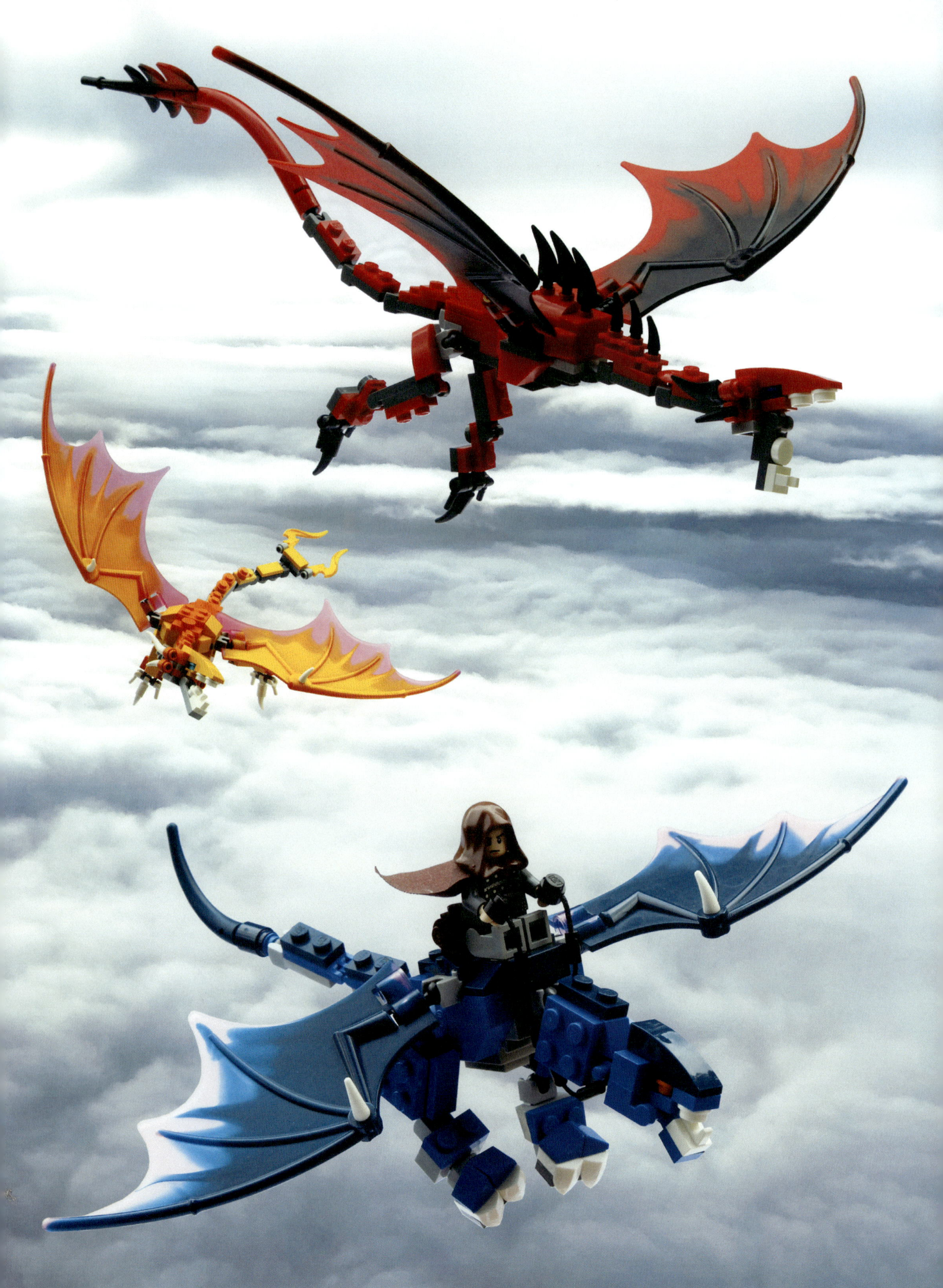

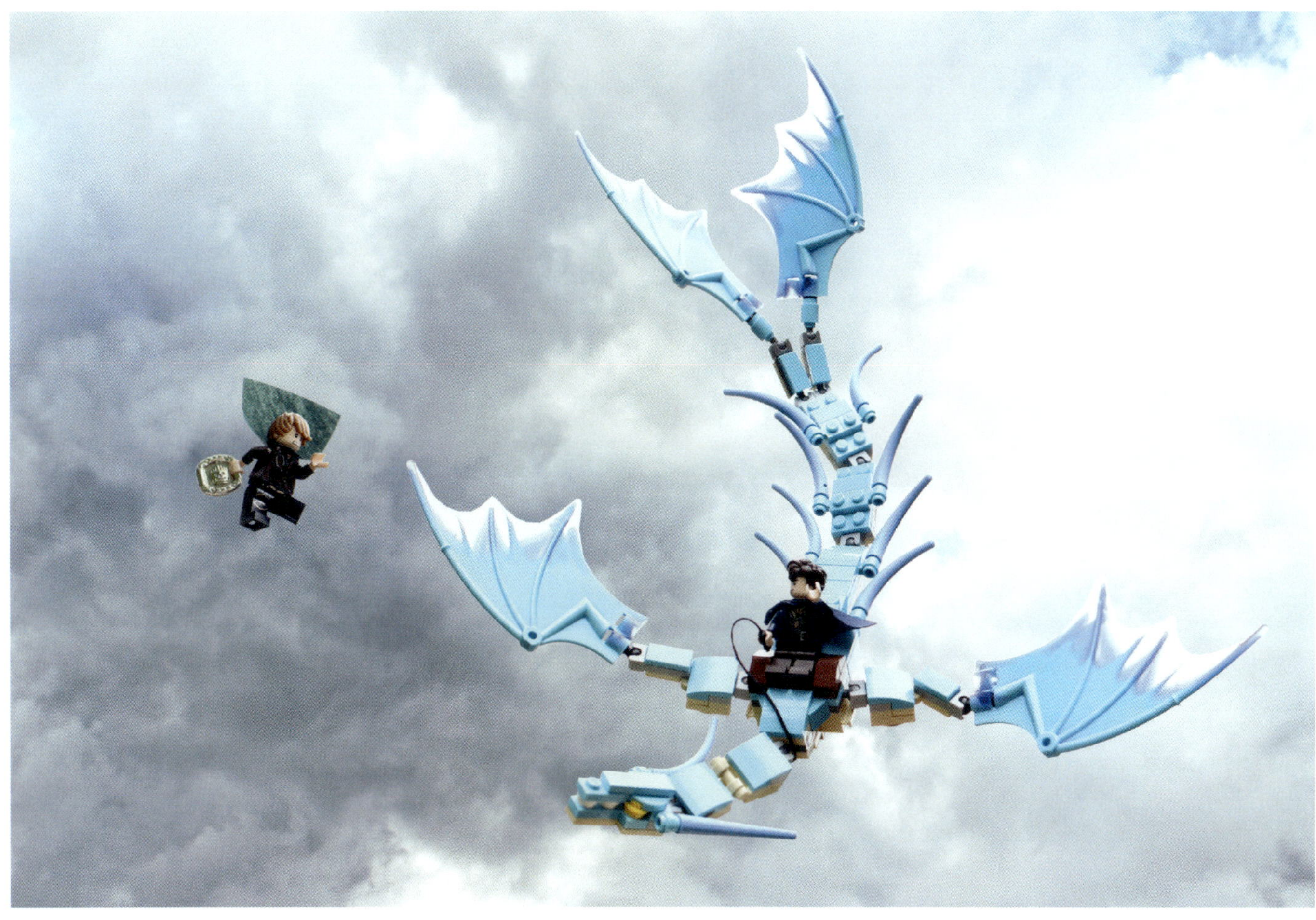

There are a lot of bizarre dragon designs. One that I really wanted to try out was the Amphiptere, or "Sky Serpent", described as having no legs whatsoever, and only wings for limbs. It swims and flies but never touches the ground. These beasts are basically a type of Wyvern but without the two legs. Light azure is a pretty rare color for the time this was built. This creature has loads of pose-ability, and it was also made for Isles of Aura.

When you build for a long time, It's important to keep things fresh and new and lively so you don't get into a rut. That's why I explore all these different designs.

On the left, we have a collection of beautiful Wyverns, and with these I'm really sticking to minifig scale size. These are some of my later dragons, and they were originally built for a big collaboration for my LUG (LEGO® User Group) and they were also part of Isles of Aura.

The dragon wings are prefab LEGO® parts, normally not used in LEGO® dragons but I think they work just fine here, and are both light and colorful. The bold, primary colors work great against the sky backdrop. I also really like their pose-ability, of the heads especially.

Even when you build a really giant, elaborate castle, at various public events, it's amusing to see how many people will instantly point out the dragons FIRST, especially kids! For some reason they are extremely eyecatching despite being a small detail of a many-meters-wide castle.

Stórhoggvi

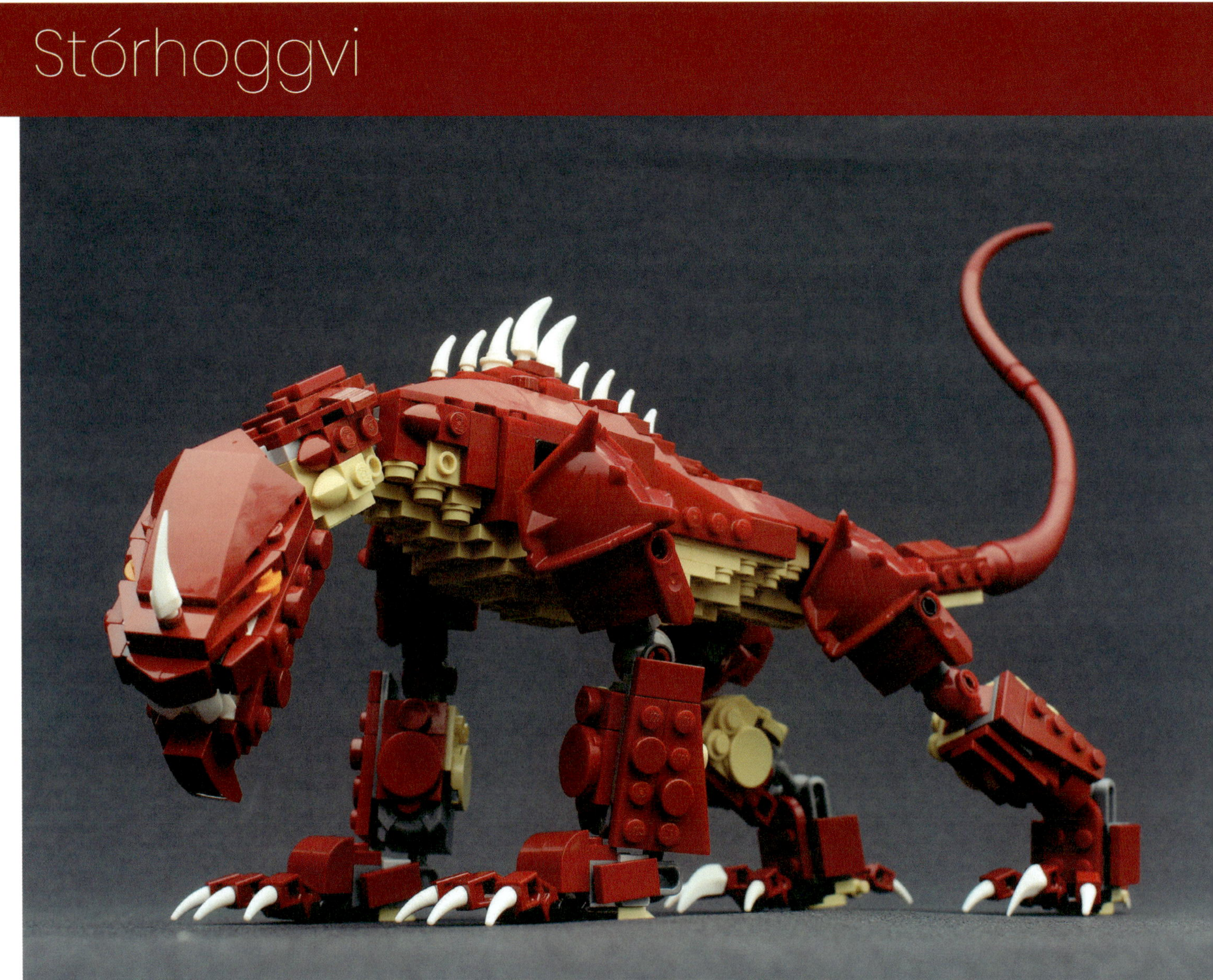

THE MIGHTY Stórhoggvi! Among all my creatures, my favorite and most popular is the mighty Stórhoggvi! (pronounced Strohg-vee, rhymes with row-bee). What most people don't know about this creation is that he originally started out life as an Allosaurus before being reimagined into a dragon. (check out the original design on the opposite page, bottom)

A partial reason for the swapout was that the **Allosaurus** design was too fragile in the legs and therefore difficult to pose. He kept falling over. But the biggest reason he changed to a dragon was because of a popular dragon contest that started up at the time - in which this beast brought home gold for first place. He went on to appear at more LEGO® conventions than any other creation I've ever made!

Interestingly, the initial dragon design was meant to be two-headed! Starting with the allosaurus head, I made an exact copy, intending to have them side by side. However, sometimes LEGO® creations build themselves, and the two-headed design just wasn't having it. After running into too many difficulties, I realized one head was plenty, and Stórhoggvi was born!

Another highlight of this build is his unusual name! The name "Stórhoggvi" is from ancient Viking and is interpreted "great slasher". Very appropriate, I thought!

90

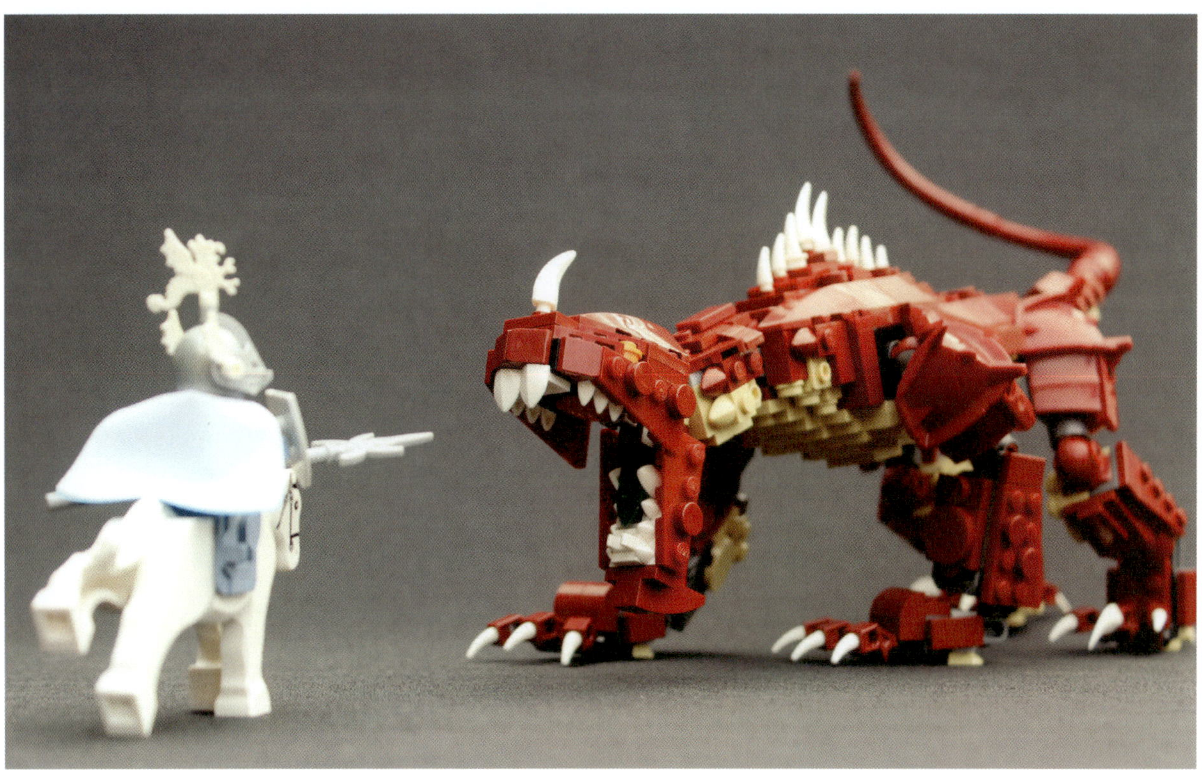

Like with many of my other dragons, I celebrate the studs - though here they're emphasized with round plates to accentuate the scaly look, and are accented by larger pieces like his shoulder pauldrons. Also, the original olive green I was going to use seemed to disappear, so I changed to tan, which has a nice contrast with the red.

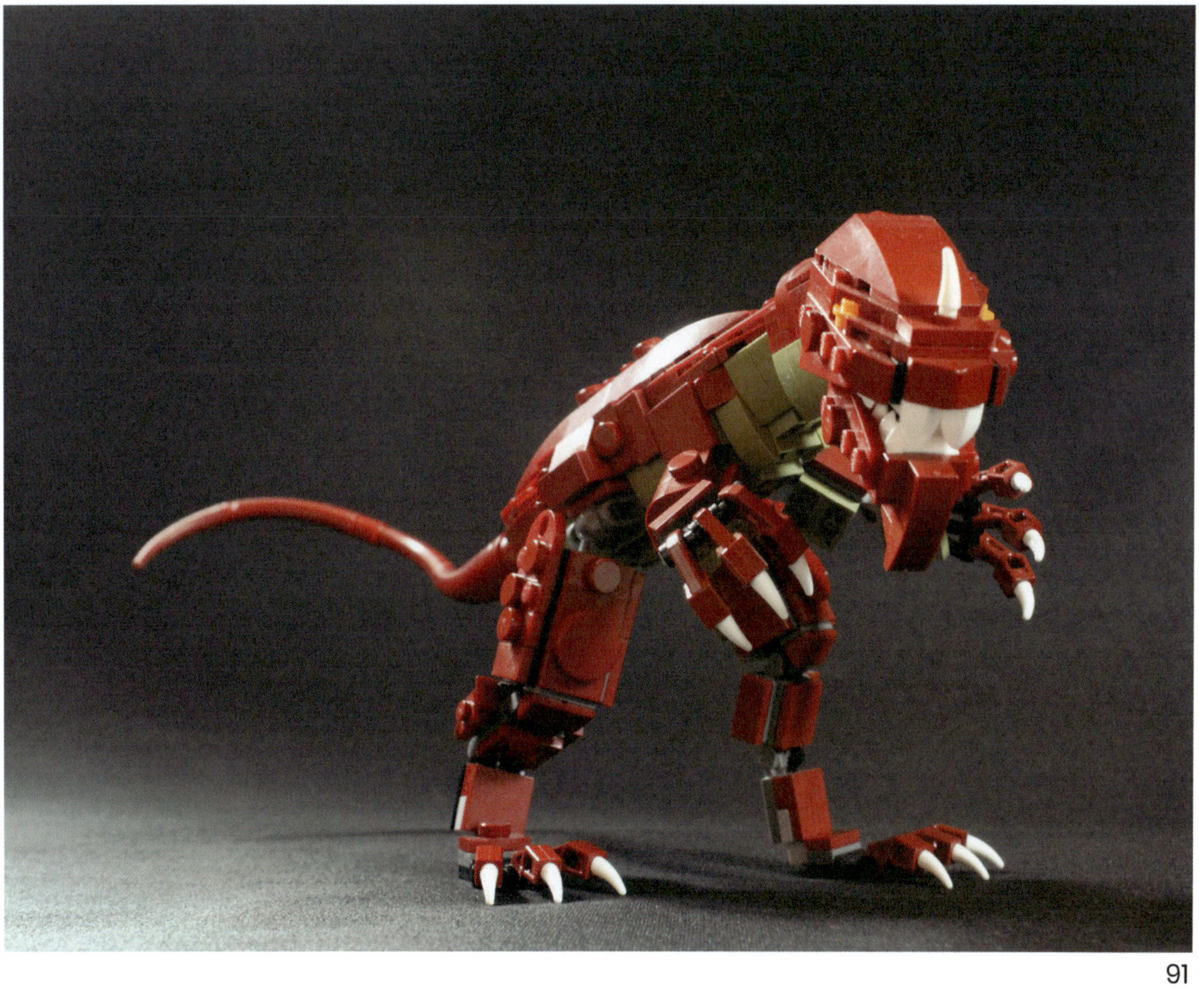

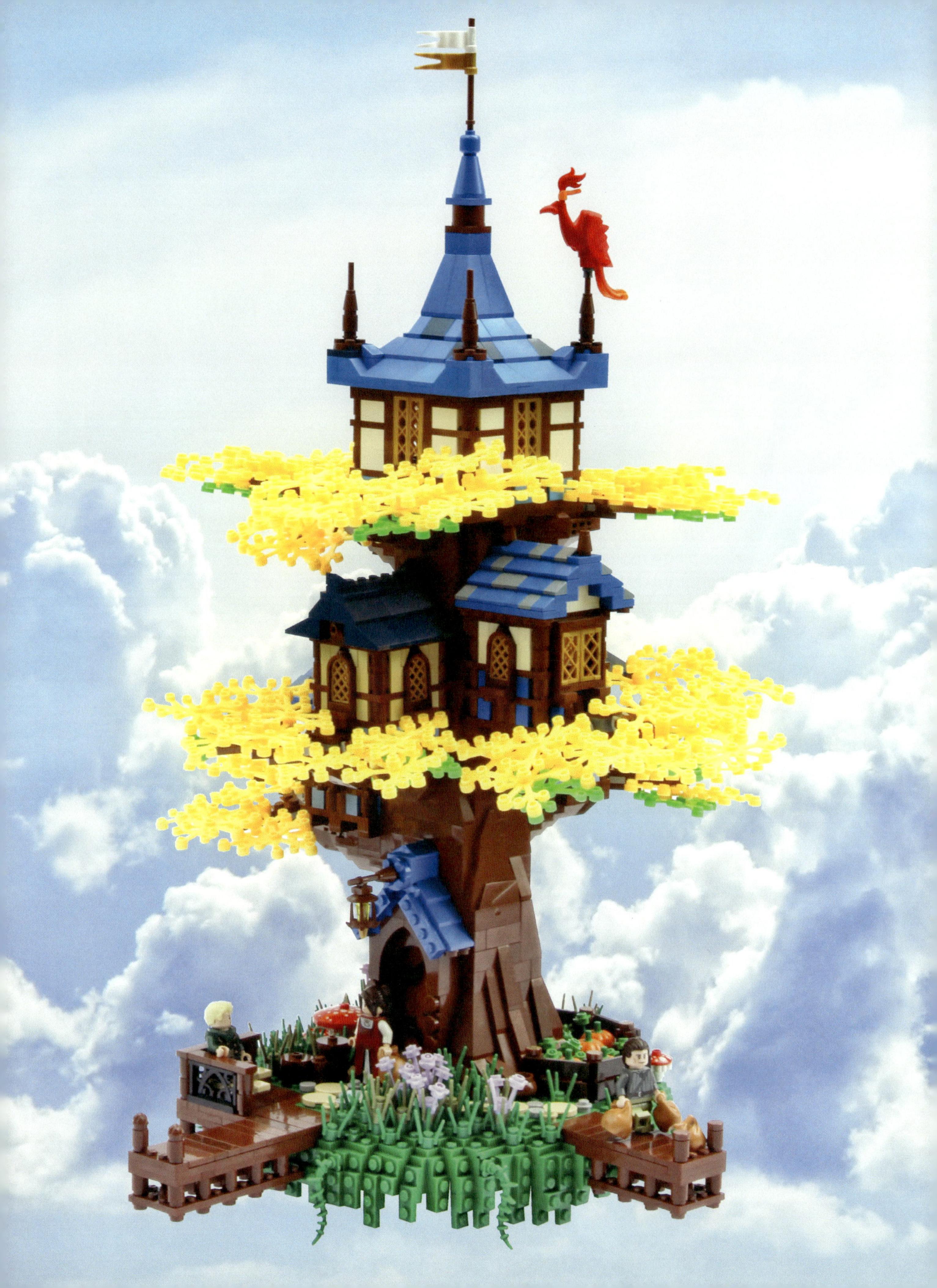

HOUSES~IN & OUT

Although Castle is my favorite theme of all, castles wouldn't be complete without houses to protect. Medieval cottages, taverns, farms, inns, and monasteries have become some of my favorite aspects of LEGO® Castle, and over the years they have become a highlight in my hobby.

Real-life Medieval houses typically use the iconic Tudor design, constructed with a technique called Wattle & Daub, a combination of clay-like mud and timber frames or woven reed panels. I interpret this style with a light color framed with a darker color in a distinctive, architectural pattern. This gives these buildings an unmistakable old-world flair, and LEGO® lends itself well to these structures.

Like castles, houses have a huge potential for variety, style, and a plethora of different techniques. **Ginko Lodgings** (seen on the left) is my favorite example of taking a simple theme and expanding it to a new level. The concept for this creation was to perch an entire village on top of a single tree which is floating in the air! This build was for a contribution for the Isles of Aura.

For me personally, I prefer a clean, sturdy, well-built design using even distribution of color, and organized elements. The intent is to present a creation with highlights and details in order and easy on the eyes, not simply heaved in the viewer's face. I try to make the details clearly pop. I can't enjoy a cluttered look as much, so I have decided to avoid what I consider "over-detailing" and the recently popular trend to build run-down, shabby, and weathered things with lots of vines and cracks.

As fun as the outside of a house is, the inside can be just as amazing! Interiors provide a unique opportunity to play with mood, atmosphere and feeling - most of which can come from tricks with lighting, character, and furnishings. Rooms range from coziness to grandeur depending on furniture. All the detail crammed into a single room can really tell a charming story. In this final section, we will be exploring a wide range of outsides and insides of LEGO® houses both large and small.

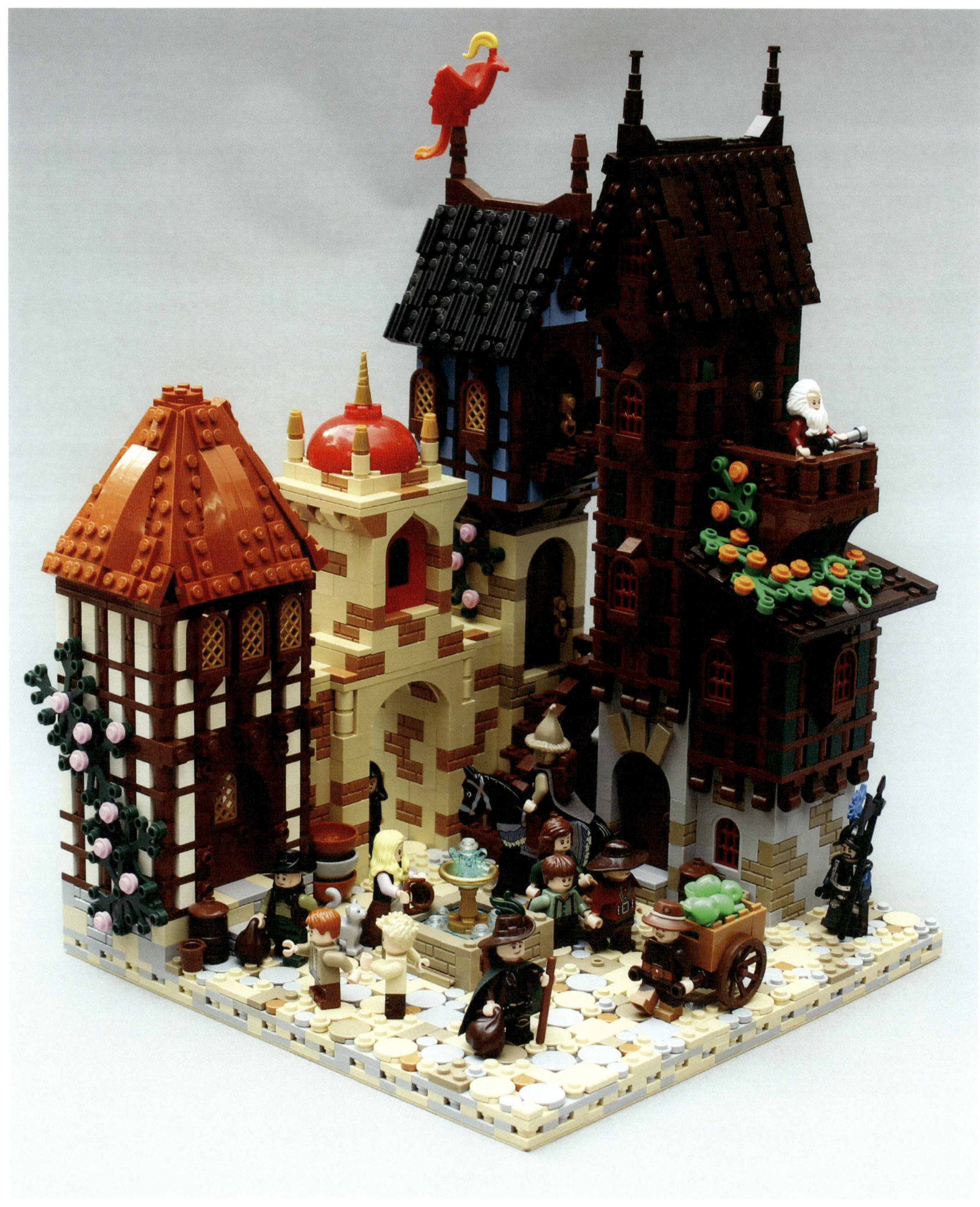

Fagimburg - What makes this build cool is the fact that it has all these diverse colors! Although they all share similarities, no two buildings are the same palette. The ground also incorporates many neutral shades in the cobblestone. All the buildings have unique architectural details. It's always nice to see unique parts used in buildings, and here minifig legs are used as timber supports of the dark green house.

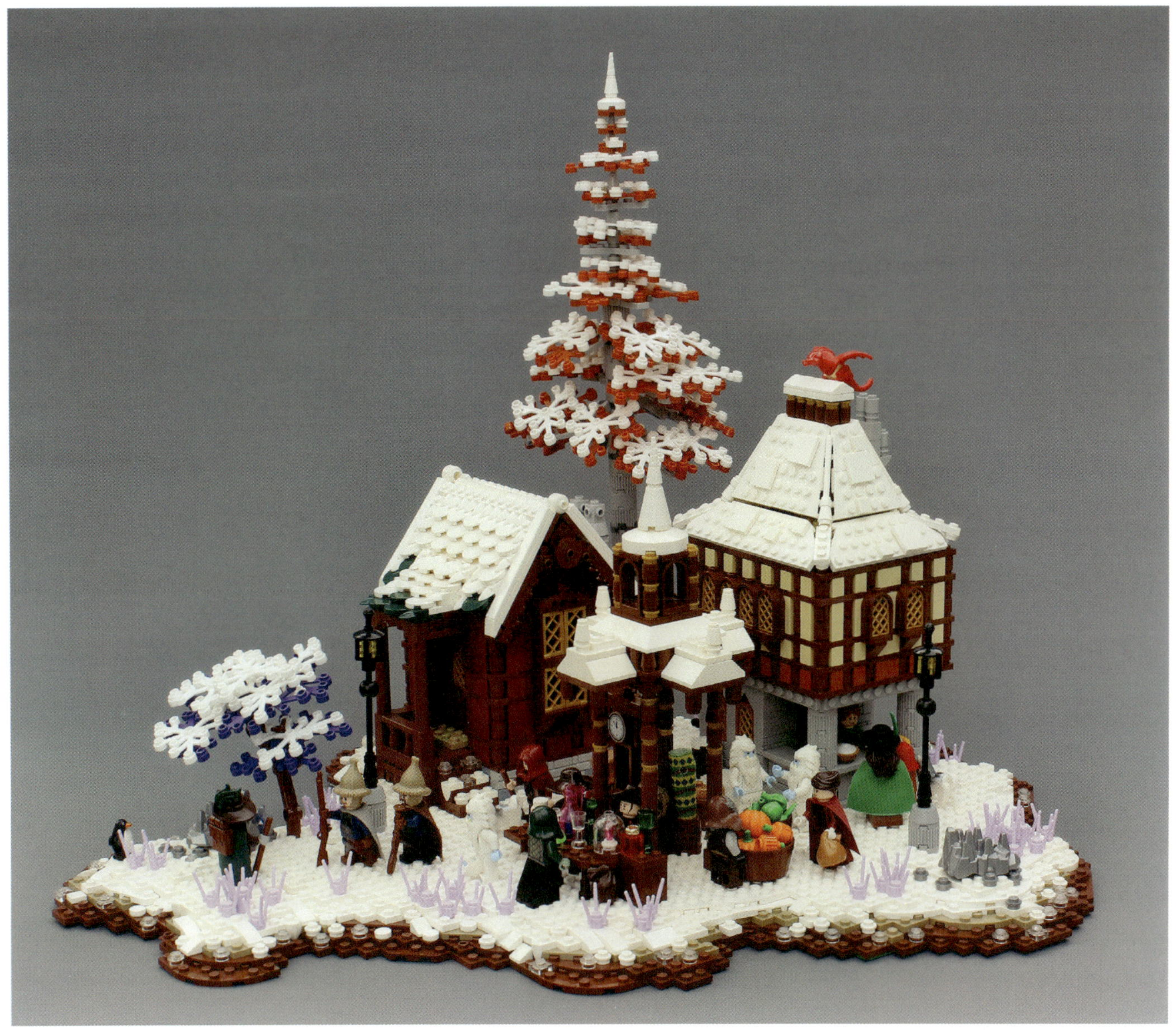

St. Yarinsburg - Plants, greenery, and foliage can really accentuate a building - they bring out extra color, life, and story to what could be an overly straightforward build. On the left, we've got creeping flower vines, and above we have more landscape. The purple tree and lavender grass contrast with the larger orange tree, a balance of warm and cool colors.

In the creation above, I also used the landscape and the white snow to highlight the color on these houses. The dark red really stands out against the icy surroundings of these village houses.

It's important to be able to frame off a creation, too. The village has an organic look with an irregular base and more quaint, cottage-like buildings, while the city has a square, straight-edged base and taller and skinnier buildings to represent a more urban design.

The roofs are really a big highlight on these builds as well. The shinglework on the red cottage (above) is made to look like the snow is sliding off the edges of the dark green shingles.

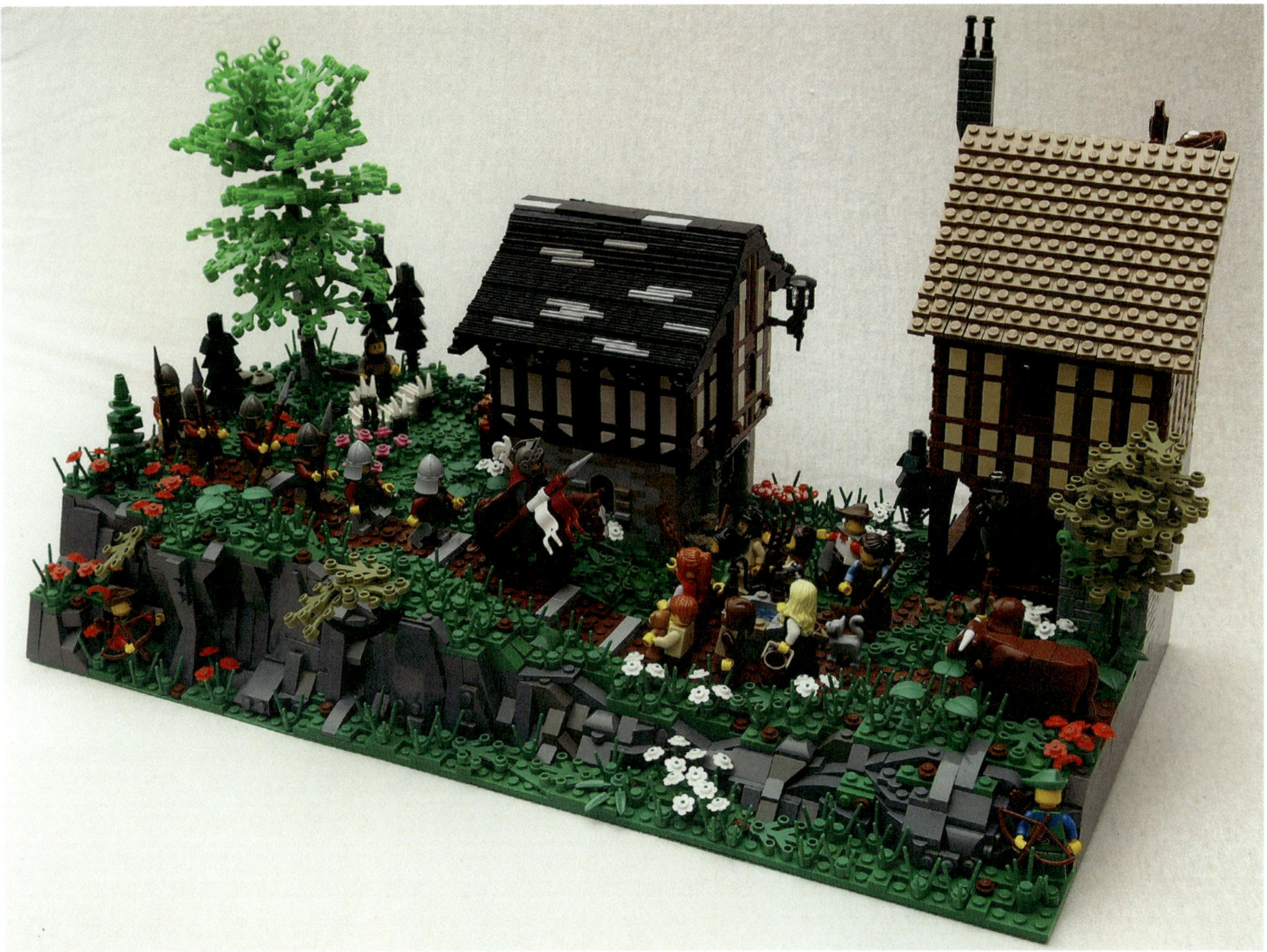

On a technical level, houses can have a lot of intricate bits and pieces that really add up quickly. In **Trouble in St. Swannick**, the center white Tudor house in particular uses Technic axle rods for its roof shingles and upside-down 1 x 1 cheese slopes for the bottom of the Tudor walls as well as plates for fine-tuned stone-work. On the next building, I purposefully arranged the plates to have a sagging, weathered look for a realistic roof.

There is a ton of landscape and foliage to go along with the structures, including lots of my favorite details like mountain goats, miniature fir trees, and retaining wall steps as well as a few hidden elements like foresters.

Built for the CCC, Classic Castle Contest. this build was centered around a saga of various knights and adventurers. For the contest, the MOC was held to stringent rules: two 32 x 32 base plate was the maximum size requirements as well as no third-party elements allowed.

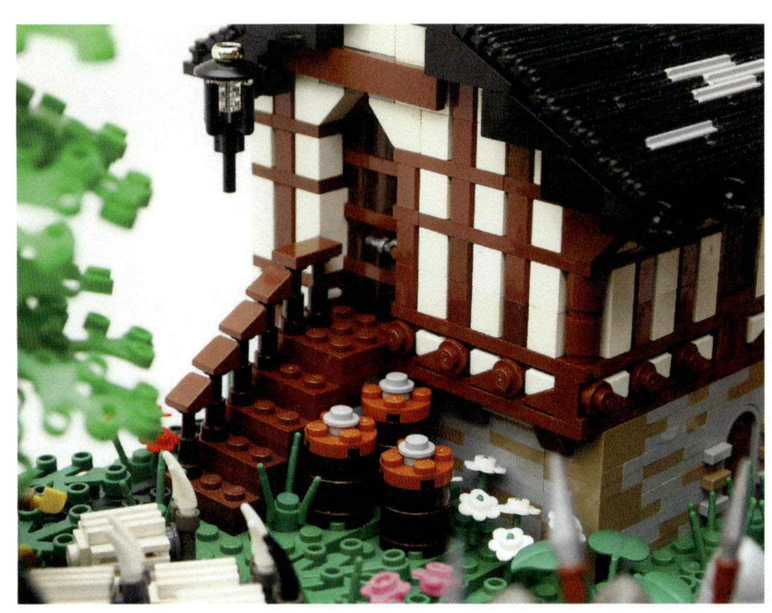

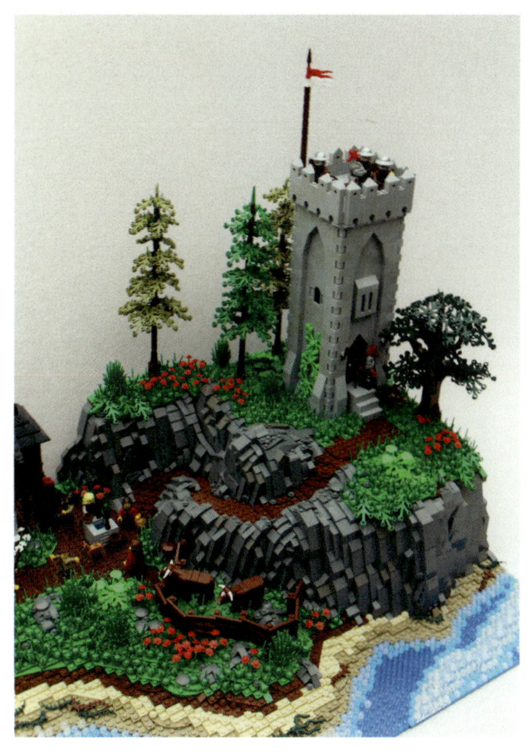

Adalgardis Keep was also built for the CCC contest. This creation ended up being a balance of fortification, landscape, and dwellings.

This was a massive build that really allowed me to explore landscapes and go nuts on the foliage. And this was one of the first appearances of my "grass-stalk trees"

At this point in my career, I was starting to hit on a style. The basic architecture of the houses (and the tower) would be carried over later on into other builds.

I had been experimenting with roofs, but started using slope bricks for more convenience. I would also continue castle architecture with 1 x 1 rounds on the corners, which made for a clearer design. There are some things that had room for improvement - the houses, tower, everything besides landscape suffers from being a little too plain here.

After this build, I would start to liven up my scenes with more color and design.

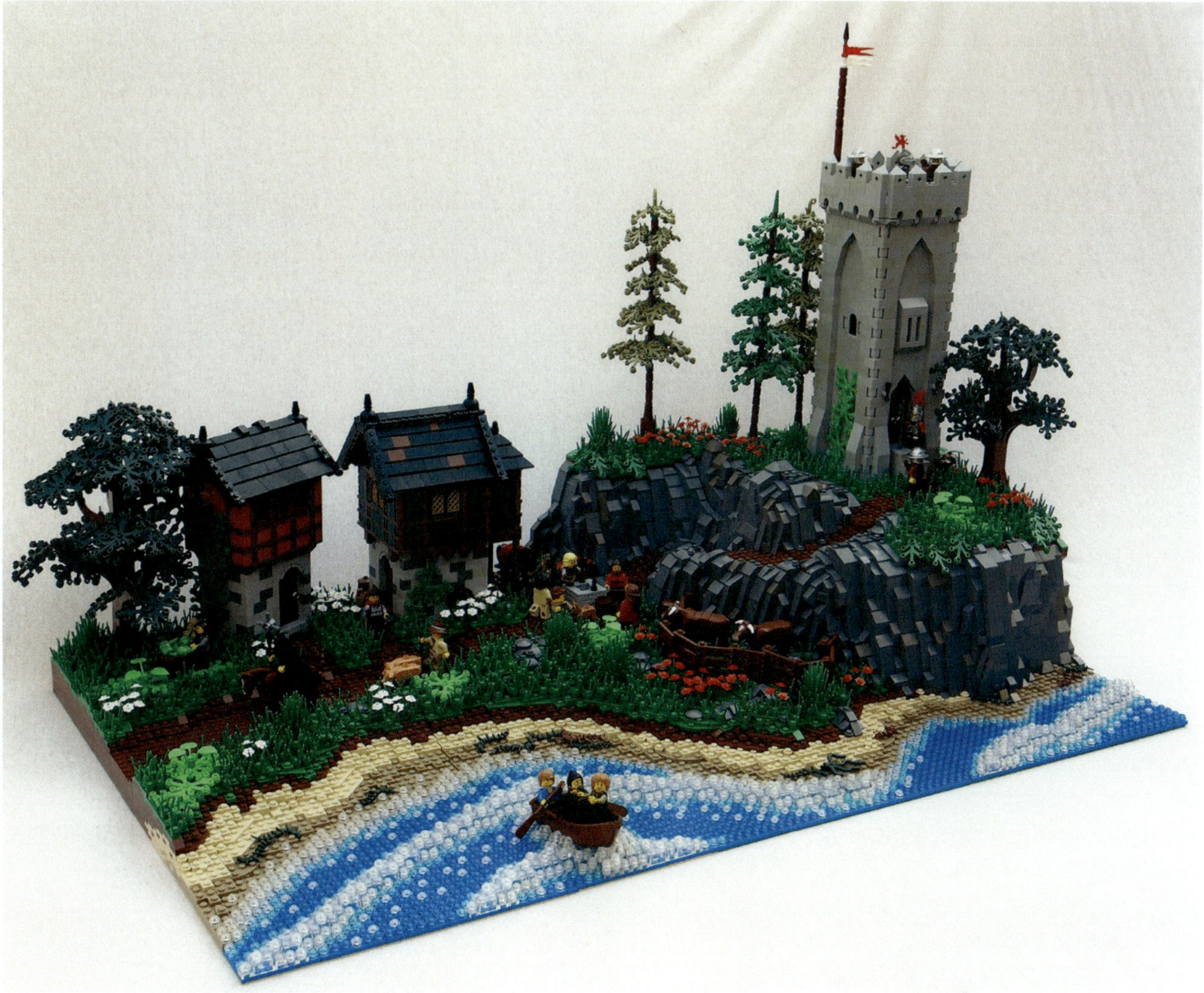

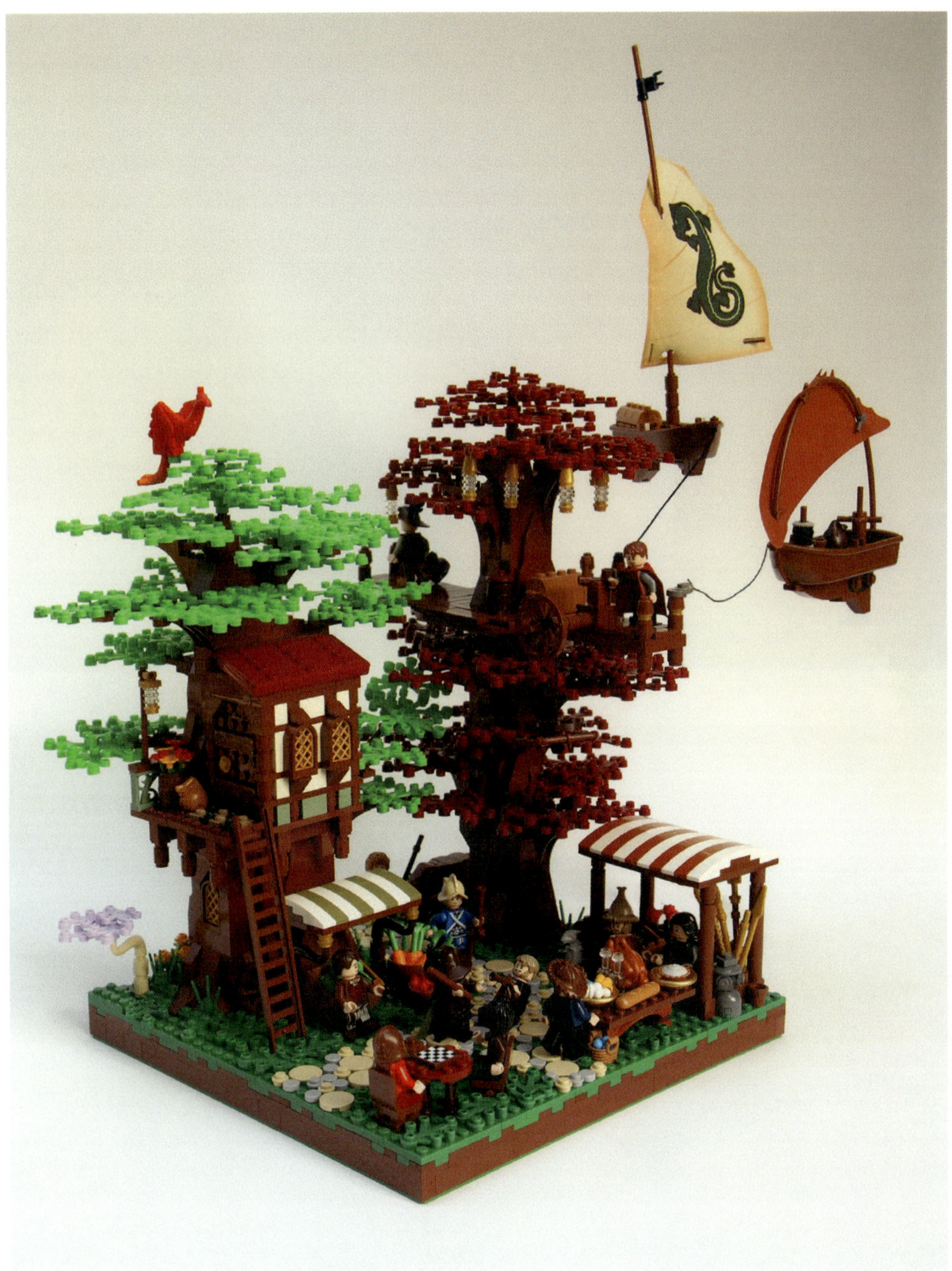

Gentleman of Fortune - Personally, one of my favorite places to build a house is in a tree! Treehouses have their own unique challenges which makes the creation that much more interesting. The biggest challenge is the limited space, but that allows for "a lot in a little" to come back into play. The treehouse on the left exemplifies this by being only 8 studs long at its widest, (Surprisingly, It's not the smallest house I've built!) but it turned out very well-proportioned.

What helps this creation really pop is the color. The whole scene has a colorful but earthy vibe. The market stalls have striped roofs that are simple but look fantastic. Green and red are again the perfect combo of complementary colors and really work here in this LEGO® forest marketplace. It's easy to pick up the atmosphere from looking at this scene, and that's always a good thing.

This build was again a contribution to the Isles of Aura - and the illusion of the flying ships is courtesy of photoshop editing trickery.

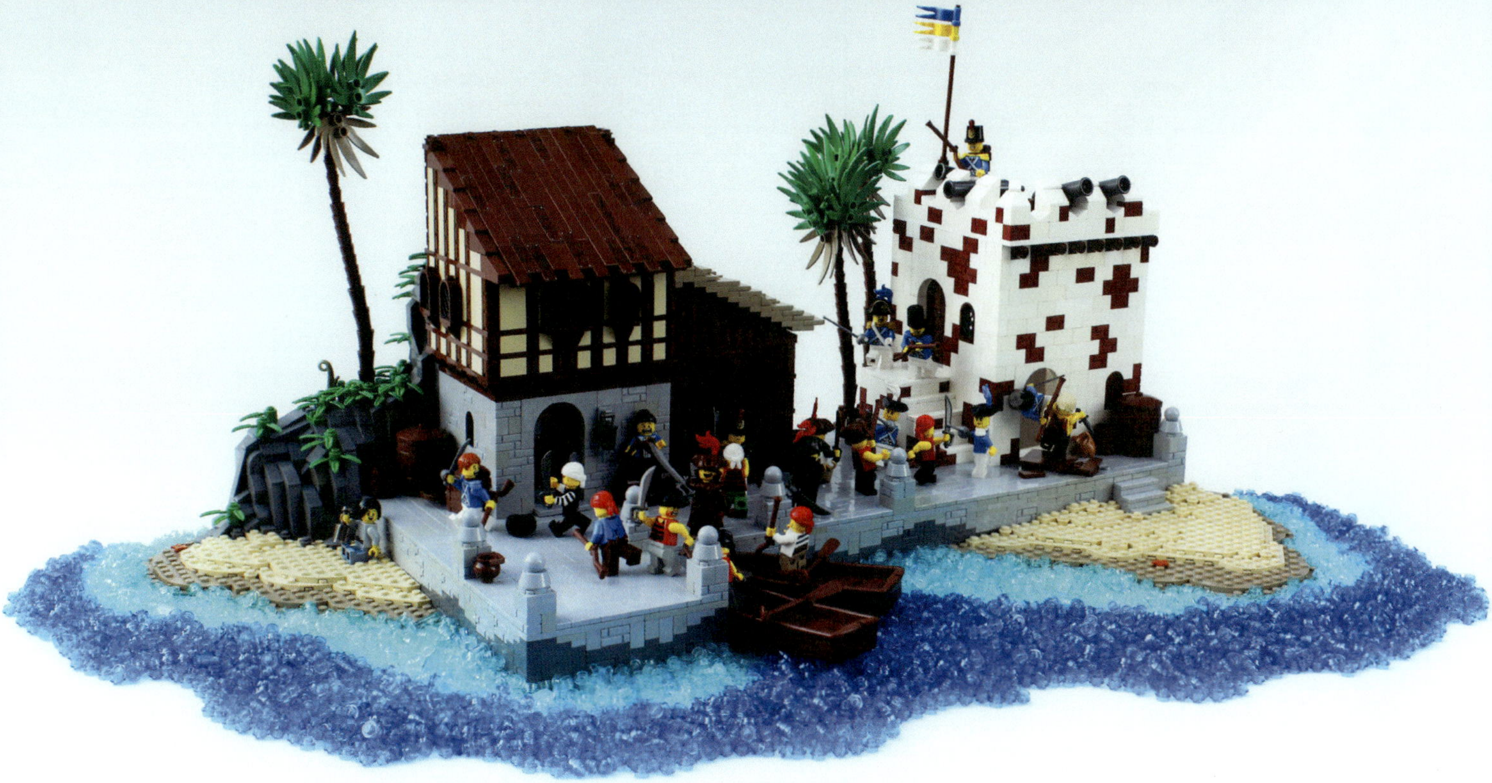

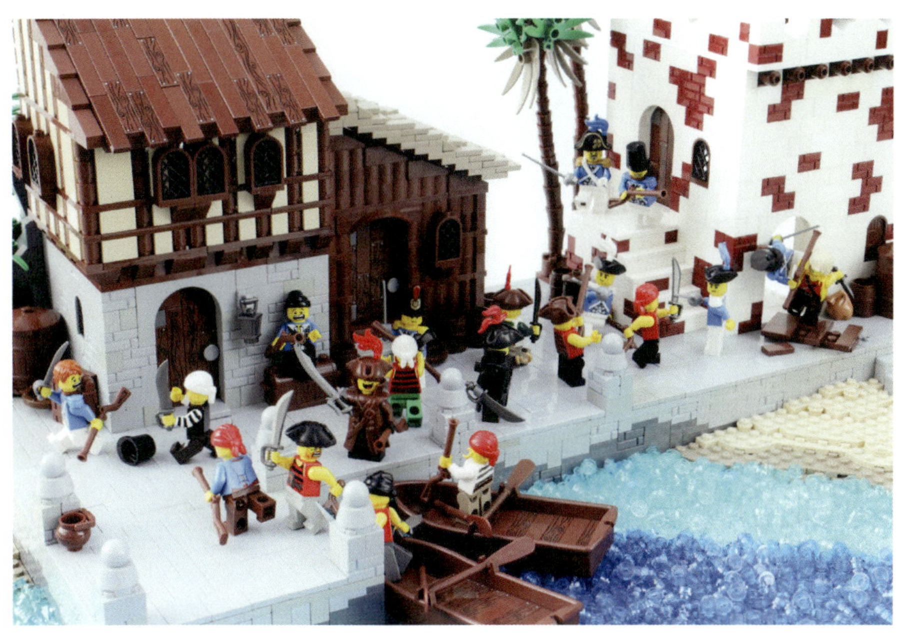

For this caribbean pirate scene **Buccaneer Brawl**, my brother and I (who collaborated with me on this creation) really got to enjoy utilizing some masonry tricks, most notably the 'wet' looking bricks at the water's edge on the dock to give the scene more realism.

Continuing this theme, the imperial block house has dark red elements to pay homage to the original pirate's theme which had white and red for the fortress walls. At the time, the dark red masonry bricks were very rare, so Mark and I couldn't resist a little showing off.

The house and the stones were a little reserved in color so we could accentuate the colorful action in this scene. The bright colored pirates were able to stand out more against the neutral backdrop.

This scene was actually sponsored by a third-party minifig accessory company and this build was designed to feature and highlight them.

This would be a recurring thing for me and Mark, and these advertisement builds gained pretty good popularity online - which was a win-win for us and the company because we got to keep the parts sent to us!

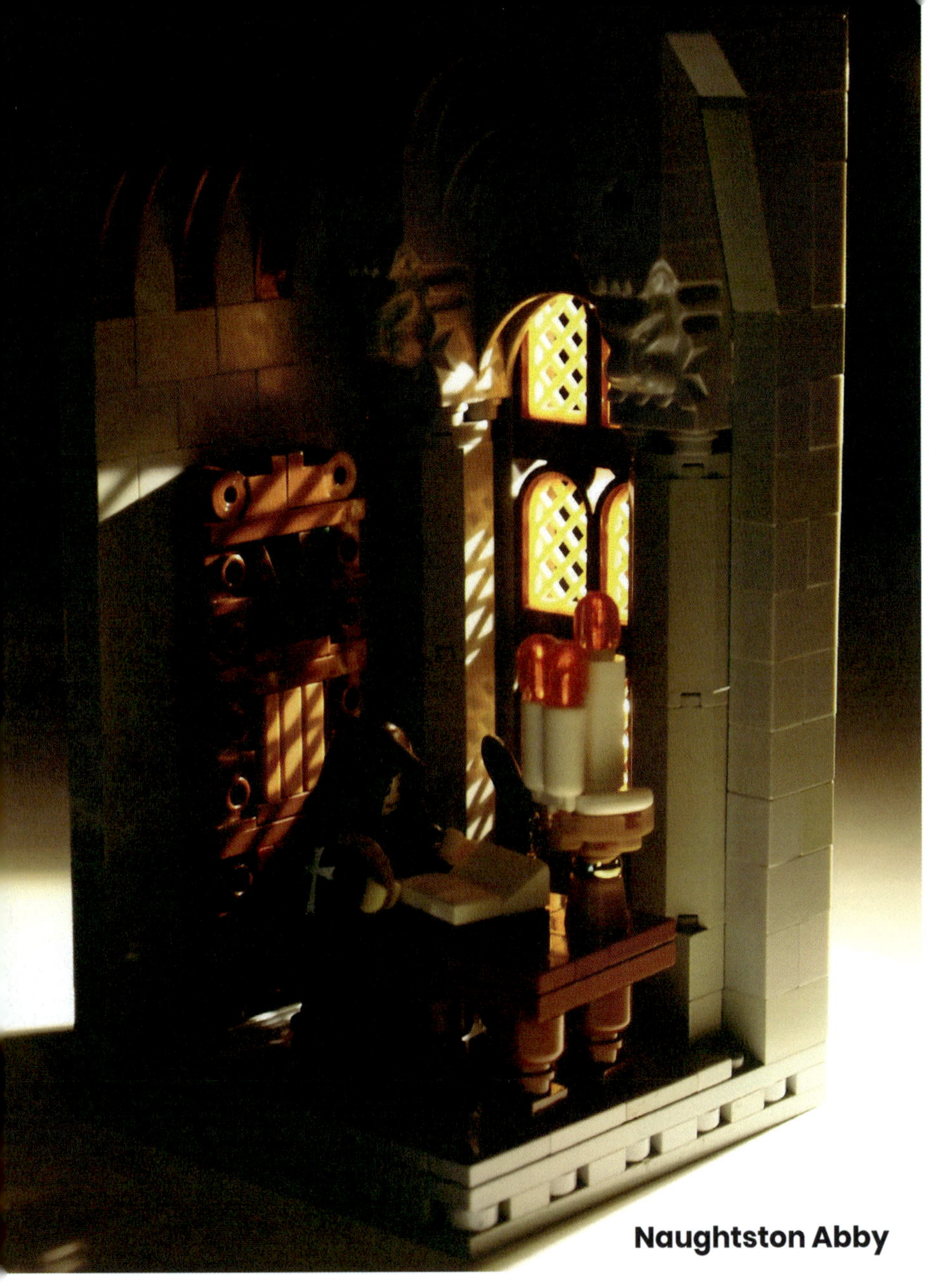

Naughtston Abby

They make up a small percentage of my gallery, but interior vignettes are some of my very favorites because nothing can capture an atmosphere in a small sliver like a warm, cozy interior. It can be difficult to achieve a cozy vibe from LEGO®, but with the right balance of details such as architecture, lighting, furniture, characters, and story, together they can create an image not unlike a painting.

On the left, we have a rare appearance from my signature avatar fig, Brother Steven the Priest. I keep this character scarce deliberately and don't share many traits about him, to add an aura of mystery. This allows the character to become synonymous with the name and the brand. More details about him would distract from the fact that he is used as my "brand logo".

(Fun fact: most members of the LEGO® online community have a signature fig).

The architecture, particularly the walls, is set up so that all the bricks are stacked on each other and overlapping like true masonry.

The lighting in this build is honestly what I'm most proud of. It really captured the gentle glow of the late afternoon sun. Most of this is thanks to the the pearl gold windows which create a brilliant shine. I have found these pieces are excellent for use in direct light.

There are a number of subtle but very interesting details in this small creation. On the bookcase, you have minfig leg assembly pieces for carved decorations and the candelabara uses technic, a lego plume, and minifig airtanks pieces. I will say this was just before they invented LEGO® candles, so this technique is a bit old-fashioned.

Other elements such as Brother Steven turning a page and the leaning book on the bookcase, really help the scene come to life.

Hilariously, despite being posted on the internet for many years, no one has ever pointed out the fact that there is a missing 1 x 1 plate tile at the very bottom corner of the floor in this scene just above the decorated base!

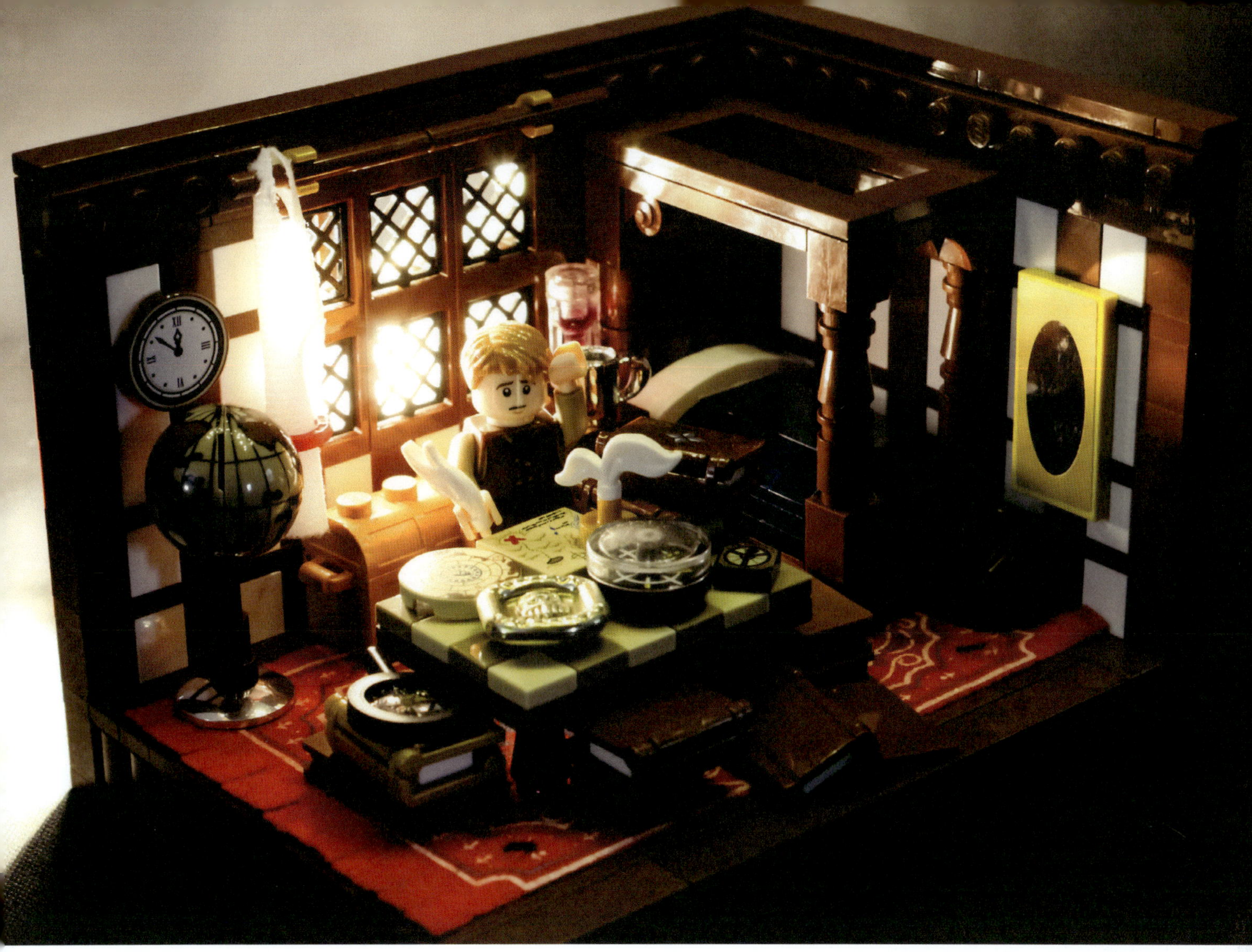

Above we have another long-running character of mine, Zenas Abbington. He stars in my Isles of Aura series with his ongoing adventures. In the creation shown here, we get a glimpse into **Zenas' Abbington's study** which is chock-full of charming details such as the hourglass by the bedside with a cup of coffee, the inkwell with a custom third-party feather plume, a curtain made from a minifig cape, a lego mirror, along with books strewn all over the floor and the old model working LEGO® compass on the table.

For a creation like this, I wanted to see how many great details I could put in a single room. All the furniture is freestanding on top of a bellville cloth rug,

One very simple characteristic can dramatically change the entire feel of any interior space, and that is the height of the ceiling in comparison to the walls. On the left, we have a smaller, taller building. Whereas above, we have a shorter room with a wider footprint, which feels more like a cozy bedroom of an inn rather than a stately medieval chapel. This basic concept can really add a pivotal effect on a creation.

I used the lighting again here for great effect, but with black window frames which evoke a more "structured" feel. At the time of this writing, LEGO® didn't sell gold square window panes, so in this design I used black ones. They are perhaps more appropriate for a humble inn anyway, as black (iron) looks less expensive than gold.

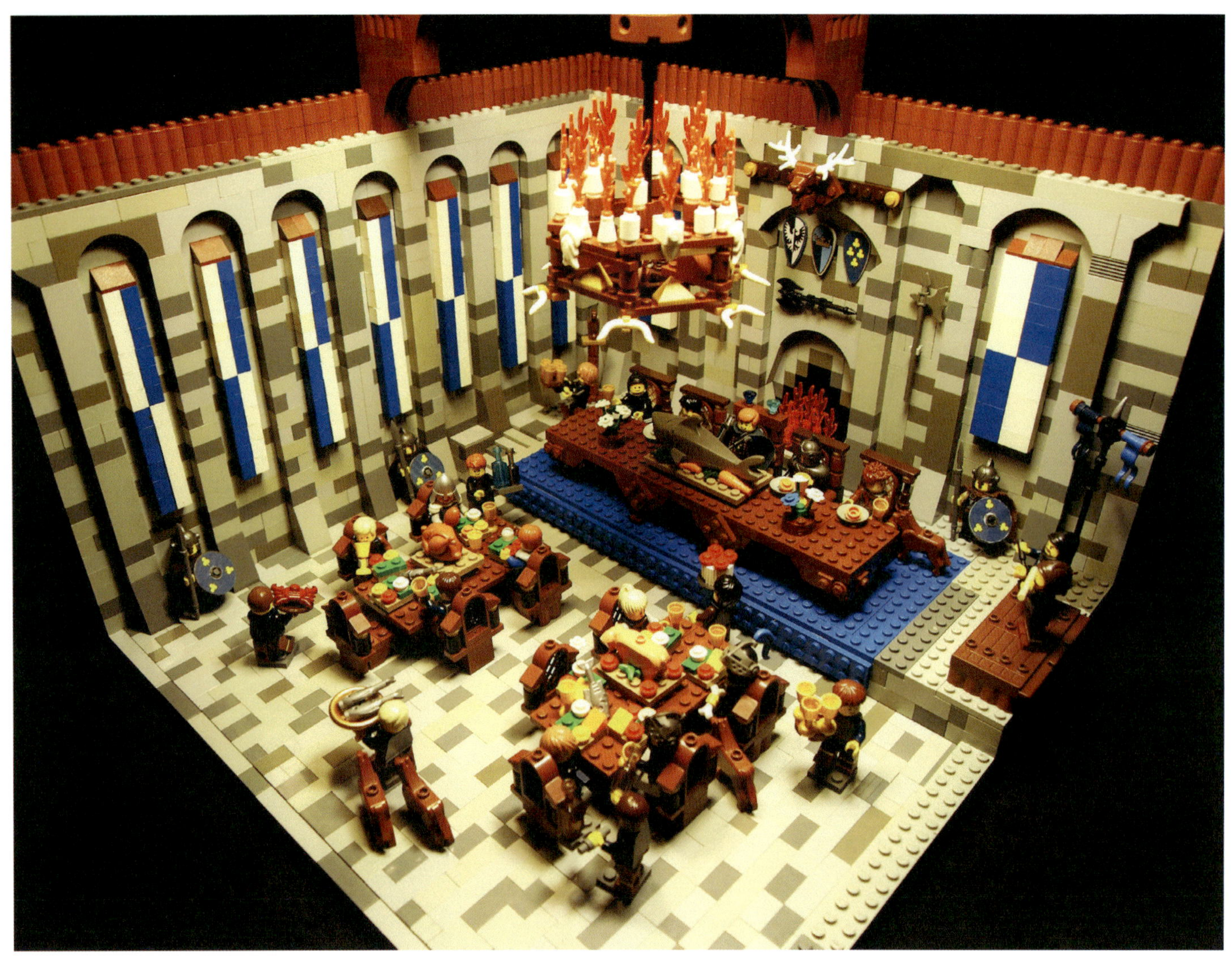

The Great Hall of Rothburg was one of the earliest creations I ever uploaded online, but it turned out to be a very pivotal build for me in my early career. Like a lot of creations in this book, it was built for a contest, specifically a "medieval feast" contest, and it came in first place.

This was one of the first builds that put me "on the map" in the online LEGO® community. I really enjoyed the layout and festive atmosphere, along with the chandelier, which was a big highlight for this creation. It incorporated some fun techniques including minifig beards which resembled dripping candle wax.

Obviously this creation is a bit... old! Some of the architectural detail is a little rough around the edges and the exposed studs mixed with horizontal bricks (as on the side and the raised dais platform) are somewhat distracting. Overall though, the build has a lot of colorful character. Highlighting this is the blue and white banners which are just a couple stacked bricks!

A fun detail about this creation was that every figure seated around the banquet tables represents an actual LEGO® builder, mostly from the online forums and community where this contest was hosted. The general theme around this great hall build was a sort of pseudo-Viking theme inspired by Nordic culture, hence the heavy emphasis on seafood (and roasted shark).

Another detail about this creation was the use of third-party minifig accessories and elements like the weapons hanging on the wall and worn by some of the characters, not to mention the third-party moose head at the top of the fireplace. Alongside these are stickers that my brother and I created. We made quite a name for ourselves with these high-quality printed stickers that we would add to shields, minifig torsos, flags and banners. The stickers were inspired by original LEGO® designs.

It wasn't just the contest that this build was created for, it was part of an online group called "The Lands of Classic Castle" later changed to "Lands of Rowaia". This was an online role-play game with separate factions, kingdoms, and empires with an overarching story which was advanced through the results of building contests. The faction I belonged to was known as "Garheim" from the cold North. This theme was one of the highlights of my career.

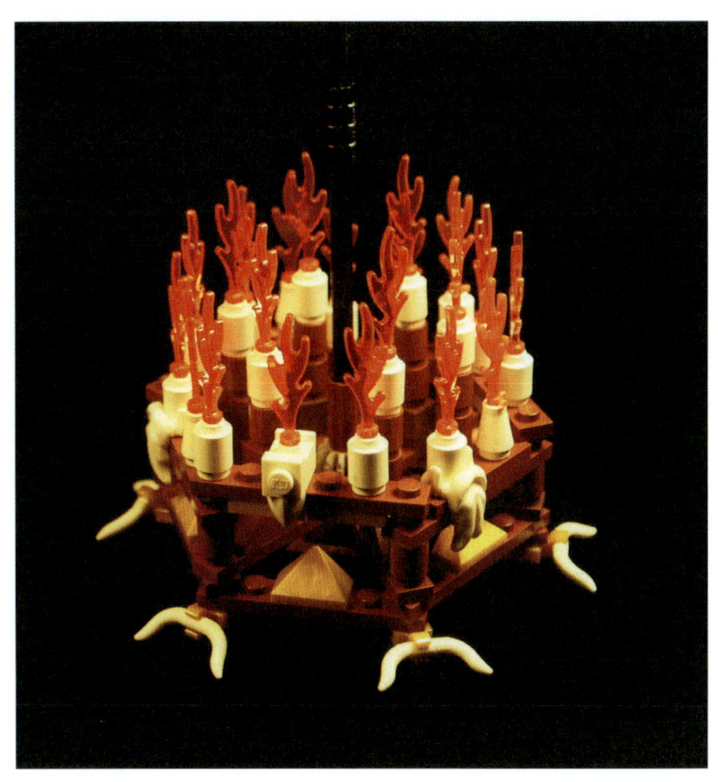

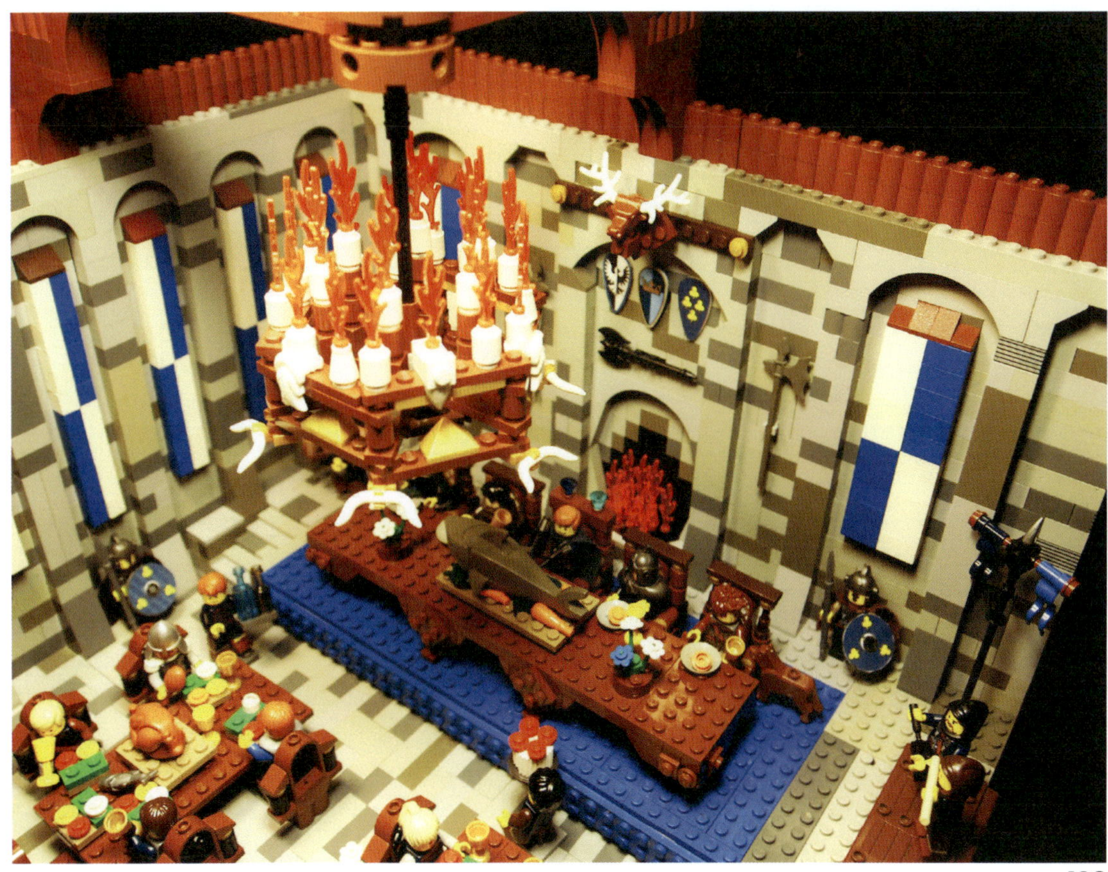

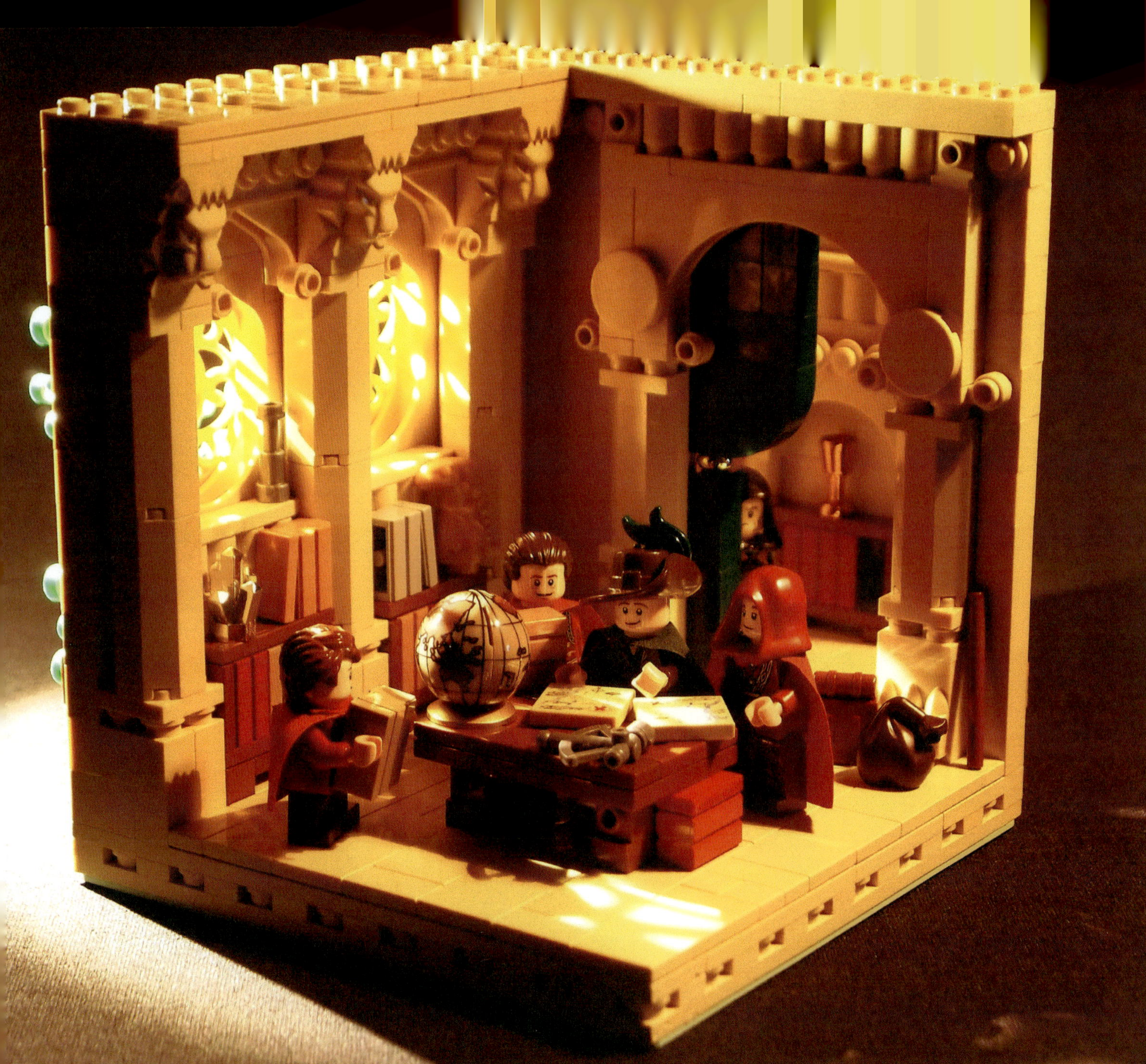

One of my best-loved interiors was the **Library of St. Ablasterio** from the Isles of Aura theme, which really contains all my favorite elements of an interior - lighting, atmosphere, and perspective. Although this is a 16 x 16 scene, on the back right I've added a second room that cannot be seen from the side, a visual trick that keeps the layout while giving the build an extra layer of depth which makes the build look larger than it is.

Possibly my favorite element in this creation was the color. The rich tans, reds, and browns give a beautiful atmosphere of warmth and charm with just the right amount of contrast in the emerald green (Zenas' feather and the curtain, specifically). So many of the tiny details in this creation help tell the whimsical story. The telescope on the windowsill suggests the library workers enjoy stargazing. For me, the silver crystal could represent geology and science, the dragon statue representing ancient lore, and the goblet in the back, history. This interior was built just before LEGO® released their now-famous book pieces, so I used profile masonry bricks and 1 x 2 tiles to resemble volumes on the shelves and floor. I enjoyed this library so much that I even returned to it later to create the exterior (seen on page 16).

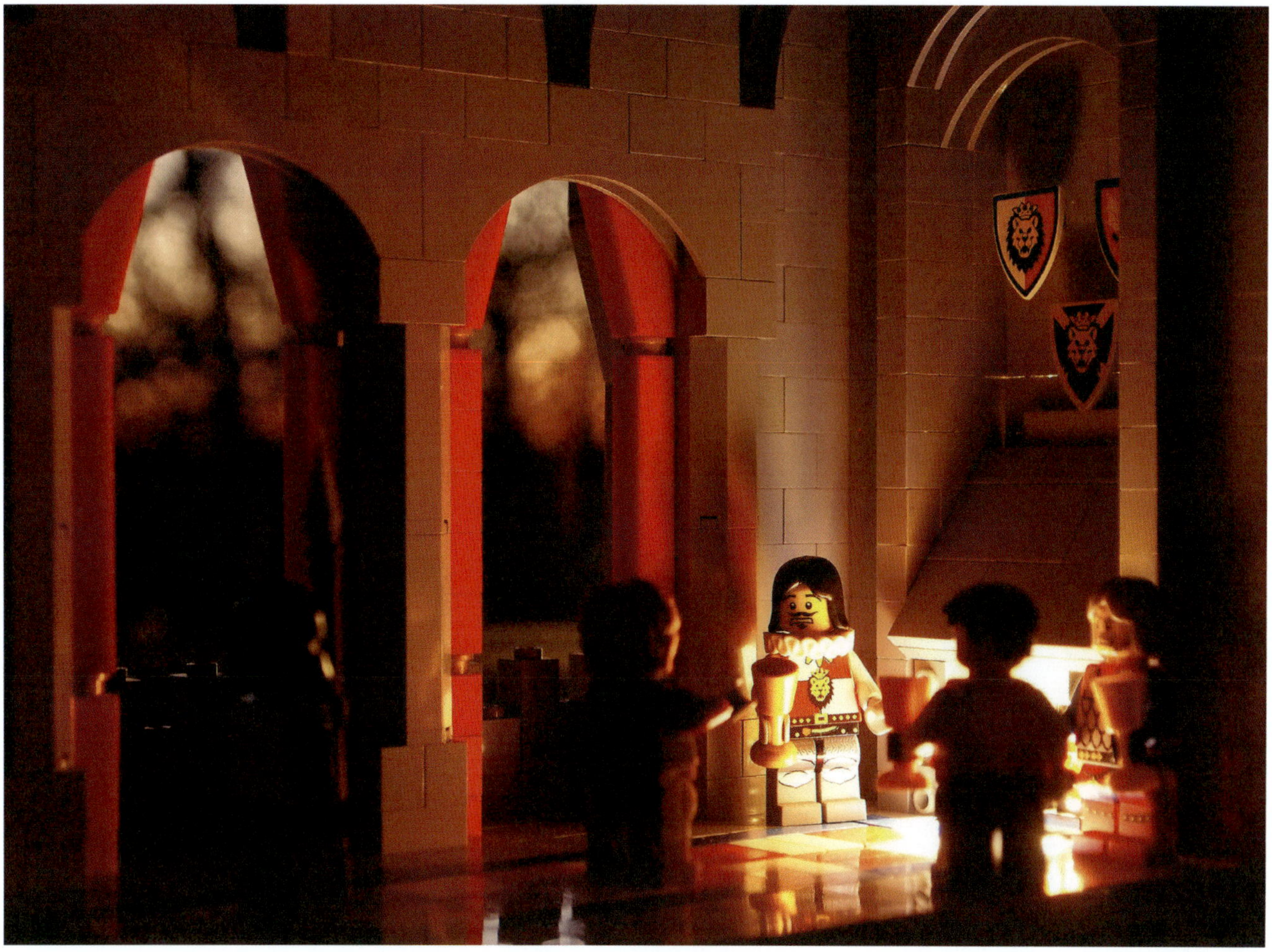

For this castle interior, **Seeking Aid** (above)
I stuck a light through the fireplace, put this
creation on a windowsill and took a photo
at sunset, with the woods around our home
as the backdrop. This creation employs
really simple techniques but together
they create an amazing environment.
The scarlet drapes in the arched windows
and the slick-looking floor are some of my
favorite details.

I played around with shadows as well
as light with this next interior, **A Nook Of
Learning** (right). The faint light source
coming from outside the creation highlights
the upper floor since the glow of the
fireplace on the ground floor wasn't enough
to light the whole thing.

There are some interesting details upon
a closer look - a green parrot is perched
by the blazing fire, and a tiny portrait of a
young lady hangs on the wall, perhaps in
remembrance of Zenas' deceased aunt.

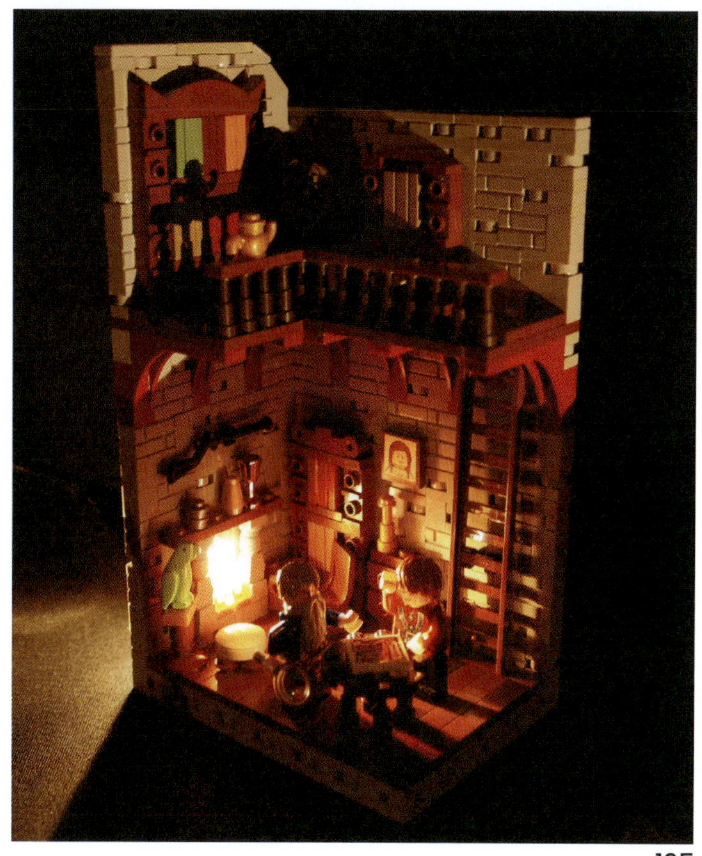

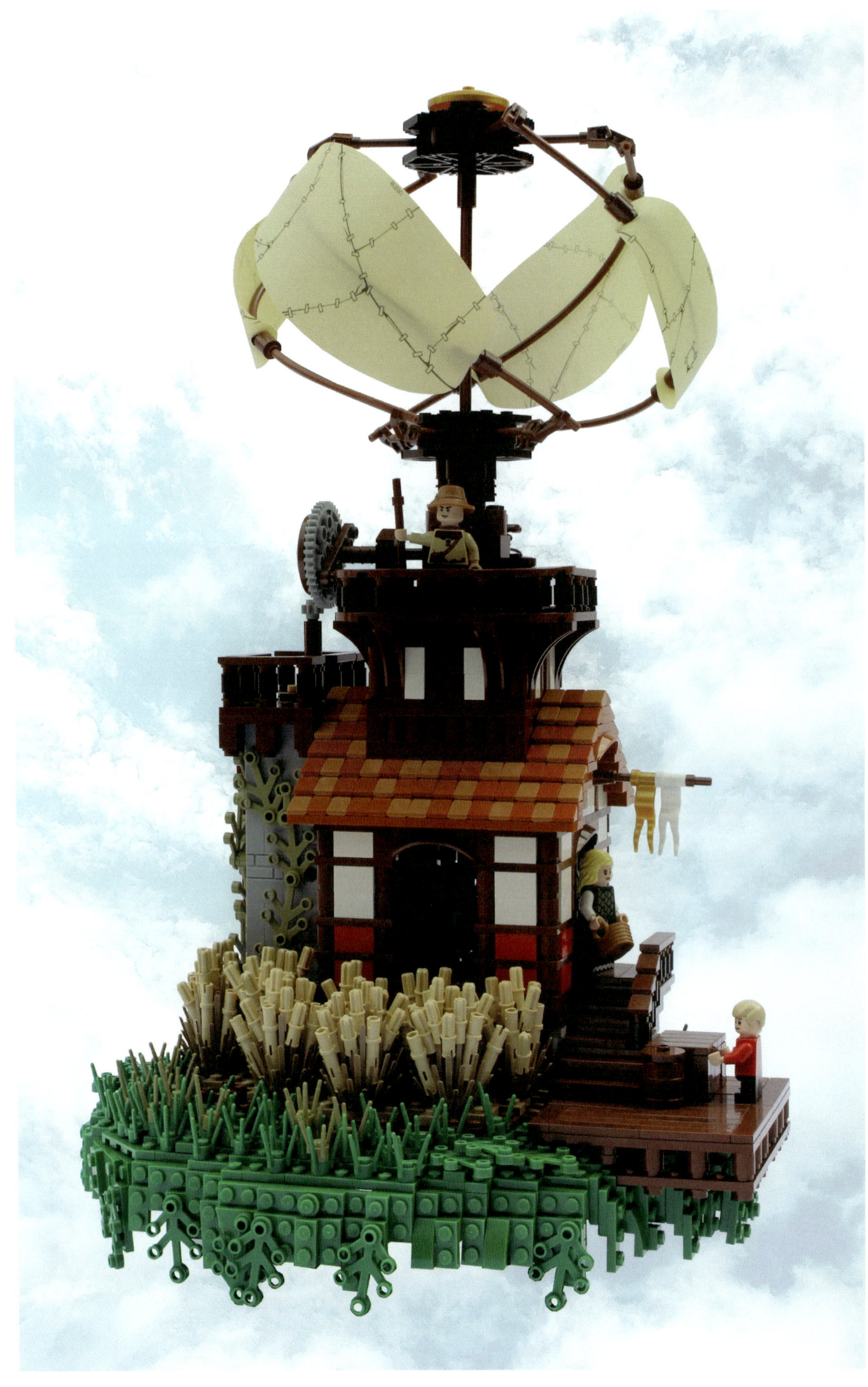

On a rare occasion, I build a creation that has a function aspect. This unpublished windmill, built to go alongside Rosewood Hall for a convention, had a power functions motor installed in the stone structure (left of the house) that was connected to the sails and which was then linked to a mill stone inside. (Note the gears on the side of the balcony.)

Something that has kept me coming back to floating islands is the challenge of putting "a lot in a little". For this build, the tiny wheat field was especially fun to innovate. Although the light tan technic pins are common, I have yet to see anyone use dark tan bushes for a wheat field.

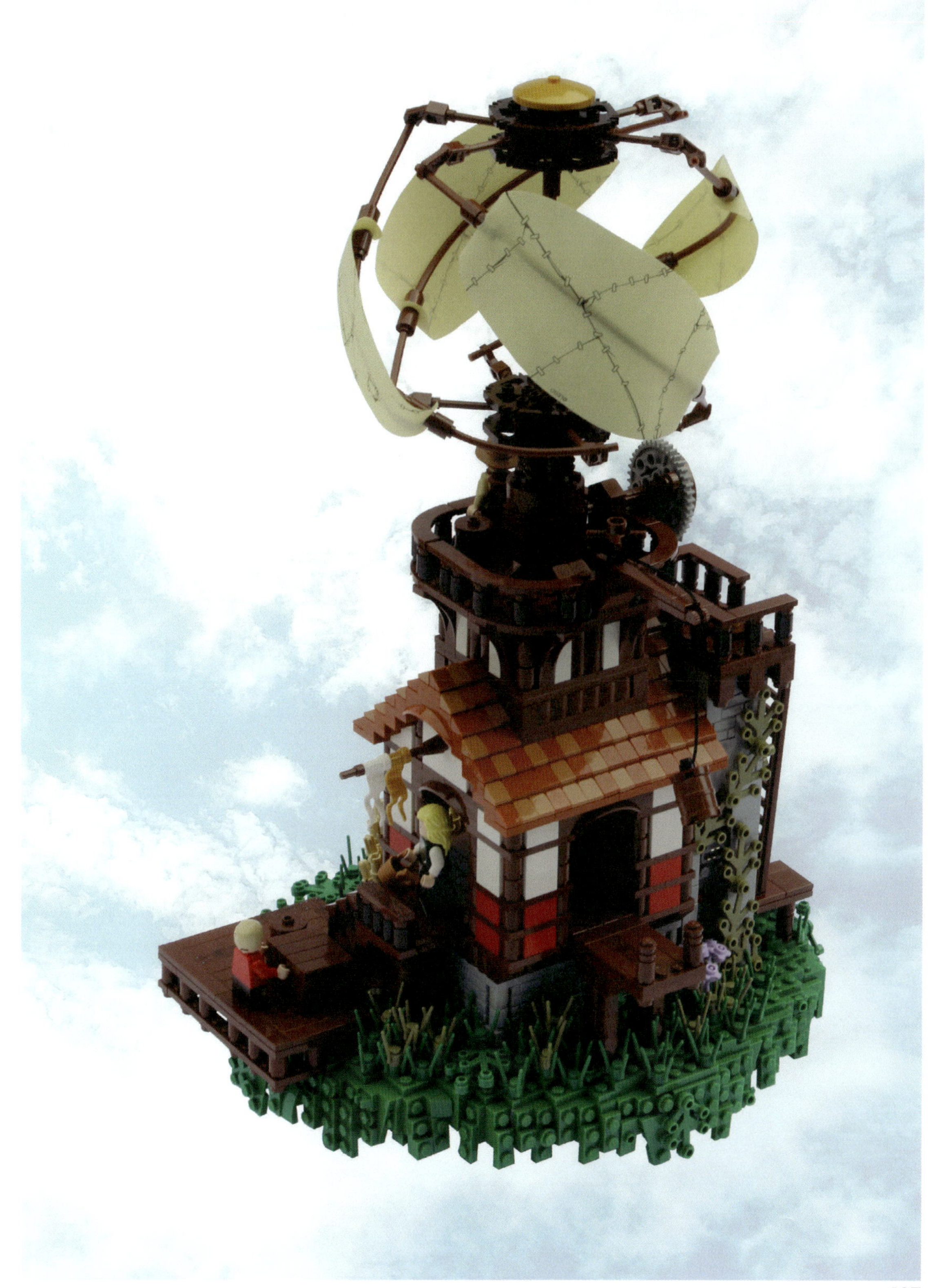

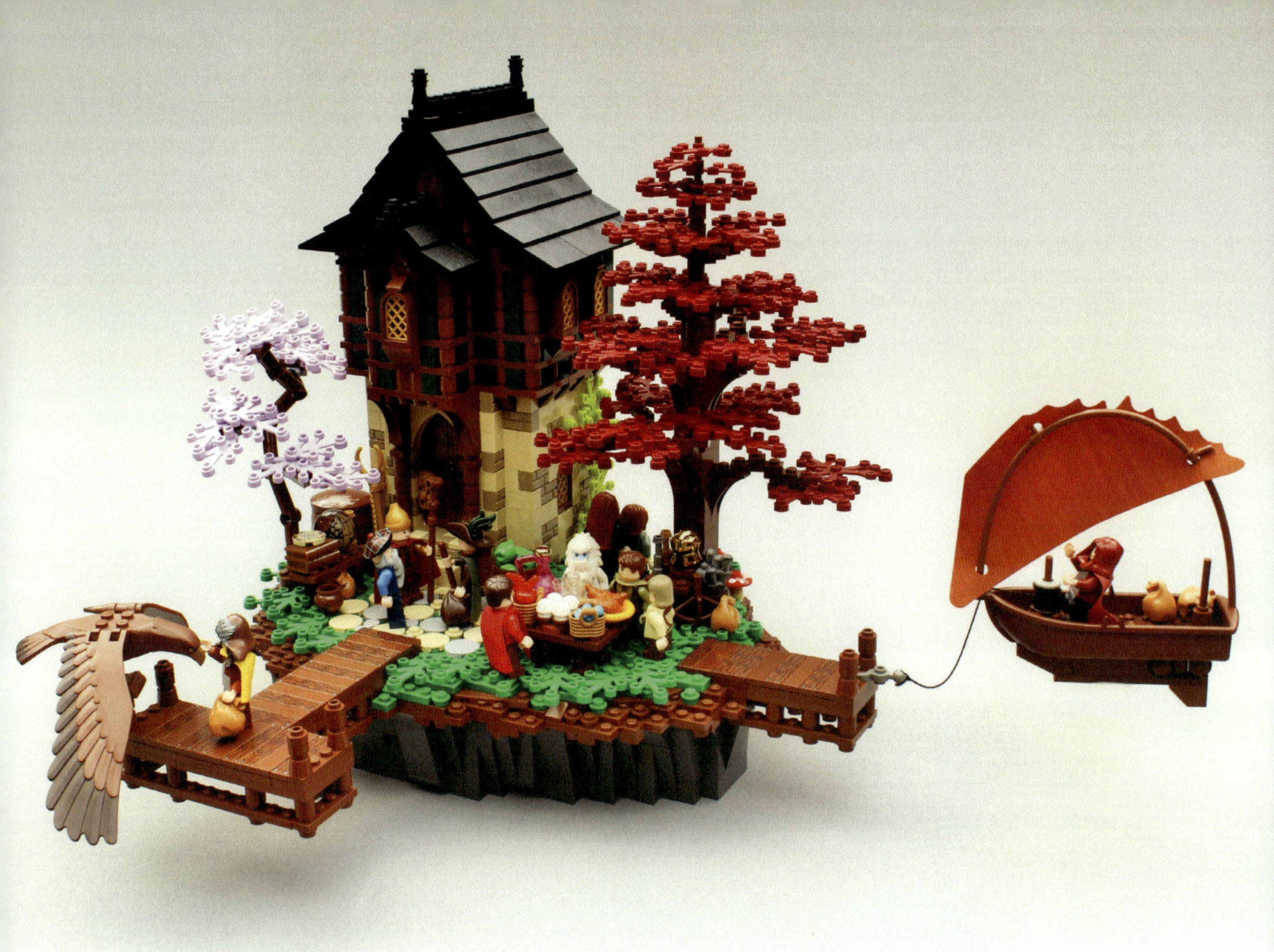

Departing from Danger is from the Isles of Aura series. The color in this creation really stands out because everything matches and works togther. The cool green with the warm brown docks, the tan alongside the house's dark green, the red with the green grass and vines, and finally a splash of lavendar are examples of how color can make a creation really pop! Seeing the diverse cast of interesting characters going about their business makes you want to explore the creation even more.

One thing I had learned later in my career is to keep the trees and ground a different color or shade. I found this very helpful in making sure the MOC wasn't overwhelmed with a single color palette.

The build itself is an excellent combination of some of my favorite themes rock work, landscape, trees, character design, and houses. And the Isles of Aura, as a theme, really gave me an avenue for expressing all of these elements that I enjoy so much.

Sometimes, the key elements of a build will be more subtle. For instance, the "power of three" comes into play in the **Coxwell Cottage** below. The lower half of the MOC has three minifigures all involved in different activites. The trail with the artistic brown bridge helps the lower half of the build stay interesting because the horizontal trail helps to draw the eye across the creation.

For the larger details, you have two trees bookending a single house which creates the three major features. However, the upper half has it's own trick up it's sleeve, mainly color. Against the large palettle of green, the red in the house really stands out. Even though the house is simple in design, it catches your eye very quickily.

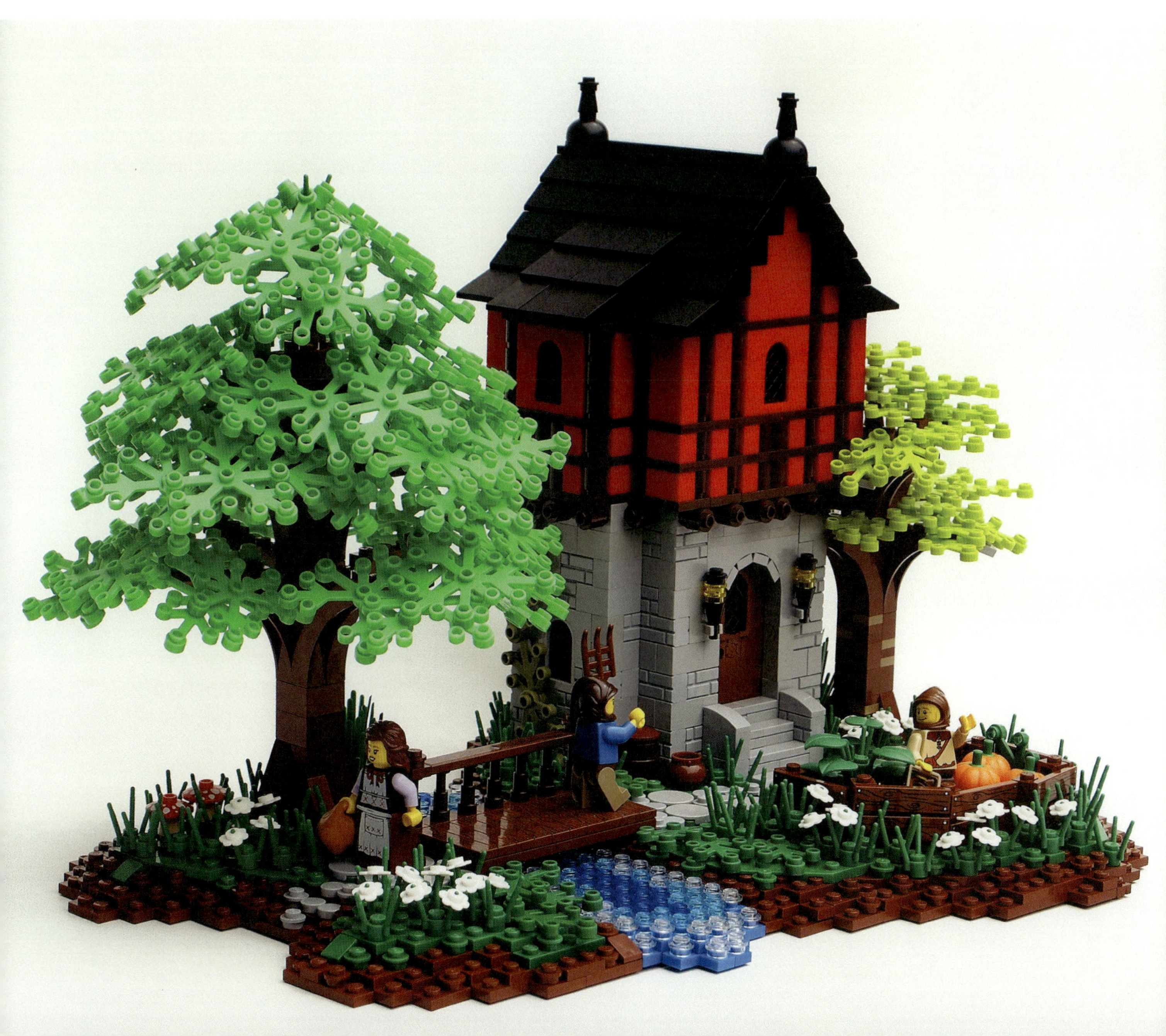

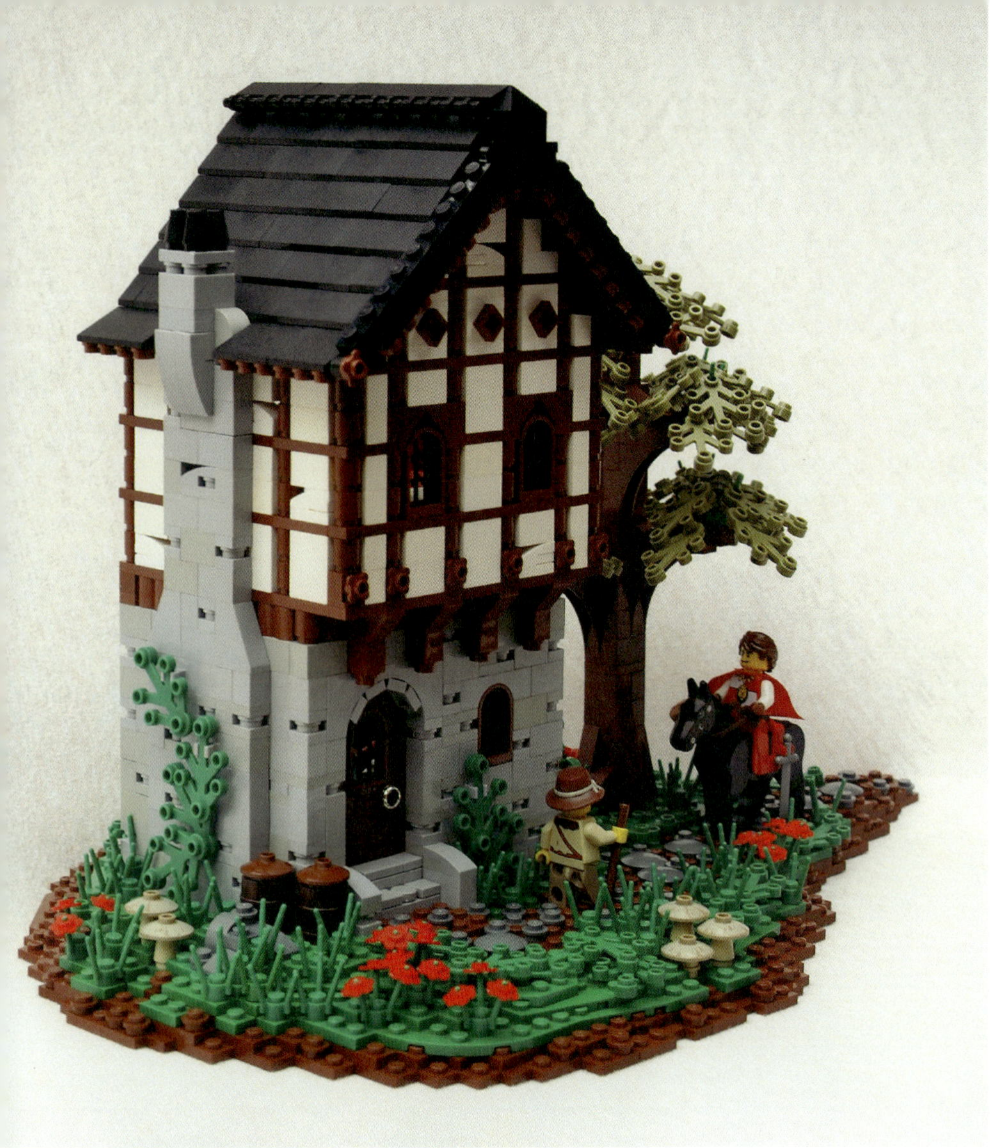

All of the previous houses in this book have relied on either interior or exterior as their main focus. There are occasions where I have combined the two into what I've nicknamed a "dollhouse".

On the left, we have **Lancly Inn** built for the Colossal Castle contest. This inn contains many details unique to the build. For instance, I incorporated a lot more one-by-one round plates and slopes to give the building a more weathered appearance. The dollhouse theme naturally left room for more inside details.

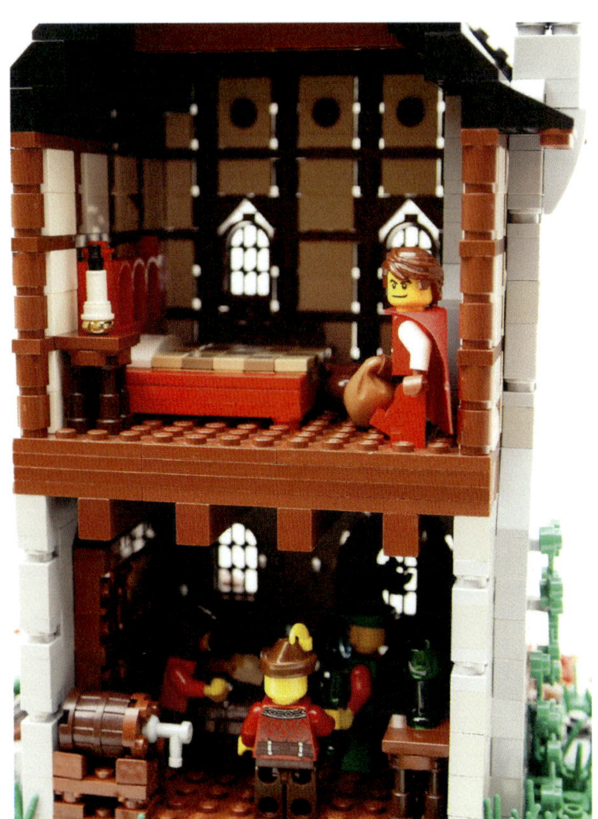

Some of my favorites details are the bed and the candlestick. Since this build, LEGO® has released an official candle piece but back in the day, we had to improvise. The candle is a technic pin with a barb for the candle wick.

Lastly, there is the color. Red and green and in this case, white have always been a reliable go-to palette for me and all are carried throughout the entire build.

Davinci's Workshop

Leonardo da Vinci's house was originally a LEGO® IDEAS project submission.

The outside is a simple tan with dark tan plate accents. I usually use tan for building structures that have a Mediterranean theme and any medieval builds that I create. Bookending the tan is a clay tile roof with green grass inspired by Italian colors.

On the inside, this color scheme is carried throughout with Davinci's red outfit and his green, flying contraption. The layout of the dollhouse provides ample space to incorporate many interesting details that help to tell the story.

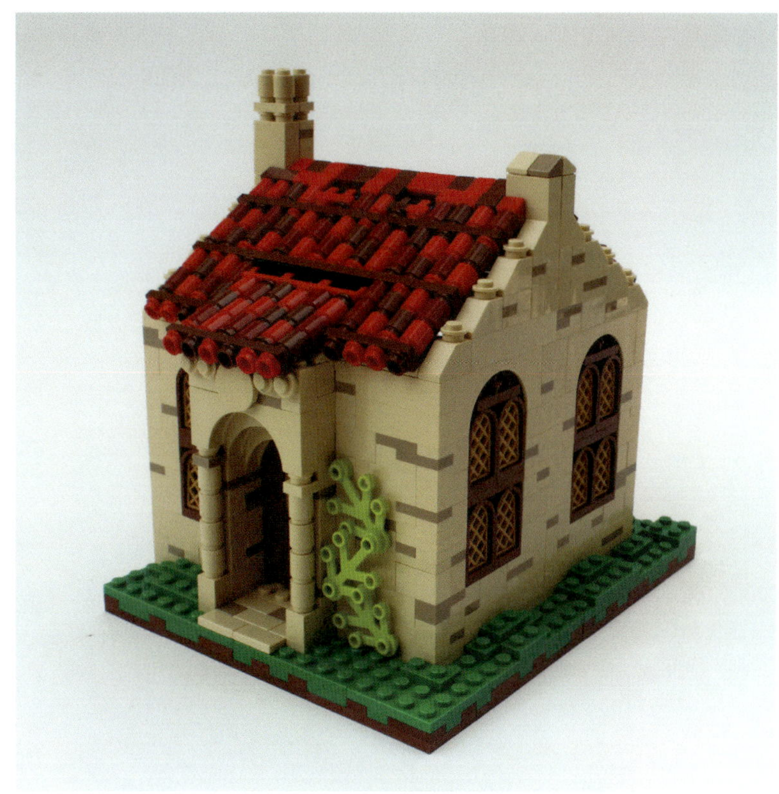

Leonardo da Vinci has always been a great inspiration for me and I've incorporated many of his signature designs in this workshop such as his flying contraption., easel, crossbow, and tank with little wheels, and some small cannonballs sitting next to it.

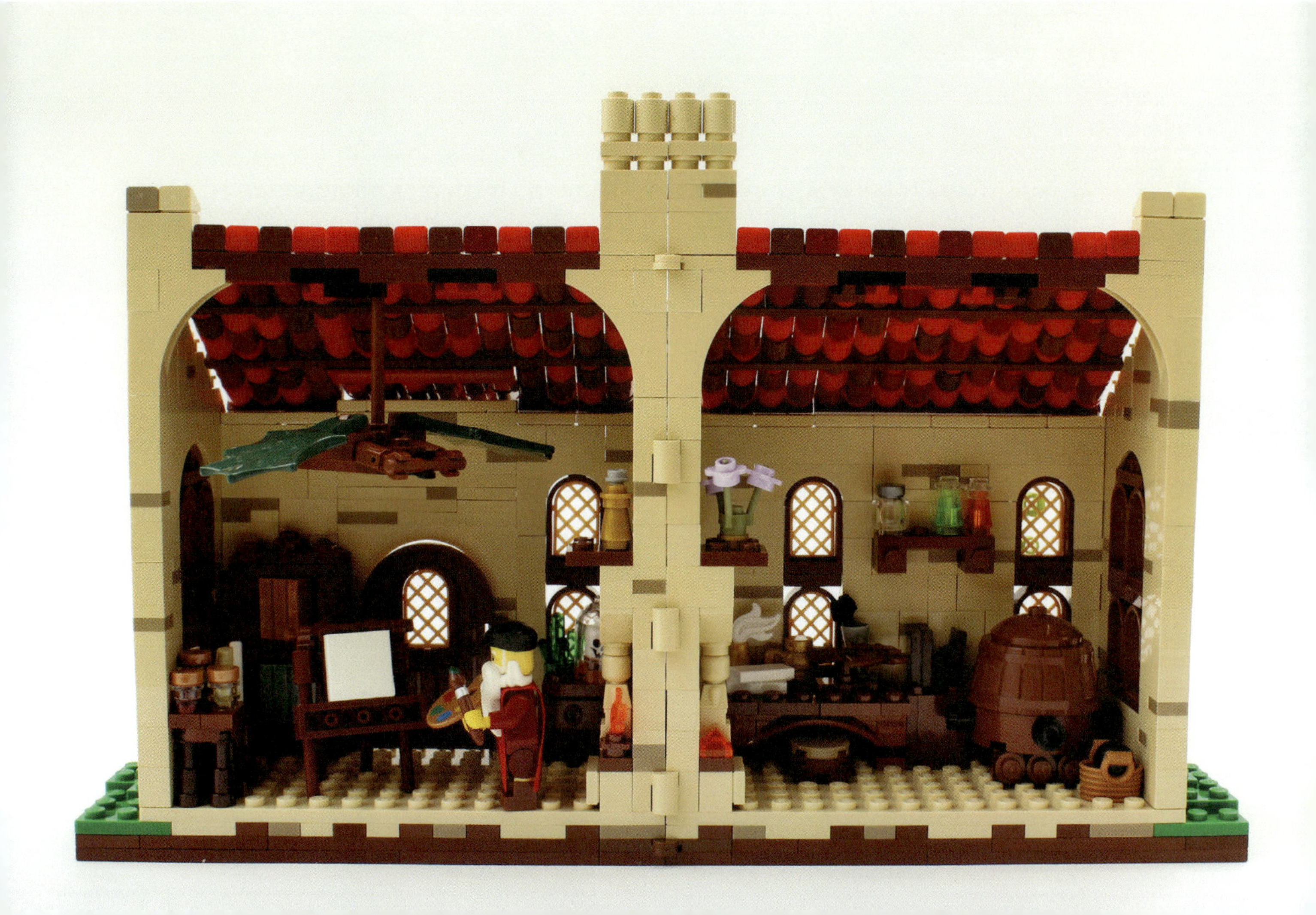

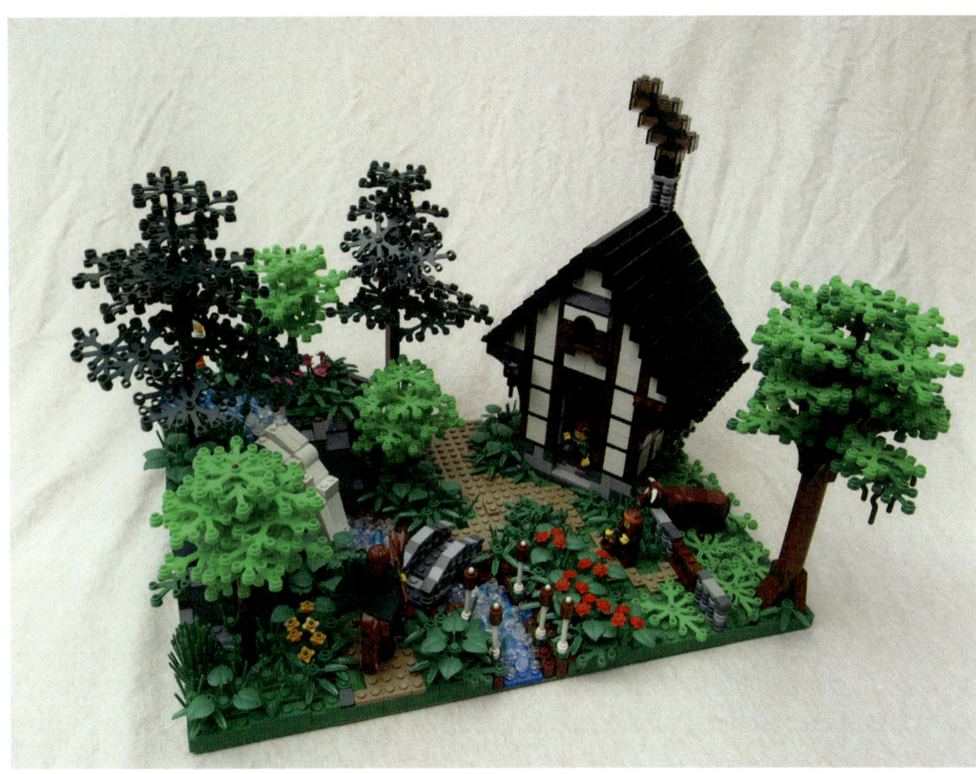

Home again
This build was one of my earliest examples of a house. Even at this early stage, I was off to a pretty good start.

Although the house itself looks good, the colors are a bit boring. It gets lost in the abundant foliage and a lack of general composition. But, at least there is a decent color palette with the flowers and water.

And considering the other progession sections, this one isn't so bad actually.

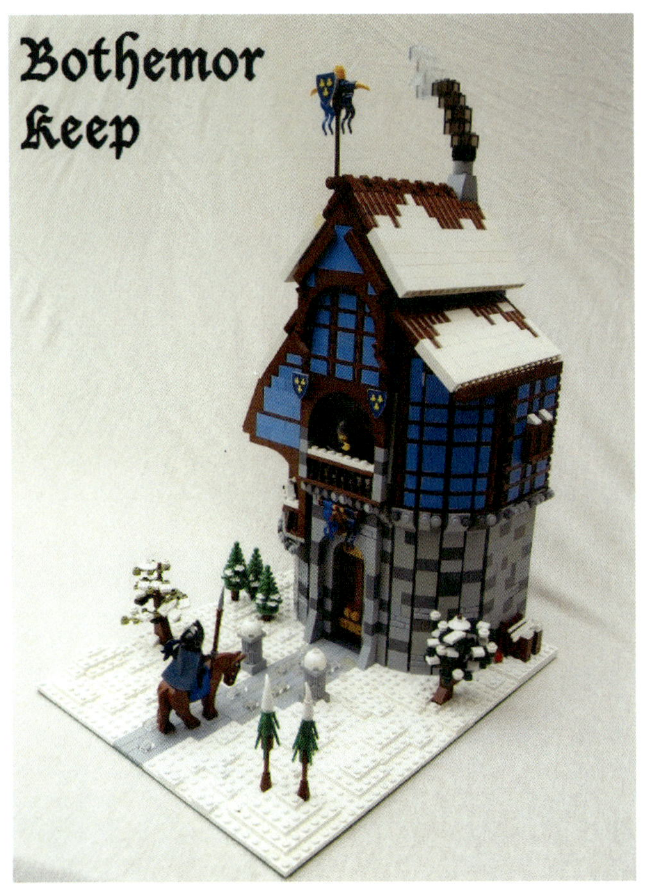

With **Bothemor Keep,** my work was still suffering from an imbalance with some details improving and others stagnating. The house itself has many improved architectural bits - curving walls, interesting roofs, and a neat looking Tudor style.

The problem is the layout. The elements are mostly there but they don't come together harmoniously. The build looks smaller than it is and a little boring. Not to mention the landscape isn't doing this build any favors. The whole thing has an appearance of being rushed. It was built for the Colossal Castle Contest and it was a later entry which meant that I didn't have a lot of time to work on it.

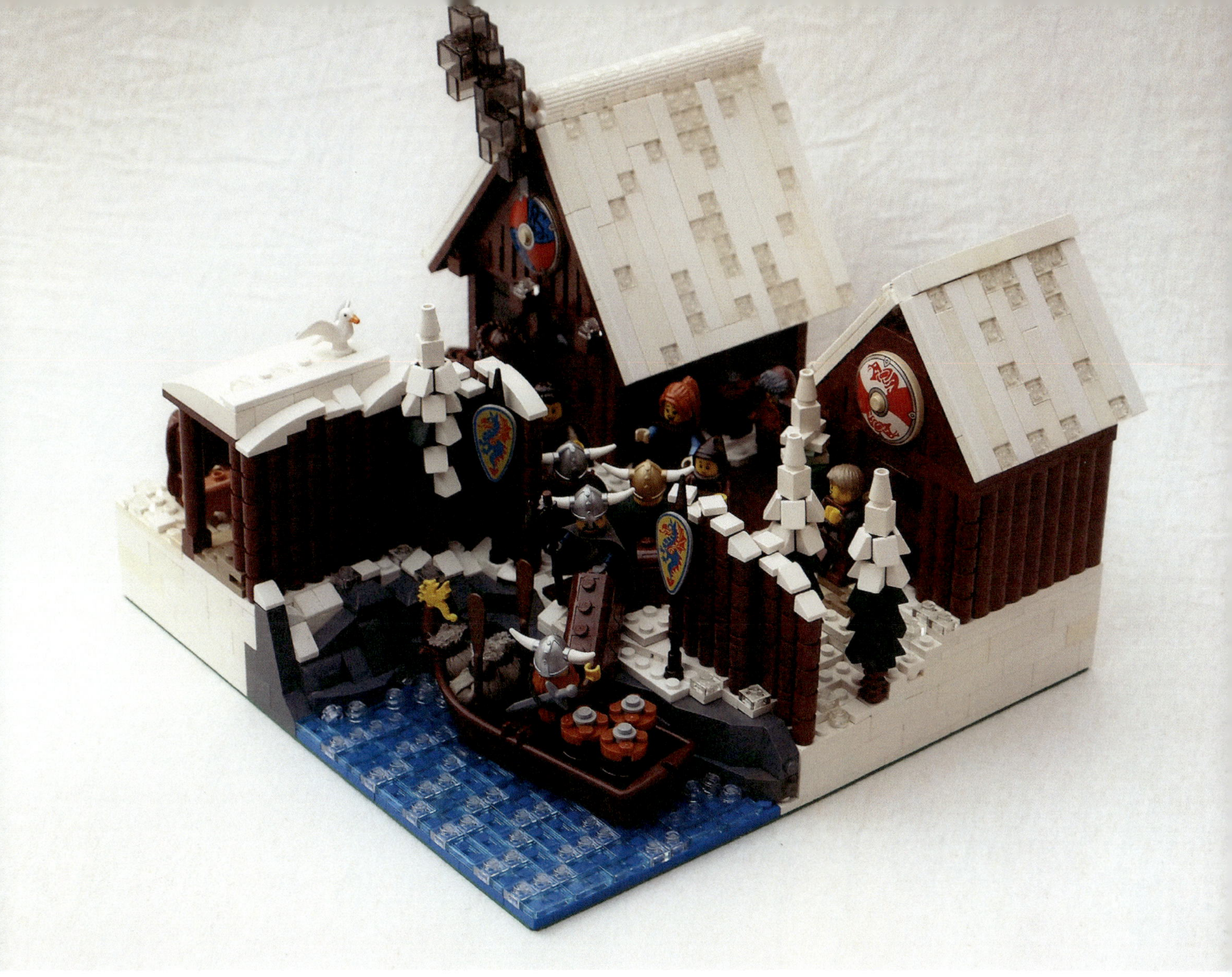

The Viking Village would start to showcase a better balance of elements and details. For example, the improved landscape is more clearly defined and has it's own importance without overshadowing any other feature. The houses themselves, although simple, have a better atmosphere aided by the warmer brown contrasting with the frigid white and blue. The characters (although a bit crowded for my taste now) can still have their "say" in the overall presentation without getting lost.

One critique I could make is that the color palette isn't quite enough. You could almost sum up the whole creation with three colors, brown, white and blue. The only thing breaking up the monotony are the Viking shields with their pop of reds, blues, and yellows.

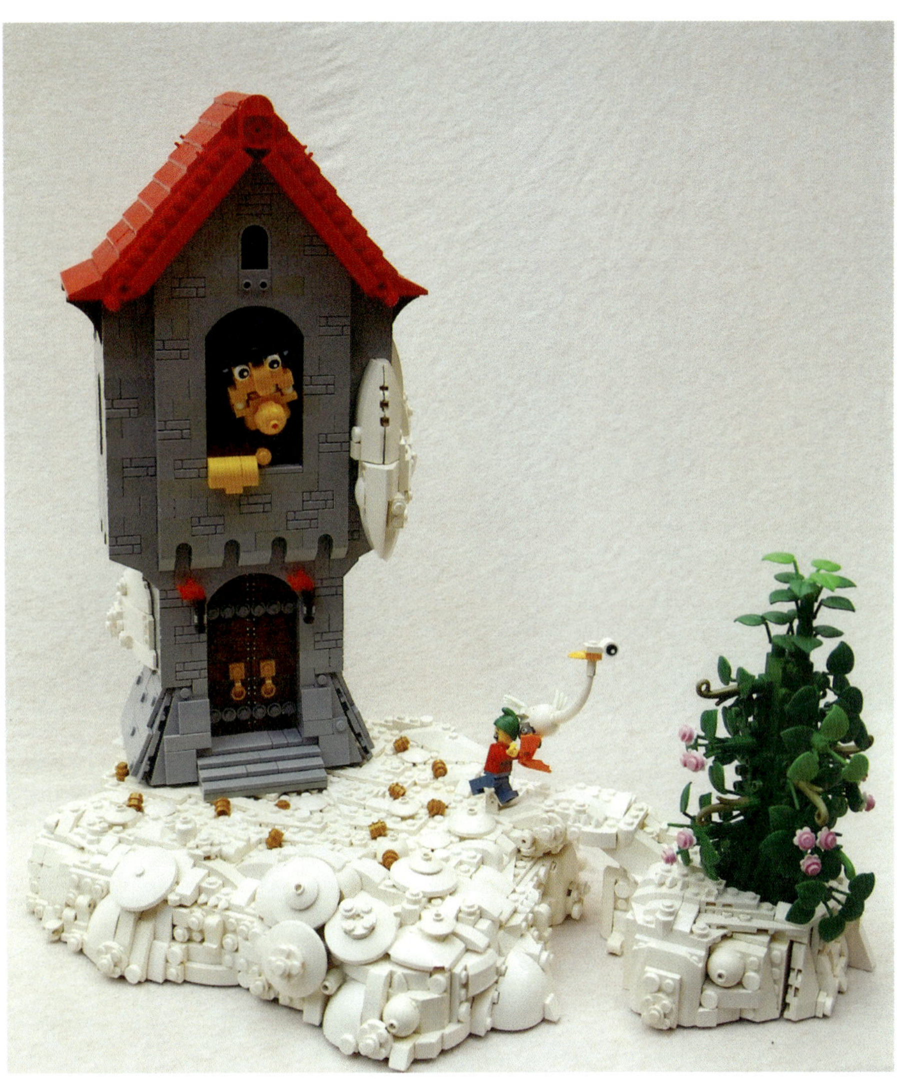

Jack and the Beanstalk was initially built for the CCCXII, Classic Castle Contest fairy tale castle category.

The layout focuses on the balance of the power of three - the house, Jack, and the green beanstalk.

Once again, this build uses one of my signature color combinations, the red and green with the white clouds. The house was an intentionally simple design to showcase the giant. I did leave room for some experimenting like the lower sloped area using plates and tiles. Although I eventually abandoned this technique, I kept going with the more detailed roof and doors especially the gold door handles.

One thing I was pleased with was the "cloud-scape". It was very interesting to look at but didn't interrupt the main focus of the build.

This is a very early appearance of my of character and creature designs. They give the scene a lot of personality. The goose is a simple design but instantly recognizable. It's evident by the expression on the giant's face that he is frustrated and annoyed with Jack and Jack is clearly terrified! The simple but effective elements bring the story to life.

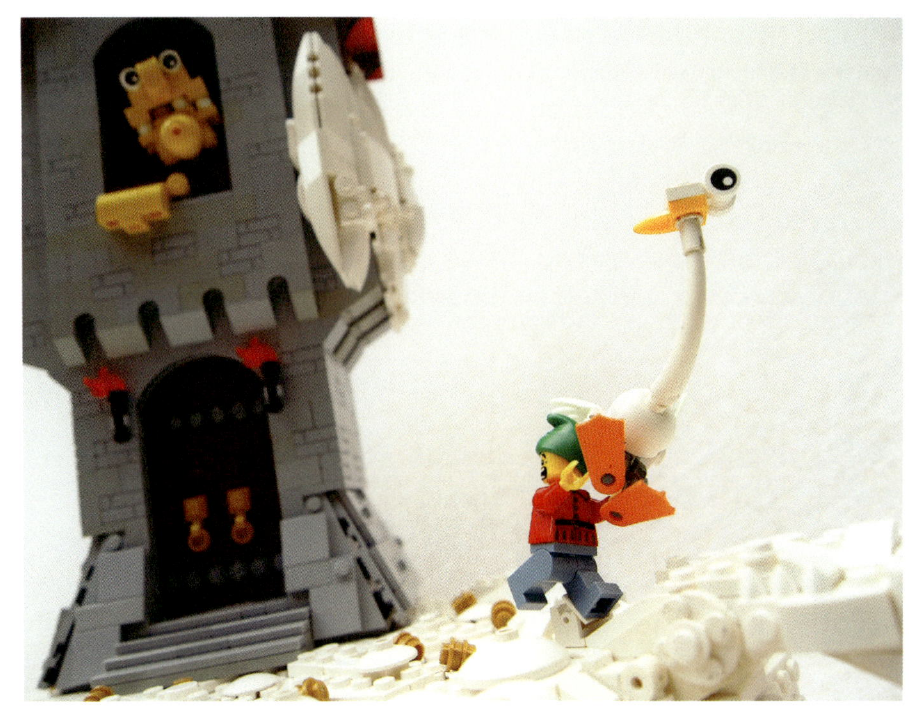

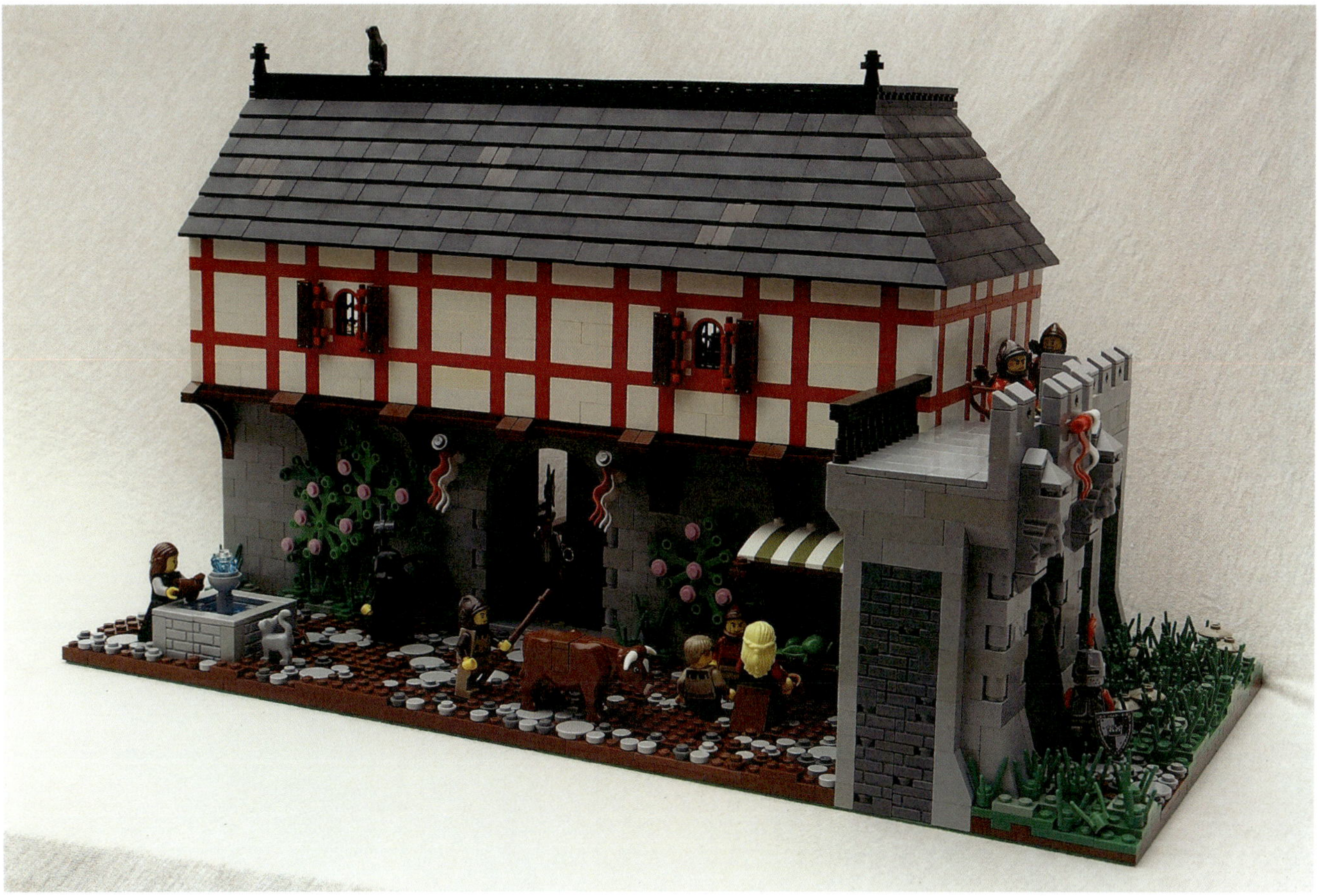

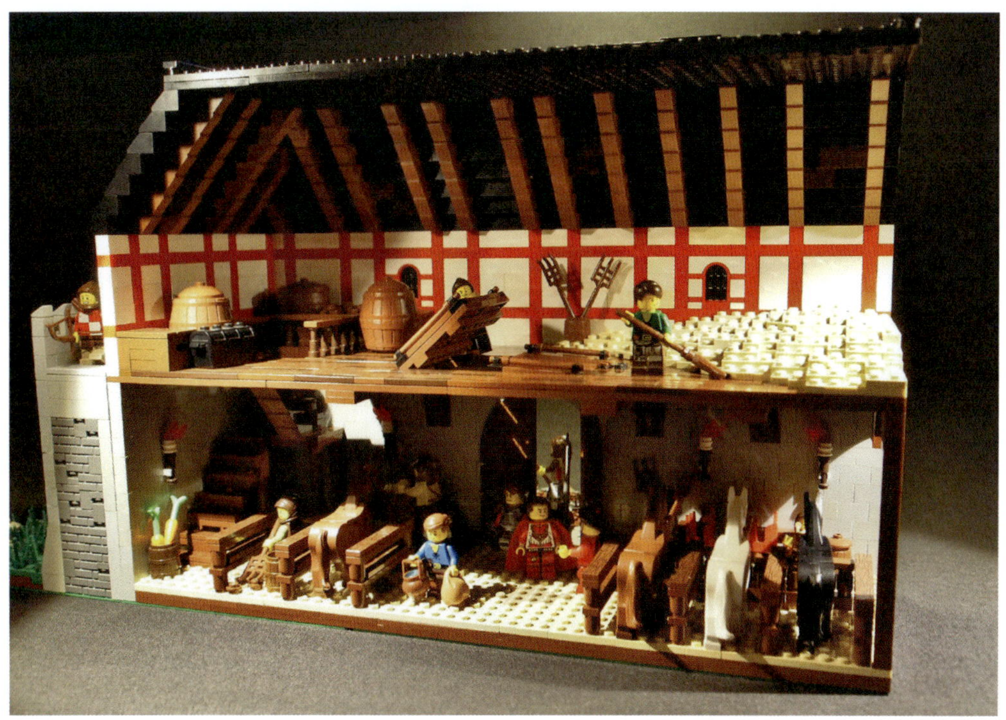

Dimarton Livery Stables

This is another doll house style building. In this build, I was playing around with different colors for the Tudor work. I was also expanding on my cleaner style with the one-by-one round studs and intricate cutaways of the stone walls. At this point, the wooden accents are starting to improve and develop. A lot of thought went into the interior elements, the stable hands, and their individual tasks. The details like the straw, the useable stairway, the barrels and boxes, and the working trap door give this setting a very realistic feel.

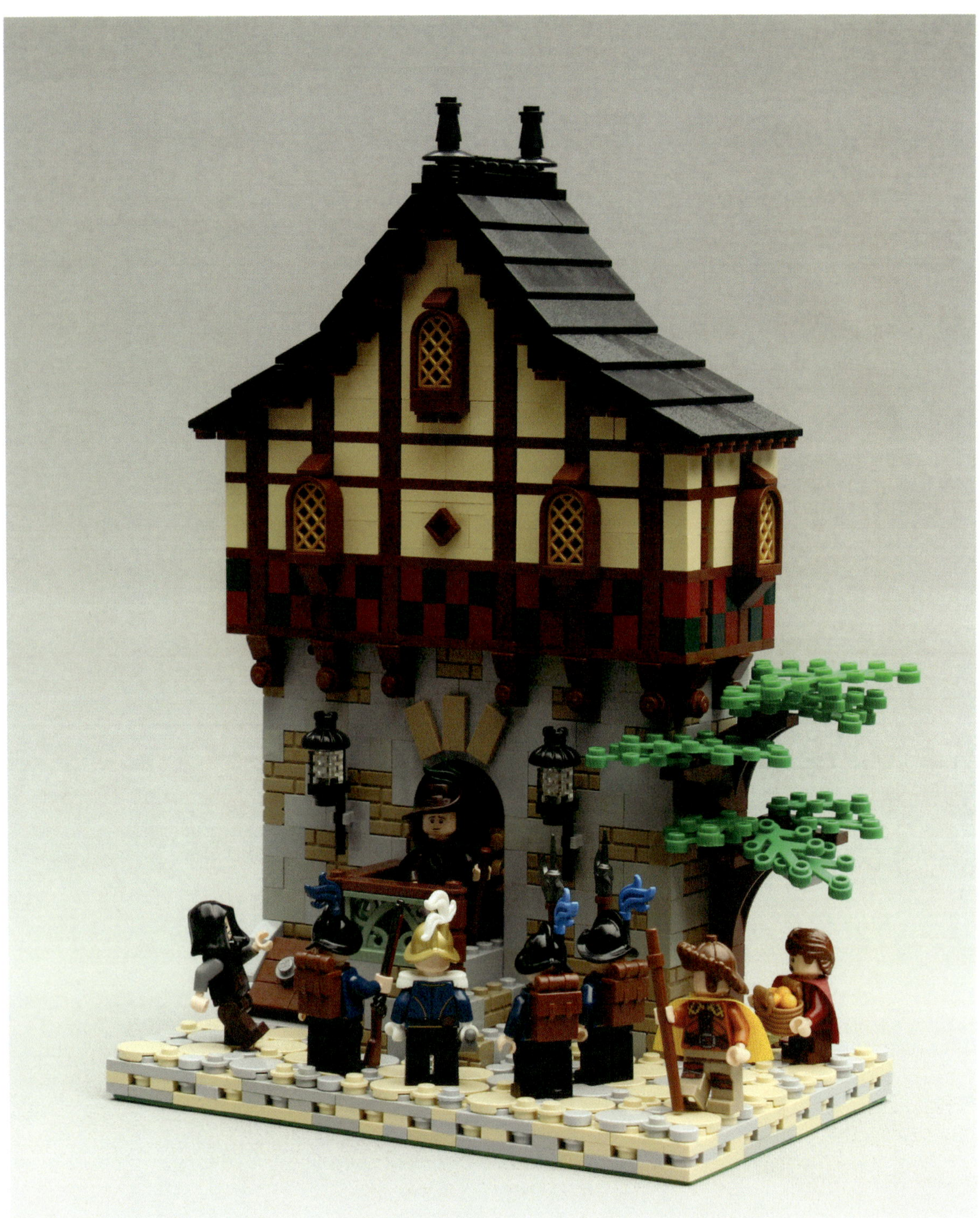

Trouble at the Tavern

When I started branching out into the Isles of Aura, I took the opportunity to explore more colors for my architecture. The best example of this is the difference of color between the layers of the build. The road uses tan and light, bluish gray which gives it a more weathered appearance. The ground floor is a dark tan and a light, bluish gray and it still looks old but perhaps built at a different time than the road giving it a subtle history. Colorful characters on the street are balanced by the colorful Tudor on the top floor. This wasn't the first time I used the checkered pattern but I really enjoyed it and would use it many times in the future. Another detail that I came to really appreciate are the outset windows. This design was far more efficient as it needs less parts and planning. A few extra interesting details like the tree and lanterns really helped to top off this creation.

116

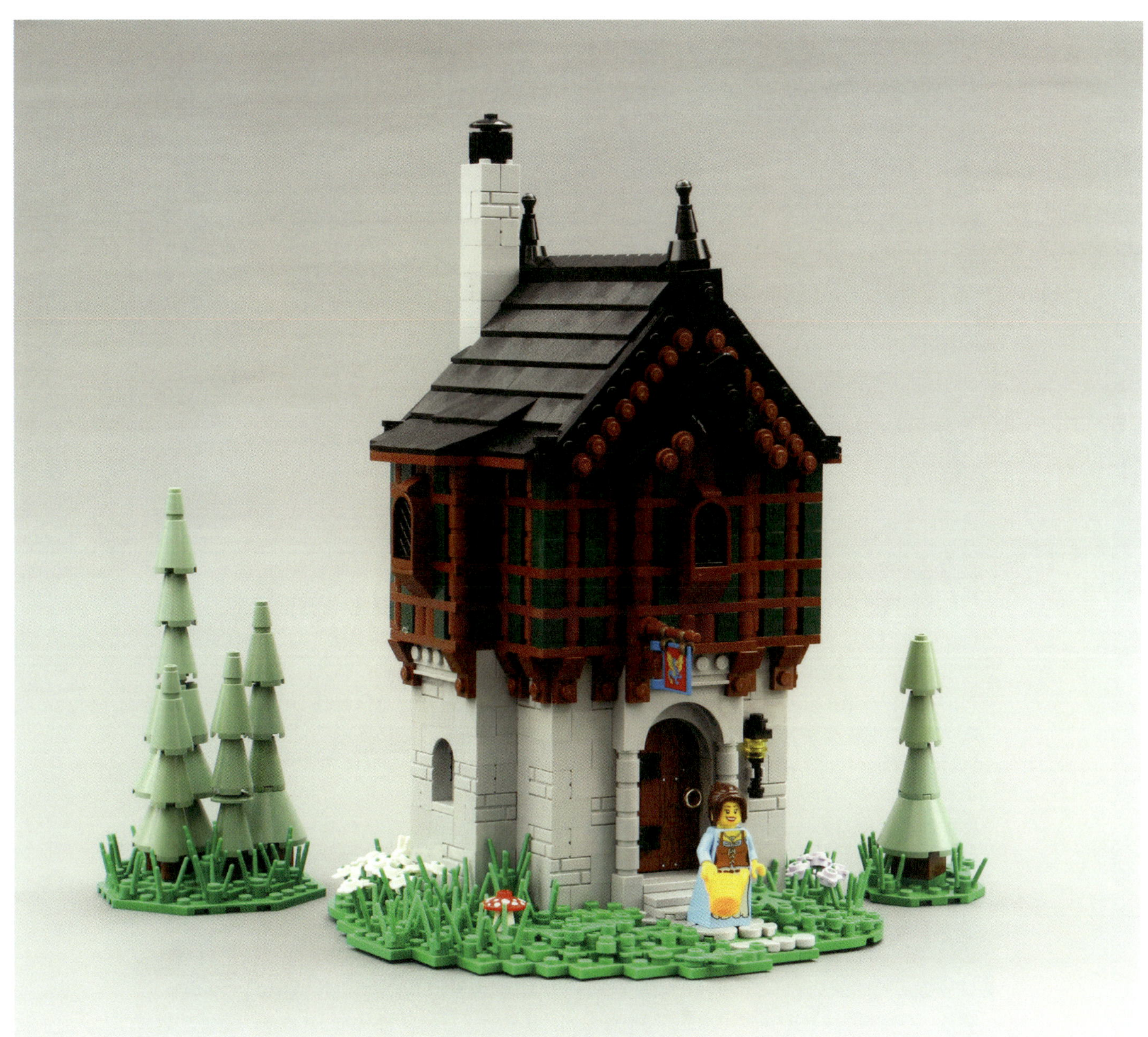

It took a long time but, in the end, I really did find my signature style which can be summarized by the word, cleanliness. But in order to achieve a clean look, I had to challenge myself to make generally simple techniques look amazing when they are all brought together. This unpublished house, meant to go alongside of Aldingham Keep (found on page 6), is a good example. The roof design is both simple and complicated with the roof trim having a similiar structure like the roof from Jack and the Beanstalk. As for color, the brown really stands out from all of the green and this contrast helps keeps the eye in the center of the picture. Another feature that I was proud of was the landscape. It frames the creation with the use of very simple trees which reflect the overall cleanliness of the build.

CONCLUSION

Inspiration

One of the most common questions I am asked is "Where do you get your inspiration?" Personally, I found this question confusing because I believe that inspiration is based on the individual. What you love to build and create and what encourages you to find your greatness is found in you. I think what they are really asking is, "How could I do that, too?"

It's not **what** inspires me, it's being able to let my mind be free to **be** inspired. I believe that everyone has innate creativity. The challenge is letting the creativity flow, letting your mind grow and develop. It takes being willing to throw yourself out there. Overcome the fear of criticism. Don't be afraid of trying or failing. Listen and observe. Develop your art to find out who you are and the best way to do that is to tell your story. With practice, the confidence grows. You want to steadily break through the boundaries in your mind that hold you back from what you can do. Continue to stretch the borders of your imagination. That's how inspiration is found.

You can see the progression of the growth in my life is this book. Now, I know what I can do. I have tried and tested myself so I know that I accomplish whatever I set my mind on.

Let yourself be inspired and share it with those you love.

Connect

◈ **Website: BrotherStevenBuilds.com**

◈ **Instagram: @brothersteven100**

◈ **Flickr: Brother Steven**

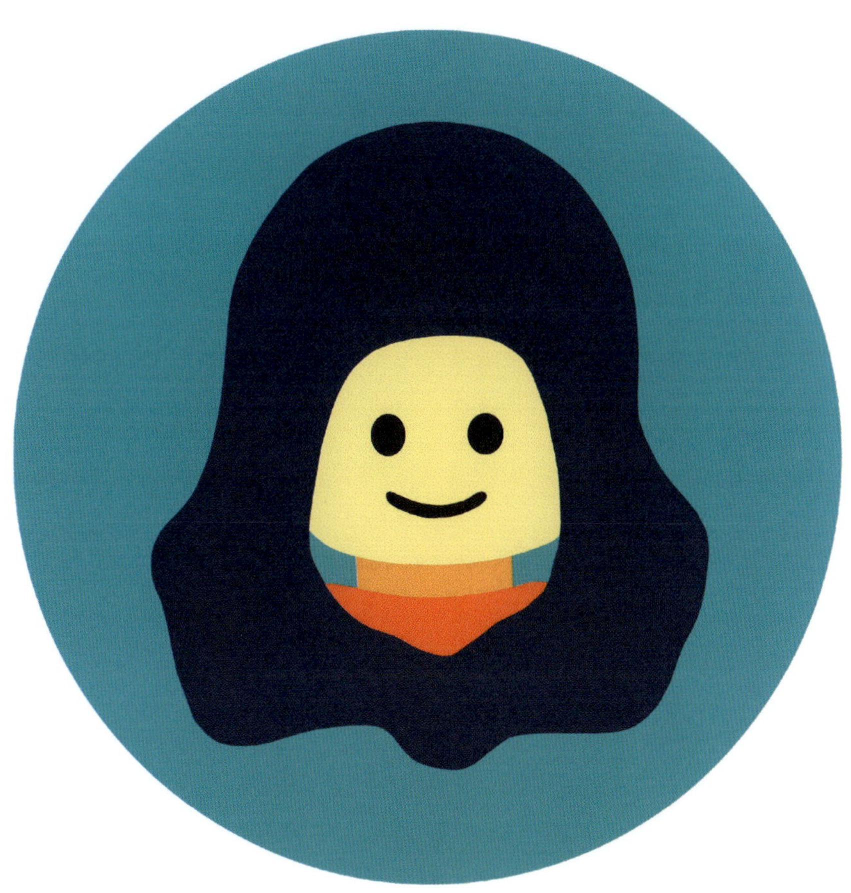

Printed in Great Britain
by Amazon